CARTAS A MI MUJER

Miguel Oscar Menassa

EDITORIAL GRUPO CERO
COLECCIÓN NARRATIVA 2001

Cuadro de Portada: «Pensando en Olga»
Óleo de Miguel Oscar Menassa

Fotografía: Carmen Salamanca
Dibujos interiores: Miguel Oscar Menassa

Índice

Cartas a mi mujer

BENALMÁDENA-COSTA
SÁBADO 4 DE OCTUBRE DE 1997

Estoy a un metro del mar, sentado en una reposera del hotel, en la playa privada. Esta mañana, precisamente, es tan privada que soy el único hombre semidesnudo frente al mar, a un metro de distancia.

Me meto hasta las rodillas en el mar y ahí me mojo con alegría la cara, los brazos, meto mi cabeza en el agua como un animalito, hasta que una pequeña ola me recuerda los grandes momentos marítimos a tu lado, tal cual dos compañeros y me enternece escribirte una carta casi metido en el mar donde tú no estás.

Hoy quiero liberarte de la responsabilidad por mi trabajo.

No fue que trabajé como una bestia para que vos pudieras vivir como una reina. Fue que trabajé como una bestia para poder soportar que fueras una reina y vivieras conmigo.

Algunos, algunas podrán decir: una pequeña reina de su propio corazón, una reina sin reino dirán otros pero frente a la poesía siempre te comportaste como una verdadera reina del mar.

Fuiste capaz de acallar el sonido de las olas para que yo escribiera ese silencio.

Después, también, tantas veces fuimos esos dos estúpidos haciendo compras en el supermercado creyendo que el problema de la humanidad era el precio de las alcachofas o el precio al consumidor del tomate de las granjas de cercanías o los putos o los negros o la crueldad con la que nos había tratado la vida haciendo de nosotros dos exiliados, dos extranjeros a todo, también a nosotros.

Sin embargo, hundimos con pasión arrebatada nuestras manos en las entrañas de la vida y algún jirón le hemos arrancado, algo de vida hubo para nosotros.

También hubo muerte y humillación, dolor y enfermedad y tuvimos que comprobar el horror de la traición por un pedazo de pan y algunos de nosotros se tuvieron que vender totalmente por un pedazo de amor pero la vida se quedó con nosotros y nos obligó a vivir despiadadamente ocurriera lo que ocurriera.

Nosotros dos estábamos condenados a seguir vivos, con los ojos abiertos, sin darle nunca las espaldas al horror.

No sólo asesinaron brutalmente a uno de nuestros hijos, a Pablito, en medio de la calle, casi delante de nuestros propios ojos, sino que todos los días, por la televisión, miles de jóvenes como Pablo morían delante de todo el mundo sin que nadie hiciera nada.

Todos exclamábamos, ¡Qué horror! ¡Qué horror! pero nadie podía hacer nada. La policía estaba comprometida en ciertos tráficos ilegales u otras yerbas. Los estados eran gobernados con el dinero del contrabando de drogas y de armas, hasta nucleares y todos nos mirábamos unos a otros y exclamábamos, ¡Qué horror! ¡Qué horror!

Y cuando no los mataban a los 20 años, los empezaban a violar a los 5, a los 7, a los 9 años. Y hay un montón de diversiones organizadas por compañías, se podría decir de turismo, donde niños y niñas de esa edad y sus mutilaciones, maltratos y vejaciones, son en algunos casos la diversión de jueces, magistrados, uno que otro presidente de algo, locutores de radio y maestros, ¿te das cuenta lo que nos hicieron ver? Los maestros de la escuela, vejaban y maltrataban a los niños, en lugar de educarlos. ¡Qué hijos de puta! Y nosotros no podíamos morir, tampoco podíamos cerrar los ojos.

DOMINGO 5 DE OCTUBRE

Nunca nos poníamos de acuerdo en el precio de las cosas.

Para mí las cosas siempre eran baratas. Estar al lado tuyo para mí, hacía poco todo precio.

Fuimos de tal manera libres que ahora eres una mujer que está cerca de mí aunque estemos lejos. Eres un verdadero invento.

Una mujer que está ahí aunque no esté. Una mujer que me permite estar allí cuando, en realidad, estoy aquí.

Un verdadero invento y no sé quién inventó el amor entre nosotros pero no nos importa y no creemos demasiado.

Lo hacemos, el amor lo hacemos y cuando no lo hacemos, hacemos otras verdades, fabricamos otros sueños que los de la especie, esos días que nos levantamos enamorados de los puentes, de las vías férreas, de las autopistas, de todo aquello que separa a los amantes para que luego se vuelvan a encontrar en otros caminos, otras ciudades, otros amantes.

Yo y vos, querida, hemos participado en esa historia universal del amor. En siglos venideros cuando se hable del amor, se hablará de nuestro amor, eso quiero decirte cuando te digo que te amo.

Ahora, hoy día, para decirlo de alguna manera, he cumplido 57 años que, en parte, son míos y, en parte, son del mundo.

Hay veces que todo me lo debo a mí, hay veces que todo se lo debo al mundo, tanto unas como otras veces sólo existen, para mí, por tu presencia. Sin vos volando por el salón de la casa como si fuera un aeropuerto internacional, yo no hubiera podido concebir que el destino de la poesía era volar y, tampoco, sin ese vuelo permanente anunciando el porvenir, nunca hubiera podido concebir la idea de Las 2001 Noches.

LUNES 6 DE OCTUBRE

Tus ideas eran todas maravillosas, se te ocurría cada cosa y yo, que era muy ambicioso, trabajaba para todas tus ideas.

Bueno así, llegamos hasta aquí.

Hoy mismo, en el acto de esta carta que, con amor y pulsión te escribo, abandono el ejército (basta de jefes) abandono la fábrica (basta de patrones) y abandono la universidad (basta de maestros).

A partir de ahora te amaré en los espacios abiertos del poema, en el mar, en las grandes ciudades extranjeras donde nadie nos conozca.

Nunca tanto amor.

Vivamos donde vivamos, a partir de ahora no nos adaptaremos a nada. Seremos siempre extranjeros. Eso vengo, en parte, a pedirte en esta carta. Un último viaje, por fin, un viaje verdadero:

Construir en los próximos 30 años, vivamos donde vivamos, digo no importa dónde sea, Madrid o Buenos Aires, vivamos donde vivamos, construir para nosotros dos y si algún otro quisiera, una muerte extranjera.

MARTES 7 DE OCTUBRE

Quiero decirte que ahora que me toca un poco de fama y cierta cuota de reconocimiento, yo no quiero nada de eso, aunque reconozco haberlo ambicionado alguna vez, ahora quiero quedarme tranquilo.

Escribiendo cuando a mí me dé la gana.

Trabajando cuando a mí me dé la gana.

Estando juntos cuando a mí me dé la gana.

Tus ganas, quiero decir, que soy yo quien descubrió lo que pasó este siglo que agoniza a pesar de mis versos o a causa de mis versos.

Pero esta vez jugando de verdad al vuelo de tus labios, al sonido estremecedor de tus caderas rompiéndose, para mostrar al mundo que en este siglo que no se pudo casi nada, nosotros dos pudimos amarnos en libertad.

Estuviéramos cerca o lejos, nuestro amor, nuestro famoso, infinito amor, no era otra cosa que una nueva manera de pensar el universo, aunque debo reconocerlo, con mis versos y algunas historias mal contadas entre amigos, le hice creer a toda la humanidad posible, que garchar era lo único que hacíamos.

Nuestros culos, tus tetas y mi pija, aparecieron por doquier. Sobre mi pija hicieron un simposio en la Facultad de Psicología de Buenos Aires, pero nadie entendía nada. Eran ejemplos de una manera de pensar, esas anécdotas no eran nuestra vida, sin embargo, sería bueno pensar que tanta pasión, tanta carne sexual entre nosotros fue, precisamente, lo que nos permitió la vida.

A veces, tratándose de la sexualidad, éramos capaces de grandes estragos, casi sin darnos cuenta.

No era que hacíamos todo el día el amor. El amor necesitaba, históricamente, que pasara lo nuestro. El mundo necesitaba saber que la "energía" (para llamarla de alguna manera) que produce el placer genital reproductivo en todos sus paradigmas, la pasión del acoplamiento de las bestias para la reproducción o sus desviaciones, no se puede sublimar. Porque la sublimación es un mecanismo del sujeto psíquico y no de la especie.

Alguien tenía que demostrarle al mundo que habían equivocado el destino de todo un siglo, pensando que la "represión genital" hacía al hombre más civilizado, mejor dotado para el arte, para las construcciones sociales. Y yo y vos, amor mío que, a veces, parecemos tantos, lo que deberíamos mostrar que no estoy seguro de poder hacerlo:

El animal no puede ser doblegado por el símbolo. Sabiendo que va a morir lo único que le interesa es acoplarse, amar, (follar, garchar en lenguas más correctas).

Por eso que lo único que se puede hacer para poder alguna cosa, es dejar de amarse a sí mismo y eso es lo que las bestias no pueden.

Quiero tranquilizarte, diciéndote que, esta vez, no será necesario sostener con nuestros cuerpos estas escrituras; porque estas escrituras ya están sostenidas.

Algo hemos logrado, nosotros, al menos, somos un escritor.

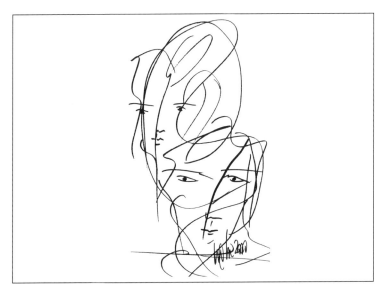

MIÉRCOLES 8 DE OCTUBRE

Desde aquí, a un metro del mar, las olas me salpican y yo trato de decirte que estoy pensando, pensando concretamente nuestros próximos o últimos 30 años.

Y no es que ahora deberemos cambiar porque hemos hecho las cosas mal. Es que las cosas a cierta edad son otras cosas y por eso deben ser hechas de otras maneras.

Nuestros hijos son grandes, tienen todo nuestro amor y algunas pesetillas para seguir creciendo, eso quiere decir que de eso ya somos libres.

Yo por mi parte he trabajado lo suficiente (aunque no haya ganado lo suficiente) como para pasarme 30 años a un metro del mar, escribiéndote. Y si consigo mantener algunos negocios que, todavía, no puedo destruir, hasta tendría dinero para invitarte a vivir conmigo.

Claro está, que todo esto, después de lo dicho, sólo es posible si vos lo desearas.

Este siglo fue tuyo y lo perdiste como una madre que se deja ganar al ajedrez, siendo campeona de eso, por su hijo. Sólo para que el niño sienta el olor del triunfo, la alegría de vencer a alguien por nada.

JUEVES 9 DE OCTUBRE

Ayer perdí todo el dinero que tenía destinado para el juego. Había aguantado lo que se dice hasta ayer sin perder ni ganar una peseta, pero ayer lo perdí todo. Me acosté pensando que algo me faltaba por aprender. Algo, evidentemente, no se había hecho carne en mi pensamiento, todavía debía pagar por mi psicoanálisis.

Ahora espero al señor de la toalla, todo me subleva.

Cualquier injusticia se hace carne en mí, aunque como vimos en renglones anteriores no todo pensamiento se hace carne en mí.

Estoy llegando a las más importantes conclusiones de mi vida. La verdad no sé mucho acerca de las cosas que hago o que, directamente, me pasan:

Cuando juego quiero demostrarme a mí mismo que fui un boludo trabajando tanto, cuando en una noche se podía ganar lo mismo que en muchos años trabajando. Entonces, en el juego, perdía.

Después, es cierto, en la vida ganaba casi siempre, porque todo lo hacía trabajando, pero cuando jugaba, negaba, yo también, como todo el mundo actual, el trabajo.

VIERNES 10 DE OCTUBRE

Hoy, que ya sabía cómo se hacían las cosas, se nubló. Nuevamente me toca un retiro espiritual.

Dejar que las cosas ocurran tal cual tengan que ocurrir, pero yo no tengo que estar en las cosas. Haber aprendido esto, este mes me costó 2 millones de pesetas. Lo que cuesta vale.

Para mí sólo existen Buenos Aires y Madrid.

Tengo que poder quedarme en mis cosas, la casa que conseguí comprar, la familia que pude construir, el trabajo que con suficiente eficacia realizo.

Pagar 2 millones de pesetas para separar lo real de lo simbólico, nunca es mucho dinero.

Amor mío, Málaga era, tal vez, mi última posibilidad de ser joven, fundando un nuevo lugar, pero no me dejaron.

Las bestias, por lo menos frente a mí, han preferido seguir bestias, como todo el mundo, pero como yo ya no era joven, sino que estaba simulándolo, me lo tendrían que haber puesto más fácil.

Pero la vida es así, amada mía, si todo el mundo está empeñado en que tengo 57 años, y que eso para la vida que hice, el pensamiento que amé y los versos que escribí, es ser muy grande, tendré que tener 57 años y ser muy grande.

Y una persona grande está sentada en algún lugar, en algún tiempo, esperando que alguien quiera saber de qué se trata.

Cuando yo era joven, como todos los jóvenes, de cualquier porquería que me encontraba por la calle, hacía vida.

A mi edad, cuando me encuentro con una porquería no puedo entender que, todavía, ocurran esas cosas y la dejo porquería.

SÁBADO 11 DE OCTUBRE

A veces me impresiona el horror de las diferencias temporales. En el mismo momento, en la misma ciudad, un hombre pertenece al futuro y otro al pasado.

Querida, querida, me molesta un poco que con todo el dinero que nos hemos gastado este mes, no hayamos solucionado ninguno de los grandes problemas de la humanidad.

Si puedo parar con la máquina triste que me quiere matar porque otros murieron, porque otros fracasaron, podré evaluar positivamente mi situación vital. No es poco lo que he conseguido y ya ha pasado la peor parte.

Una vez más lo único que deseo es quedarme en lo que pude construir con mi trabajo. El resto no me pertenece.

Libros, amores, hijos, una manera de decir.

También me doy cuenta que lo ya conquistado no se puede dejar. Es sobre lo que ya tenemos que quiero más:

Si ambiciono vivir por lo menos hasta los 80 años, algo tendré que modificar de mi vida actual.

Hay algo que no digiero bien, hay algo que me duele haber perdido.

Amor, amor, yo quiero vivir y no me importa lo que haya pasado, yo quiero seguir viviendo, aunque reconozco que estos años anteriores, muchas veces, tuve culpa de seguir viviendo.

Ahora, sólo quiero vivir, ahora sólo quiero que todo el tiempo que me quede por vivir se llame con mi nombre y apellido.

No me gustaría que dijeran: "Menassa hacía el amor así" y estuvieran hablando de mis amantes más torpes.

No me gustaría que dijeran: "Menassa hace así con el dinero" y estuvieran hablando de algún socio mezquino.

Y tampoco me gustaría que dijeran algo del Grupo Cero sin haber leído antes mi escritura.

Pero tengo que saber, y por eso te amo, que todas esas cosas que no me gustaría que pasaran, pasarán.

DOMINGO 12 DE OCTUBRE

Estuve en la suite escribiéndote y ya había llegado a la página diez, ahora espero al señor de la toalla y la colchoneta.

Estoy sentado en las escaleras, el sol me da de lleno en la cara. Las otras personas que esperan como yo, están impacientes, un poco por la espera y otro poco porque me ven escribiendo.

Ahora te escribo ya sentado en la reposera a un metro del mar. Hace airecito pero el sol está fuerte.

Te hablo de estas cosas para que se sepa que un hombre como yo, se tira en una reposera, espera por una toalla para secarse a la salida del mar, se deja besar la punta de sus delicados pies de bailarín, por las olas más generosas que llegan a la orilla. Y, a veces, tengo ganas de cagar y cago y me duele la barriga y, a veces, me tengo que cuidar en las comidas y siete veces en mi vida no tuve erección. Una vez por cada deidad de cada día de la semana. Siempre me sentí inferior al universo, en general, y frente a cada planeta en particular.

Recuerdo aquellas encrucijadas de mi infancia donde todo lo grande era lo divino. Por eso fue que de adolescente y, a veces, ahora mismo me pasa; cuando una mujer dice que soy un Dios, yo inmediatamente lo relaciono con el tamaño de mi pija.

Bueno el tamaño que ella, en realidad, otorgaba con su grandeza y quitaba con su crueldad.

Ahora dejo de escribirte y no porque vaya a hacer ninguna revolución o conquistar ninguna amante imposible, te abandono para ponerme crema en la piel, para durar más años. Es decir, me alejo de ti un instante, para tenerte todos los instantes.

LUNES 13 DE OCTUBRE

Así fui escribiendo mis versos, y si no, nada hubiera sido posible. El sol juega conmigo, hace como que está pero no está. Todas las cosas, me digo, están pero no están.

Es cuando nos dejamos usar por las palabras que las cosas existen, aun, las imposibles, como el amor, el goce.

Abandoné un poco la escritura y miré el mar, un largo rato, porque había sentido que esta carta podría ser un libro y eso me detuvo y descubrí el mar en esa detención.

57 años no es moco de pavo, como queriendo decir, en mi barrio, que 57 años era una cosa respetable.

En mi barrio hasta los delincuentes obtenían cierto perdón, cierto prestigio a los 57 años.

Sé que ya no vivimos en mi barrio, pero, quiero decirte, amada mía, que a mí, eso, no me importa un carajo. Porque mi barrio soy yo y el que no quiera o no pueda tenerme un poco más de respeto, ahora que tengo 57 años, lo mandaré a tomar por culo, en buen porteño, a la concha de su madre.

MARTES 14 DE OCTUBRE

Justo en este momento se me ocurrió una frase un poco rara pero igual la pongo, por las dudas: "Viva Perón aunque Menem decaiga" y en esa frase sentí que había comprendido algo del peronismo, algo de nuestro exilio, algo de la vida en general, también me di cuenta que Menem comienza con las letras de Men-assa y que la partícula separada es capicúa como el nombre de la frase.

Espero que me permitas, amada de las tiernas horas donde todos éramos gloriosos porque un destino grande nos esperaba, recordar cuando todos éramos jóvenes y valientes, cada uno a su modo y luchábamos por una patria peronista: Pan para todos, trabajo para los peronistas que éramos todos, educación para todo el mundo también para los niños. Los niños en la Argentina antes de Perón, no existían. A los niños en Argentina, los inventó Perón.

Y, eso sí, fundamentalmente por eso éramos muy peronistas: una mujer sería nuestra mente.

Una nueva mujer poblaría la historia de mujeres. Su grito de libertad e igualdad, arrancaría al hombre de su letargo.

Ella, entregada toda ella al mundo, para nosotros nació con el peronismo, se llame como se llame, esa mujer, nació con el peronismo.

Vos también sos esa mujer.

MIÉRCOLES 15 DE OCTUBRE

Yo había nacido en un barrio periférico, nunca tenía fuerzas suficientes para imponer mis ideas, siempre prefería inventar una nueva idea.

Después, como ya te dije que no tenía fuerzas para imponer las ideas, las dejaba ahí, ahí, donde estuviera, a la benevolencia o malevolencia de los caminantes del viento.

Te amo y te recuerdo, aun en estas tontas digresiones, tan importantes para la humanidad que no termina de enterarse, porque ni yo mismo, hago los esfuerzos necesarios, porque estoy amándote o recordándote todo el tiempo.

Y el mundo se hunde, el siglo se termina, pero nosotros no. Nosotros estaremos atados, por mis versos, a las vertientes del hombre que no desaparecen.

Por eso que cuando yo te digo que habrá alguna luz para los hombres, te hablo del futuro.

De nosotros, de nuestra oscuridad ya se habló hace cien años. Nosotros sólo podemos padecerla.

JUEVES 16 DE OCTUBRE

Me vuelvo a meter en el mar y pienso que viviendo en España, es para mí todo un récord bañarme en el mar a fin de Octubre y gozo con meterme en el mar y gozo al salir con el sol y el viento, muy parecido a las playas de nuestra juventud, pero debo reconocerlo, siempre me atraviesa un dolor, una incomprensión dolorosa.

Como te decía en páginas anteriores: Millones de jóvenes asesinados delante de todo el mundo, millones de jóvenes drogados porque no hay trabajo ni educación para tantos, millones de jóvenes educados mal, por orden de los gobernantes, estupidizados hasta más no poder.

Hoy día, cualquiera podría decir con sencillez, "menos mal que existe la familia". Y algo de razón tendría.

El sol es abrasador. Me muero de contento pensando que estoy en el mar a un metro de distancia. Me vivo de contento pensando que muchísimos colegas de todo el mundo están trabajando y yo aquí tomando el sol.

Bueno, me digo, alguna vez me tocaba a mí y si me gusta mucho, que me está gustando, habrá que repetirlo.

VIERNES 17 DE OCTUBRE

Hablé con Carmen, están desmontando la sede Málaga, en unas horas más yo seré libre y Málaga será del Grupo Cero.

Estoy contento con todos los trabajos realizados y si, a veces, no estoy contento es porque algún trabajo no se ha realizado.

La ambición de las olas: hablar como Freud, cantar como Gardel y garchar como nosotros dos, hace unos días, en el baño del hotel, contra el lavabo, mirándote al espejo me metí entre tus nalgas y algo te resististe.

No quiero hacer alarde de esas virtudes vegetales, pero mientras te la metía, sentí que murmurabas entre dientes, canciones, melodías lejanas, abiertas notas de cantos insondables y te reías, feliz, enamorada. Mientras te la metía te miraba por el espejo y murmurabas entre dientes: manifestaciones de millones de hambrientos pidiendo pan. Millones de niños infectados pidiendo piedad.

Lugares, amada, tiempos del hombre actual, donde las enfermedades que, generalmente, se producen por las vías reproductivas ocupan un lugar preponderante en las oficinas del Estado y nadie se ocupa de nuestro amor.

Estamos condenados, te lo dije, estamos condenados a demostrar la importancia del trabajo. Para que haya amor entre nosotros tendremos que hacerlo.

Y esa es nuestra condena y nuestra dicha. Existir, apenas, cuando el amor brilla para nosotros. El resto, todo el resto, es producir el surgimiento de un poema.

SÁBADO 18 DE OCTUBRE

Muy jóvenes, como Paul Eluard, abrimos nuestros brazos a la pureza, pero nosotros escapamos enseguida cuando nos dimos cuenta que lo puro era ciego.

Después vino el exilio y era todo muy divertido. Vos seguías siendo una reina como en Buenos Aires, bueno vos no podías dejar de ser una reina. La diferencia con Buenos Aires, que casi se hace una cuestión entre nosotros, era que en Madrid yo, todavía, no tenía trabajo.

Pero tampoco fue como creimos en su momento, que tú me pedías algo que yo no tuviera, por envidiosa o cruel. Era que yo, no tenía lo que todo hombre tiene que tener: Un trabajo, billetes de 10.000 pesetas en el bolsillo, y sobre todo confianza en sí mismo, en sus cuentas bancarias.

Al principio yo me decía, un hombre así no escribe un verso ni que se cague en Dios.

Así, que cuando te ponías así, yo no te pegaba, porque en esa época era un libertario, pero no te daba pelota.

Después, cuando me di cuenta que la gente que me rodeaba no tenía ni para darle de comer a sus hijos, comencé a mirar la idea con simpatía.

Había una vertiente de la idea que me enloquecía, si yo conseguía trabajar, hacer efectivo mi trabajo, como ella decía que era efectivo mi sexo, ella me amaría dos veces.

Me amaría porque ya me amaba, tal vez, por mi grandiosa pija marinera, tal vez, porque yo siempre escuchaba sus gritos de libertad y si, ahora, tengo dinero, me amará por segunda vez por mi dinero o por mi manera de gastarlo aunque ella no esté o el modo de ganarlo o la planta llamada de la moneda que, con tanto amor, regábamos en nuestra juventud.

De golpe pensé que aunque yo no lo quiera o no lo ambicione, algún joven, algún hijo nuestro, alguna criatura incansable, puede querer aprender algo de mi escritura y esa posibilidad, guía todo el sentido de mis versos.

JUEVES, 30 DE OCTUBRE, 10:00 H.

Querida, amor mío, amor en general, juntos abiertos en todas direcciones:

Hoy es el último día de playa de este viaje, mañana a esta hora estaré viajando hacia Madrid. Espero cosas normales, viajar bien, sin problemas.

El saldo, como diría un general victorioso a quien la victoria le haya costado perder muchos hombres, lamentable.

Hemos triunfado pero, también, hemos perdido.

Pérdidas irreparables, inolvidables, heridas siempre semiabiertas a punto de abrirse en cualquier momento pero, también, hemos triunfado.

Dentro de cuatro días habrán pasado cuatro años de la trágica, inesperada muerte de Pablo, nuestro hijo Pablo.

Esta carta, en realidad, parece un pliego de condiciones:

Es necesario, después de cuatro años, dejar morir a los muertos para que ellos, a su vez, nos permitan comenzar a vivir nuevamente: Con libertad, con soltura, llevándonos al mundo por delante, porque seguimos siendo hermosos y valientes, cualidades que no envejecen ni con la muerte.

Dar por muerto a Pablo, que está muerto hace cuatro años, permitirá que nosotros, que aún estamos vivos, podamos resucitar.

Abandonar las tumbas, esa melancolía errante.

Hagámonos sospechosos delante de todo el mundo de querer vivir. De querer plasmar en una vida plena todas nuestras muertes amadas.

Una vida, mi amor, donde haya sitio para todo el mundo, también para los vivos, para nosotros.

Una vida, querida, que será contada con orgullo por hijos y nietos y biznietos y algún que otro intelectual enterado del fenómeno.

A veces éramos los puntos cardinales opuestos para poder amarnos con mayor libertad.

Llegamos a ser aristas de triángulos diferentes para poder amarnos en esa nueva dimensión.

Nuevos decires atravesarán nuestra vida para siempre. Ya nunca más en nuestra familia se olvidarán del mar.

Este mar, por ejemplo, desde donde te escribo, esta carta perdida y encontrada, sentado a un metro de las olas.

No aguanté más y me metí en el mar, 30 de octubre, en España y, ahora, estoy contento y quiero que todo el mundo esté contento y me doy cuenta que estoy a punto de cometer el mismo error, una nueva vez, y rectifico diciéndolo de la siguiente manera:

La felicidad, lo poco de felicidad que nos permite la vida actual, depende del trabajo de cada uno.

El que no sea capaz de trabajar por su felicidad no tendrá ninguna felicidad.

Y esto es, a la vez, querida mía, una mala noticia: Nuestra felicidad depende de nuestro trabajo y, al mismo tiempo, una esperanza: con mi trabajo, sin esperar la ayuda de Dioses que, en general, no existen y sin esperar la ayuda de ministerios que no existen para mí; es posible algo de felicidad, con mi trabajo.

Sin duda es una esperanza. Espero que el siglo que viene los poderosos no utilicen estas frases para dominar, con el asunto del trabajo, con mayor eficacia a un número, siempre, mucho mayor de trabajadores.

JUEVES 30 DE OCTUBRE, 11:00 H.

Escuchad, el mundo es, verdaderamente, de quien lo piensa.
Escuchad amada.
Escuchad amadas.
Escuchad damas en general.
Lo nuestro fue posible porque venía en un poema.
Un poema, os explico: una manera diferente de concebir el horizonte, el límite, la zozobra, la caída.
Lo hemos aprendido todo, mi amor, casi todo, porque venía en un poema.
POEMA: potro alado, yegua volcánica, mujer sostenida en el aire más de dos siglos por la vertiente oceánica de un verbo enamorado, hombre declinando, sin poder caer nunca del todo, sin poder tocar fondo jamás. Y un poema, también, es una pequeña ola, sin corazón, sin vientre, acariciando suavemente a una piedra muerta.
Fuimos alcántaras, nueces perdidas, hojas de periódicos olvidadas.
Te digo, mi amor, quiero que entiendas, exactamente, lo que te digo mi amor:
Si llegamos a sentirnos viejos, estamos perdidos.

Uno debe sentirse un hombre de su edad (una mujer, se entiende) y si alguien me confunde con un joven, será para faltarme al respeto con menos trabajo, aunque yo no lo tenga y si alguien me trata como a un viejo, es porque considera que soy descartable, pero yo, tú si quieres, sigo siendo un hombre de mi edad.
Juventud y vejez son dos argucias de los sistemas del Estado moderno.
Sabemos que un niño de 8 años puede considerarse un experto en matemáticas, llamadas por algunos, superio-

res, o problemas de la lógica emparentada con la producción de conocimiento y un viejo de 80 años puede dar una conferencia de 7 horas de duración, en pie, o echarse un polvo, tranquilamente, en esta misma playa desde donde te escribo.

Cuál es la diferencia entre un niño y un viejo cuando un río de lava hirviente baja de la montaña, cuáles las diferencias entre un hombre y una mujer frente a un tifón marino o frente a una borrasca loca y sedienta.

Adiós mar, ahora volveré a hacer las maletas y mañana partiré, espero encontrarme contigo, en algún mar perdido, en Diciembre en alguna playa argentina, aquella de mi juventud.

Te amo, mar, y después de haberte descubierto te entrego, para que ella haga su deseo.

Amor mío, amor mío, amores, estrellas, lejanas soledades, tierras fértiles, amor mío, amor mío, ¿serás algún amor?

Hoy me termino de dar cuenta que la vida misma tiene su oscuridad.

Todo fue bien, entonces, podemos comenzar.

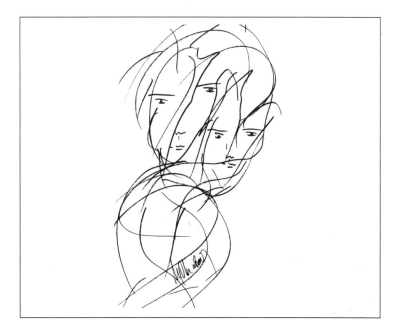

JUEVES 30 DE OCTUBRE, 14:30 H.

Hoy me cuesta más escribir que días anteriores. Hace más de una hora que estoy a un metro del mar y, todavía, no he comenzado a escribir, ya me metí dos veces en el mar, pero escribir me cuesta.

Pienso sarcásticamente, lo que cuesta vale, frase que me lleva por un lado, a la publicidad que hace actualmente el Grupo Cero, tratando de enseñarle a la gente, en general, el valor del psicoanálisis y por otro lado al segundo apellido de Amelia, a la cuesta de San Vicente, a de Lucia Vicente, que sos vos, a "questa" ragazza é molto bella; partiendo la palabra, la C, podría ser la concha de mi madre, y las "huestes" de amores parecidos para desprenderme de tanto amor.

Y amor, amor de mis amores, poesía y tus piernas abiertas, siempre abiertas al sonido espectral de los tambores. El valor, terminé pensando, es lo que no se ve, por eso es fácil suprimirlo del pensamiento.

El valor de las cosas, el valor del trabajo, eso ya nadie, casi nadie lo tiene en cuenta.

De última, mi amor, lo que cuesta vale, equivale a decirme: ya soy un poeta, todos los esfuerzos, todos los sufrimientos, todo el goce, todo fue necesario.

Una mujer desnuda se introduce levemente en el mar. Cuando pasa a mi lado, me mira, sonríe, dice palabras, en un idioma desconocido, a las cuales yo contesto: Sí, muy frío, muy frío… Y ella se mete, como decía, levemente en el mar.

Siempre tuve que ver con mujeres extranjeras, hasta vos fuiste para mí una mujer extranjera. Yo había nacido en medio del asfalto, vos habías nacido en medio de la pampa. Yo era un hombre, vos eras una mujer, siempre fuimos extranjeros a todo.

Y, después, te lo digo, cuando te escribo, otros nombres me vienen a la mano, pero no los escribo, no tanto por lo que vos o yo podamos sentir o pensar de no ser únicos, que ya lo sabemos sino, precisamente, por lo que puedan sentir las no nombradas. Por eso sólo te nombro a vos y sé, al decirlo, que he caído en la trampa.

Tú podrías decir o declarar, según las circunstancias, que todas esas mentiras fueron publicadas sin tu autorización y cualquier otra podría decir que de no ser que algunas hubieran sufrido por no haber estado, ella hubiera estado.

Me sobrepongo de mi caída mirando al mar, hay algo infinito aunque no eterno en el mar.

Algo me sobrecoge en el mar y lo abandono.

JUEVES 30 DE OCTUBRE, 15:45 H.

Te escribo, ahora, desde la terraza de la suite. El sol es abrasador y, por otro lado, tengo que terminar la carta. Sólo me queda hoy, lo que falta de hoy, ya es la hora de comer, y mañana.

Dos días y una misión, terminar la carta pero, también hacer las maletas, volver a guardar los cien libros que traje para entretenerme, las 1.000 páginas que traje para corregir, las camisas, las corbatas, los calzoncillos sucios, también, de amor y terminar esta carta y despedirme del Casino.

Ahora espero la comida. ¿Quién me ha visto y quién me ve? Voy a almorzar una tortilla de espinacas y una ensalada de endivias. Brutal. Lo que me ha pasado a mí en la vida, mi amor, debe haber sido brutal. Terminé comiendo espinacas como Popeye, quiero ser fuerte, quiero ser fuerte pero, también, soy un viejo boludo. Cualquier pibe de 20 años lo podría decir.

He comido, he zanjado cuestiones fundamentales de mi cuerpo. Puedo ahora volver al sol, a la escritura, a esa tierra mansa que, siempre, fue el poema para mí. Esa infinita llanura sin principio, sin fin, sin esperanzas.

Esa mujer perfecta sin halagos, sin concesiones, siempre fue mía.

Y yo que, en definitiva, era un muchacho de barrio yo te amaba a vos, en ella, permanentemente. Y siempre éramos millones cuando hacíamos el amor. Hasta las estrellas envidiaban esa titilación incansable.

JUEVES 30 DE OCTUBRE, 18:15 H.

Un mes rascándome los huevos, escribiendo, buceando en lo insondable. Y se lo debo a todo el mundo y sólo me lo debo a mí. Eso es lo gracioso, lo divertido de la vida humana:

Todos, cada uno por separado somos el centro del universo. Por eso, amor mío, que la mayoría de las veces no hay universo.

Amor mío, amor mío, oye cómo ruge la mar contra los muros del torreón, oye amor mío, amor mío, el ruido benéfico del goce venidero, por ejemplo de este mismo viernes a la noche, al encontrarnos en el pasillo de la casa o en alguna mirada furtiva y nos daremos cuenta que ya no somos los mismos y que podríamos, de desearlo, vivir otras vidas, amar otras realidades.

Me gusta convencerte de nada pero sólo a vos.

Sé, lo he comprendido, cuando pueda convencerte a ti, millones de mujeres y algunos hombres querrán comprar lo que sólo existió para convencerte.

Si tú no me denuncias por injurias, hasta seremos ricos de tanto vender lo que no existió nunca y yo te llevaré por los grandes salones y te garcharé a cada momento con los ojos, con las palabras precisas, necesarias, te garcharé en cada momento en cada poema de amor, en cada ceremonia, en los funerales, en las pequeñas catástrofes de todos los días y, también, te follaré, en las tristes hebras desprendidas de los grandes dolores de la vida, aún con nosotros.

Bella de tierras extranjeras. Bella de mi país, me gustaría asegurarte que a los 80 años, también, leeremos, tranquilamente los periódicos y nos quejaremos, como cuando éramos jóvenes, del precio de las bebidas sin alcohol.

Y alguien nos mirará a los ojos y ahí viviremos un pasado, vibrante, que esté ocurriendo hoy.

Me despido, beso tus nalgas, cariñosamente, sin intención segunda, pero sí con intención tercera.

Hundo mis manos en las constelaciones del sur y arranco estas palabras con luces estelares que entrego, con serenidad, a la carne plena para sombrear tu sexo iluminado.

Me doy cuenta, me doy cuenta:
HABLÉ DE MÍ, HABLÉ DE MÍ TODO EL TIEMPO.

6 DE NOVIEMBRE DE 1997, MADRID

Querida, querida, llueve en Madrid y estoy muy triste, muy triste.

Ya murió Pablo, una vez más, ya murieron como todos los años los muertos por la lluvia, una vez más. Ya el periodismo como todos los días se cebó con los cuerpos despedazados, los rostros sangrantes, los corazones destrozados, una vez más.

Yo estoy aquí, vivo, me salvé de los recuerdos, me salvé de las inundaciones y me salvé del periodismo, pero estoy triste, muy triste. Sigo en pie, creo que todavía estoy vivo, en esa creencia te amo.

Cuando quiero escribir estrellas luminosas, me alejo de Madrid, me alejo de Buenos Aires, me coloco fuera de toda posibilidad y escribo, amor mío, sé que nos esperan grandes días, grandes noches de gloria. Por eso te escribo con intensidad, por eso descuelgo del universo este pedazo de gloria y fabrico, con todo eso, este pequeño ramillete de flores campesinas en plena ciudad, este dolor amado en el corazón de la noche.

3 DE DICIEMBRE DE 1997, MAR DEL PLATA
PLAYA PRIVADA DEL GRAN HOTEL PROVINCIAL,
DESAYUNANDO

Un correntino afincado en Mar del Plata hace 21 años, me dice que si no tengo en regla los papeles él no me podrá servir el desayuno (hasta dónde, me dije en voz baja, éstos son todavía después de 12 años resabios de la dictadura). Primero no le quise decir nada, después, con relativa calma pude decirle: Y por qué no averigua usted si yo, el gran poeta Miguel Menassa, merece o no merece un desayuno, en este día jueves inolvidable.

Y en lo del jueves, tengo que decir la verdad, me parezco a César Vallejo, pero después fue todo distinto.

Él se moría en París con aguacero. Yo me rasco los huevos en Mar del Plata y un sol tibio me acaricia la frente atravesando la ventana.

A él le dieron duro con un palo y duro. Yo me agarré la pija endurecida con las dos manos y ella me la chupó hasta desmayarse.

LAS 2001 NOCHES
UN LIBRO QUE LEERLO DUELE
Y
NO LEERLO ES IMPERDONABLE

3 DE DICIEMBRE, 12:00 H.

Estoy en la ventana frente al mar. Llueve, el frío llega hasta mi habitación (que de paso lo digo, no se parece en nada a mi suite de Málaga).

El mar en este lugar del mundo, es marrón y vive en permanente agitación. Los niños corren por la playa bajo la lluvia como si el sol iluminara brillante.

Hoy desayuné con ella y me di cuenta mientras desayunábamos que ella es una joven y hermosa mujer. Mientras yo me daba cuenta, ella se fue a trabajar. A ver libreros, periodistas, a comerse, literalmente la ciudad.

A mí me alcanza con ver la garúa detrás de la ventana de la habitación del hotel "solo y triste por las calles" y me bebo de un sorbo una naranja paraguaya y miro detrás de la ventana llover sobre los jóvenes.

Que el mar sea marrón le quita infinitud, inmensidad.

Cuando joven hace más de 30 años yo me lo imaginaba rubio al mar. Rubio y esbelto con unos ojos abrillantados de locura.

En el mar, cerca del mar, hablando del mar o jugando en el Casino de Mar del Plata, desde donde se oyen las olas del mar, escribí mis mejores versos, produje mis más grandes amores.

La garúa del tango se ha transformado en una lluvia torrencial a orillas del mar. Insoportable.

Enciendo una estufita eléctrica que el conserje me subió a la habitación cuando ayer noche, al borde del congelamiento, reclamé por la calefacción.

Hace dos días que tengo inflamada la panza. Hoy me siento mejor. El cuerpo sólo lo padezco.

Cuando joven creía tener algún dominio sobre mi cuerpo, nunca, hasta hoy, pude pensar, que el cuerpo ejercía sobre mí, un dominio total.

La lluvia torrencial ha espantado a los jóvenes que jugaban al fútbol desafiando la garúa.

Dos enamorados caminan torpemente por la arena mojada y ella en lugar de estar aquí, conmigo, en pelotas, tocando la flauta dulce, para entretenerme mientras escribo, está en la calle, corriendo de un lado para otro, debajo de la lluvia, sonriendo, tratando de vender alguna ilusión, un libro.

La vida me fue deparando infinitas sorpresas. De golpe aunque me molesta la diverti-culitis (divertirme con el culo), me da hambre y pido un lomito de pan árabe y agua para saciar mi sed de venganza.

Sigue lloviendo, eso me da rabia. Toda la historia dependía de que yo, después de 30 años, mojara mi cuerpo en el atlántico sur.

Me doy cuenta que en Mar del Plata, el mar, a lo lejos es verde como en todos los mares.

Ayer estuve "después de tanto tiempo" en el Casino de Mar del Plata. Jugué a todo, ruleta, punto y banca y pase inglés. Gané 300 pesos.

Argentina me produce sensaciones ambivalentes. Por momentos parece un país en crecimiento, otras veces me parece un imperio que cae irremediablemente.

Ni siquiera las olas del mar son las olas de mi juventud.

Me doy cuenta, viajaré sin rumbo por el mundo, buscando mi lugar, mi patria y nada encontraré.

5 DE DICIEMBRE, LA CALLE, EL MAR

Buenos Aires es tan difícil para mí, como lo fue España hace 21 años.

Así que nada de nuevos exilios. A Buenos Aires, seguiré viniendo como un potentado que le gusta gastarse su dinero en libros, en poesía, en esas cosas y que eligió Buenos Aires, para gastarse su dinero, porque en Buenos Aires su mamá bailaba el tango en Pompeya en la crisis del 30.

Nadie podrá dudar de mi honestidad. Todo el dinero que gano en Europa lo invierto en Buenos Aires, en poesía.

Creo que he inventado un negocio que no existía.

Vivir de la poesía, darle de comer a más de cien personas con la poesía. Si no soy un genio, poco le falta.

La primera multinacional de la poesía. A la larga viviremos todos de vender el alma que no existe.

Aquí estoy, aquí estoy en Mar del Plata, la costa Atlántica de América del Sur y te recuerdo.

El trato que me dan en Buenos Aires no es mejor, es sencillamente, más realista. Soy un escritor importante y así me tratan.

7 DE DICIEMBRE DE 1997, MAR DEL PLATA

En Buenos Aires, me pasa lo mismo que en Madrid, soy un extranjero y encima, parece que eso va con mi personalidad.

Extranjero: Extraño, también a sus cosas.

Ella me ama, me ama y me lo dice con furia contenida.

Yo ya no doy más, vivo todo el día fingiendo: Hago de cuenta que me arrastro y así, consigo que me dejen volar.

Extranjero, extranjero, me gritan por la calle, en el Casino me gritan extranjero, el playero, la mina de la esquina, todos me gritan extranjero. Yo, a veces, me agarro los huevos con las dos manos y otras veces, me pongo a llorar, directamente. Pero nunca digo nada. Algo de razón llevan. Algo de verdad miente en sus labios.

Voy a comer en Buenos Aires y pido un puré de patatas, después voy a Madrid y me peleo con el mozo (que se llama camarero) porque todavía no consiguió el dulce de leche para mis postres.

Soy un extranjero.

A los hombres les hablo de amor.

A las mujeres las mando a trabajar.

Pienso que los poetas deberían psicoanalizarse y que los psicoanalistas se tendrían que dejar atravesar por la poesía.

Y las dos cosas son sumamente graves:

Un poeta enfermo puede llegar a confundir su enfermedad con el mundo y querer transmitir eso, su enfermedad.

Un psicoanalista sin poesía puede empobrecer la vida de todo quien lo ame. Familiares, amigos, colegas, pacientes.

Ayer en la presentación en Mar del Plata me pasó como me pasaba en Madrid al principio. El público estaba formado por tres mujeres que me acompañaban, 4 ó 5 personas interesadas en algo, un loco, dos imbéciles y tres amantes epistolares de El Indio del Jarama.

He triunfado, he triunfado, sólo sobre mí mismo.

Hoy, por fin está el sol y, sin embargo, no me dan ganas de bajar al mar.

Las tres mujeres que me acompañan, están comprando el pasaje de vuelta. A mí me gustaría quedarme aquí, en esta ventana, frente al mar, esperando el verano, el sol abrasador, la lujuria de las olas atlánticas.

He jugado 40 boletas de telekino. Si gano 600.000 dólares podría quedarme a vivir en Buenos Aires aunque, en verdad, si yo fuera un señor de 57 años, no necesitaría ganar ningún dinero en el juego como para poder vivir, de mi trabajo, en Buenos Aires.

To be or not to be, Oh Hamlet inmutable, decía Claudio de Alas y luego creo que el boludo se pegó un tiro en la calavera.

Me gustaría que todo lo que me pasa sea una fanfarronería, producto de mi megalomanía, como siguen diciendo ciertas amantes de mi juventud, cuando hablan del tamaño de mi pija, pero me doy cuenta que mi escritura lo tocará todo.

Nada de lo que se ve, tiene el valor que se le da.

Treinta, cuarenta años más, como siempre bromeo en mis escritos, son los años que necesito para que los psicoanalistas cuiden la salud mental de los poetas y para que la poesía sea la encargada de transmitir el psicoanálisis.

JUEVES, 11 DE DICIEMBRE DE 1997
BUENOS AIRES

Estoy cansado, ayer llegué a sentir que no escribía muy bien que digamos y que bien podría dedicarme a otra cosa. Lo reconozco, estoy como deprimido, como todos los intelectuales de Buenos Aires y de Madrid, a mí las cosas se me pegan. Hago esfuerzos por sobresalir, mas no consigo nada.

Todo es paso a paso, lo entiendo, para mí, así que nada de querer ganar de la mañana a la noche ningún campeonato de nada, mis cosas se arrastran en el tiempo, son cosas de larga duración, no se pueden fabricar de un día para otro.

En cuanto al reconocimiento oficial, Clarín, en Buenos Aires, El País, en Madrid, el Ministerio de Salud, la Policía, otros diarios encumbrados, las esposas de Dios, los que se cayeron del Grupo Cero, quiero decirles a mis amigos, del momento, que todo eso a mí, particularmente, no me interesa aunque, a veces, lo tome y el Grupo Cero, directamente, no lo necesita, llegó hasta aquí, uno de los grupos psicoanalíticos con más obra publicada, sin ningún reconocimiento oficial.

No quiero vanagloriarme pero quiero recordarles a los amigos, que publicamos tres revistas de difusión gratuita: una en Buenos Aires, ONDA CERO, 15.000 ejemplares; una en Madrid, EXTENSIÓN UNIVERSITARIA, 15.000 ejemplares y una revista en BUENOS AIRES Y MADRID, LAS 2001 NOCHES, 45.000 ejemplares mensuales*.

---

* En la actualidad, 125.000 ejemplares para Extensión Universitaria y 125.001 ejemplares para Las 2001 Noches.

Estos son nuestros medios de difusión más importantes y no deberíamos sorprendernos que sean ellos los que quieran aparecer en nuestros medios para poder existir, algo, el siglo que viene.

Así que pido por favor, que no me rompan más las pelotas con eso del reconocimiento, que por otra parte es una cosa hegeliana y no freudiana.

Ahora podrán decir lo que quieran, diarios, amigos renegados, mujeres extraviadas haciendo cosas de hombres y, sobre todo, los que, pudiendo haber sido Grupo Cero, ahora son una pequeña caca sin discurso.

Ahora podrán decir lo que quieran, pero en apenas diez años, para poder hablar tendrán que tener publicadas más páginas y mejor escritas que las que nosotros tengamos publicadas.

Y si no pueden eso, irán a parar a la basura, se trate de quien se trate y eso pasará en apenas diez años.

26 DE ENERO DE 1998, MÁLAGA

He pensado estos días en el mar, que no competiré más con los grandes diarios ciudadanos, las cadenas de televisión oficiales o de las otras, los Estados modernos y, tampoco, competiré más con otras escuelas o con otros grupos que, en realidad, lo único que podrían hacer bien es comenzar a estudiar conmigo.

Yo, en realidad, compito y creo que ya he ganado, con mis amigos de juventud, con otros colegas similares, con algunos grupos de pensamiento, la mayoría de los grandes poetas y en lo que respecta al vivir, ya lo hago mejor que mis padres. Algo es algo.

Después, todavía, queda que quiero ser un escritor. Eso, todavía, no lo tengo solucionado del todo. Y eso no quiere decir que tengo que ser bueno o grandioso. Como soy, para ser un escritor tengo que ser como soy, amar lo que me tocó ser, vivir de eso.

Hacer escalas en mí mismo y decir: Yo reconozco este lugar, hablo las palabras de este sitio y cuando alguien me llame por mi nombre de pila, reconoceré con un saludo ese pasado y aceptaré haber vivido.

Haber sido todo tripa, todo corazón, pero el resto del tiempo, os aseguro, me la pasaré volando más allá de mis versos, para encontrar algo de paz (pan para todo el mundo), un poco de esperanza (algo de poesía con el pan) y cantaré y con mis iguales aceptaré cualquier tipo de competencia y aceptaré perder, cuantas veces sea necesario perder, para aprender algo de la vida, algo del goce.

Con los poderosos, con los verdaderos dueños del mundo, y no hará falta que los enumere, no competiré nunca más con ellos, es decir, no gastaré ningún dinero en que los poderosos me reconozcan.

A partir de ahora con los poderosos, sólo dos cosas serán posibles, someterme o, cuando sea grande, hacer la guerra.

El resto de las cosas, imposibles, educar, escribir, amar, andar por los aires, todo eso lo haré con las mujeres, con los hombres como yo, como tú, quiero decir, como mi mujer, como el frutero de la esquina o el camarero o la muchacha de la blusa azul, o la adolescente perversa que después de chupar con fruicción, durante quince minutos, la polla de un hombre maduro le acusa, en su fantasía, de acoso sexual.

28 DE ENERO DE 1998, MÁLAGA

Todavía, a pesar de todo lo que trabajo, sigo pensando que, algún día, podré vivir sin trabajar. Es decir para que se entienda, tengo ilusiones que, algún día, dinero y trabajo no tengan nada que ver, eso quiero decir cuando digo vivir sin trabajar. Trabajar en sentido estricto es maravilloso, producir con los instrumentos precisos, transformaciones en una materia prima determinada.

El alma, por ejemplo, el lenguaje.

Hacer del acero piedra y de la piedra cántaro.

He aprendido, y he gozado con ello, que lo que tengo es una pequeña suerte que me ayuda a no perderlo todo, a ganar un pedazo. Esa es mi suerte, el resto lo tendré que hacer trabajando.

El sol me llama la atención, me hace bien, me gustaría vivir en el sol, adentro del sol, iluminando el mundo, haciendo del mundo luz.

Me dejo estar como los sapos o los cerdos, pero me siento un hombre trabajando por su libertad.

Trabajo día y noche estudiando cuales son mis encadenamientos y esa es mi libertad. Saber a qué, a quién, debo mi vida, mi propia inteligencia.

Un suave viento me hace sentir que estamos en pleno invierno. Esto de escribir al sol me parece un invento, más que verdadero, real.

Siento haber retrasado mi gloria más de 30 años pensando que yo era un hombre de ciudad y resulta que, ahora, me doy cuenta que, yo, soy un hombre de mar.

La presencia del mar, del sol, reordena toda mi vida de manera diferente, cambia, a veces, de manera radical mi pensamiento sobre las cosas.

Cerca del mar, garchar, follar, es lo menos importante de mi vida, cerca del mar mi único amor es la poesía.

Tengo, francamente calor, esto es extraordinario. Estoy descalzo, en bañador y la parte superior de un pijama de tela invernal.

No tengo ninguna dimensión de mi grandeza como tampoco tengo ninguna dimensión de mi pequeñez. Y así voy por la vida, sin saber cuántos escalones subí y, tampoco, a qué abismos bajé.

El verdadero drama de mi vida es que nunca me pude dedicar plenamente, a la escritura, porque siempre tuve que mantener a alguien. Proveniente de capas populares de la población tuve siempre que trabajar el doble para conseguir la mitad.

Ahora, por fin, me doy cuenta que me hace bien vivir como un escritor.

Garchar y jugar se empequeñecen frente al mar, sin embargo, me conmovió sentir que podría festejar mi cumpleaños número 100 corriéndome en el mar alegremente, rodeado de mujeres extranjeras.

Cuando se nubla en el mar todo es peligroso. Pienso en esos grandes maremotos del alma que pueden ahogar el amor para siempre.

Darme cuenta que necesito el sol para vivir cambiará mi vida.

Desde hace unos días no me resulta difícil pensar ir en busca del sol. Algo así como una primavera permanente.

Si lo puedo hacer enseñaré a todo el mundo las virtudes del mar, del sol, de la escritura.

Ahora escribo detrás de la ventana. Estoy desnudo y escribo con una pluma de ganso fabricada en serie.

Veo lucir mis partes morenas al sol.

Es invierno. Es invierno, me repito a cada instante, pero el dinero hace relativo todo clima, toda soledad.

29 DE ENERO DE 1998, MÁLAGA

Querida Olga:

Moderación era, en definitiva, una manera de poder pensar en vivir 200 años.

El problema no era que los órganos o el alma no aguantaran. Lo que realmente pasaba era que no había dinero o nadie quería gastar su dinero en vivir 200 años.

Cuando haya dinero los órganos aguantarán y el alma será libre.

Mientras en el resto de España nieva, aquí está un poco nublado pero detrás de la ventana, escribiendo, mirando el mar y con una manta cubriéndome las piernas, todo parece verano, verano intenso, lujurioso verano. El mar está sereno y pequeñas barcas pescan pequeños peces, pero nada se mueve, todo es quietud en este mar, como en los crueles veranos de la pampa argentina.

Hago de cuenta, haber llegado a algún lugar y, por ahora, dejo de escribir.

30 DE ENERO DE 1998, MÁLAGA

Hoy he decidido, económicamente hablando, vivir 200 años y un temblor ha recorrido toda mi mirada futura.

Quería comunicarte que ese era mi deseo y esperaba que tú, también, desearas para la poesía lo mejor.

Ahorrar, no era ahorrar, era no gastar en fanfarronerías, en falsos reconocimientos. Yendo a lugares cada vez más caros, nos alejamos de nuestro pasado.

Los fantasmas raquíticos y sin documentos no pueden acceder a lugares cada vez más caros.

Con estas teorías me imagino que un rico puede terminar viviendo en una cloaca, sólo para alejarse de su pasado, de su familia. Qué barbaridad.

Le digo que me duele todo y, ella, plenamente, desnuda comienza a recitar en voz alta poemas de Vicente Aleixandre.

Me conmuevo, mientras me con-muevo no me duele nada. La miro de reojo por el espejo. Ella recita en voz alta... "Un paisaje de corzas suspendido" y detiene su respiración varios minutos hasta que yo la vuelvo a mirar de reojo por el espejo.

Ella lee cosas terribles, la misma muerte habla en voz alta por su voz. Aleixandre crece a medida que su voz se levanta más allá de los sonidos del mar.

Ella termina de leer y suspira, levemente, agitada. Se aclara la voz, pero siente latir en su propio sexo la carne alada del poema. Suspira y calla y lee en voz alta: "Así la muerte es flotar sobre un recuerdo. No vida..."

Déjame aquí, le dije, yo bajo en esta esquina.

Hoy basta de volar.

Volar eternamente es tan aburrido como no volar eternamente.

Las molestias han desaparecido, pero mantengo la sensación de no poder moverme. Ella lee en voz alta, tercamente, "no se evaden las almas..." y calla y suspira y yo me acuerdo haber bailado el tango con alegría, con mucho sentimiento, con todo el mundo metido en la muñeca.

Oh, bella del mar, bella de las tinieblas, nadie te escuchará y, sin embargo, sólo habrá futuro, en tu voz que nadie escuchará.

Varón, creo que fui un varón, espléndido, en tus brazos.

Cuando ninguno de nosotros sabía conseguirse su pan para comer, tú me mirabas a los ojos y yo arañaba la corteza de la tierra y extraía todo el pan necesario y, después me quedaba mirando la lejanía y en el temblor de una noche cualquiera amaba, sin límites, la vida que vivía.

UNA HORA DESPUÉS

Yo mismo soy el que no tolera todo lo que se transformó mi vida.

Yo mismo soy el que no tolera separarme de la gente para escribir, para pensar.

Yo mismo soy el que no tolera ganar y gastar tanto dinero en mantener mi propia inteligencia.

Yo mismo soy el que no tolera ser amado por tantas personas a la vez.

El psicoanálisis, también, habla para mí. Estoy contento.

Un pequeño sol ilumina todo el mar. Así me gustaría que fueran mis versos.

UNA HORA DESPUÉS

Se van encadenando soledades.

Trato de explicarte, tal vez, sin conseguirlo, que el amor cuenta poco para llegar a viejos.

Que hubo grandes amantes que murieron antes de conocer el amor y hubo garchadores crónicos que nada les importaba y vivieron más de cien años y hubo señoritas vírgenes que cumplieron 120 y mujeres grandotas con más de seis hijos pasaron la barrera de los cien. Hubo vírgenes que murieron violadas antes de los 25 años y madres de familia que después de dar de mamar a 15 hijos, murieron de un cáncer chupador en pleno pecho.

Decidimos, entonces que, una vez instalada la vejez, el amor es, también, un entretenimiento, pero el amor no sabe cómo llegar a la vejez.

Ayer disfruté con mi pequeña suerte y perdí con mis grandes ambiciones de tener una suerte mayor.

Gasté con la fantasía lo que había ganado con mi trabajo. El resultado, una paridad exasperante.

Me gustaría ser el niño bien de una condesa enamorada. Yo podría vivir sin remordimientos, sin culpa. Alejado de todos, estudiando la inclinación exacta de la caída del mundo occidental, bebiendo naranjas heladas y una voz, una ilusión, un amor, siempre habrá en mis ojos.

Dirán de mí: No se aburría ni consigo mismo. Toda realidad era apasionada. Todo misterio tenía su alegría.

Recién es enero, la gente apenas puede con la cuesta y yo ya estoy volando por las nubes.

Me empiezo a dar cuenta que tengo una vida que, a primera vista, no parece para nada una vida interesante. Algo así como un hombre trabajador que después de 40 años de trabajo consigue llegar al mar como lo ambicionaba a los 17 años.

Algo he podido y, sin embargo, no estoy conforme. Y esto no quiere decir que he trabajado más que lo que recibo sino que prometo, comprometo mi vida en ello, trabajar más fuerte, mejor encaminado para ver si esta vez merezco más.

No estoy conforme pero estoy contento, alegre de haber podido, esperanzado por haber comprendido que otros, también podrán.

Alcanzo cierto poder sobre mis cosas pero no sobre mí.

Cuando me hacen sufrir con alguna guerra, con la prepotencia armada de los poderosos, me siento al mismo tiempo de sufrir, un animal herido, un caballo marchito, una vaca sin leche.

Tal vez pueda arrancar de mi débil garganta un murmullo de paz.

Quitad vuestras sucias manos del tesoro. ¡Bestias, fuera de Babilonia!

75.000 EJEMPLARES POR MES NO SON NADA

Lo que necesito es un buen administrador. Alguien que haga las cuentas a mi favor.

Alguien que me pueda decir:

–Mire Don Menassa, 75.000 ejemplares para una revista mensual de poesía de difusión gratuita, son muy pocos ejemplares. Teniendo en cuenta que cualquier periodicucho que produzca 300.000 ejemplares diarios estaría produciendo 9.000.000 de ejemplares al mes; podemos decir, una riqueza ostentosa frente a nuestra miserable pobreza. Sólo 75.000 ejemplares por mes. Así no iremos a ninguna parte.

Y yo sé que molestar al personal, cuando el personal ha hecho sus esfuerzos, no es cosa buena.

Sin embargo, precisamente, ahora, donde más de 30 sujetos del inconsciente (por su condición de candidatos al psicoanálisis) han decidido apropiarse con su trabajo (tiempo, dinero) de una de las revistas más importantes de fin de siglo, "Las 2001 Noches", precisamente, ahora, es cuando arremeto como los vientos huracanados fuera de estación para decirle a esos valientes:

–No habéis comprado nada, casi nada.

La verdadera libertad para una revista de poesía acontece cuando se publican 500.000 ejemplares por mes y se distribuyen eficazmente.

Es por eso que en el mismo tiempo donde agradezco vuestra llegada al mundo de los vivos, os pido que comprendáis que aún no hemos realizado nada, casi nada.

75.000 ejemplares por mes de Las 2001 Noches, comparado con el poder de la prensa contra la cual tiene que luchar una revista de poesía, es como un pequeño eructo en una noche de tormentas eléctricas.

La verdad, no sé por qué cometo este error, pero tengo muchas ganas de decir:

– La idea de Las 2001 Noches, es una idea vigorosa, por lo tanto para que progrese como tal, idea vigorosa, es necesaria una infraestructura económica poderosa.

Cuando tendría que ser feliz, soy feliz; pero en el mismo momento de ser feliz, me doy cuenta que mi felicidad no es la felicidad del mundo.

Entonces, gozo mi felicidad, me digo: 75.000 ejemplares por mes, qué barbaridad, qué maravilla. Todo ocurre como soñé toda mi vida y veo a mis amigos contentos, felices, por lo que hemos conseguido y sin dejar de gozar por mi pequeña felicidad me pongo a trabajar en una felicidad más grande, para más gente y me imagino grandes cartelones por televisión que digan: HACIA LOS 500.000 EJEMPLARES DE LIBERTAD y miraré a mis amantes y todos sonreiremos y algún periodista despistado dirá entre amigos: "Ahí va Oscar Menassa, el magnate de la poesía" y hará alardes de haberme conocido cuando leíamos a viva voz nuestros poemas en los barrios populares de Madrid y nosotros, pobres criaturas embelesadas por la belleza, por los terremotos y las borrascas y el olor a pan quemado, en las mañanas. Criaturas, absolutamente atadas por el amor a las palabras.

Toda nuestra vida será esa grandeza, volando de un confín a otro confín de la lengua castellana.

Antes de comenzar el próximo siglo, algo habremos hecho con el amor y estará escrito.

Antes de comenzar el próximo siglo, algo habremos hecho con la escritura y estará todo publicado.

Lo único que sé es que el bien que tenía que hacer con el psicoanálisis ya lo he hecho o lo estoy haciendo con los candidatos que, actualmente, están en formación, en la Escuela de Psicoanálisis que dirijo.

Ahora me gustaría dedicarme a otra cosa.

Un violín imparable. La música de fondo de un corazón cayéndose en el lago del amor.

Atolondrado, eso quiero ser, un atolondrado, alguien que algunas cosas se lleva por delante y que otras cosas lo llevan por delante a él.

Un juguete roto, en las manos ansiosas por jugar.
Escaparate vacío, ancho como el mar.
Ya fui el médico que mi padre deseaba para mí, ya fui el
poeta que mi madre ambicionaba a su lado.
Ahora me gustaría dedicarme a otra cosa.

Humo de viento alcanzando el paroxismo de un amor.
Zarpa dolorida, herida dulce, alegre, caprichosa herida
recordándote.
Poeta sin aviso previo. Poeta de golpe.
Poeta que, rabiosamente habla del amor.
Poeta buen equilibrista, poeta volador.
Poeta del pueblo para todos los pueblos.
Poeta dulce, agazapado, tigre del alma.
Hambriento por los verbos desorbitados.
Poeta contestador automático. Poeta sin rumbo.
Poeta encantador de serpientes perfumadas.
Abridor de caminos. Poeta del tiempo.
Poeta humanizado, viento de luz,
yo fui toda la grandilocuencia del amor.
Ahora me gustaría dedicarme a otra cosa.

Yo fui su amante cruel. El tipo de dinero que mantenía su
locura.
Su dama de compañía a la hora del té,
la tierna amiga de las largas conversaciones
y fui su macho,
tantas veces fui su macho,
todo cuerpo, baba sin fin, bujía esperpéntica
y la amaba y hacíamos el amor como los animales.
Después, también, están esos días como muertos, como
sin nada.
Esos días donde a uno le dan ganas de comenzar todo
de nuevo.
La poesía de nuevo, el amor de nuevo, la vida misma
comenzar de nuevo. Aunque no se pueda o no se deba,
cambiar todo de lugar, de tiempo.
Yo también fui un amante infernal y cuando ella reía yo
me la comía a besos y cuando ella lloraba yo me la comía

a besos y nos poníamos a jugar y yo la chupaba con frenesí y ella gritaba: Diablo, diablo; somos esta locura extraterrestre, este amor sin fin y yo la chupaba y, después, me la comía y hablábamos de mi potencia viril mientras la chupaba y me la comía y ella se ponía triste, muy triste, cuando yo dejaba de escribir.

Amor amante amor, también conozco a quien por hacer el amor contrajo enfermedad y, también, conozco a los amantes crueles que dale que dale todo el día haciendo el amor y no enferman nunca.

Alto albaricoque inalcanzable por la lujuria del recuerdo, estoy como la vida misma está, desordenado.

Tengo que sostener dos grandes amores: Madrid, Buenos Aires, y el alma se me encoje en lugar de expandirse.

Loas, entonces, para el hombre que se levanta en mí y grita, otra vez, empecinado, LIBERTAD.

Ahora me gustaría dedicarme a otra cosa.

España se equivoca siempre en política internacional.

Cuando el asunto de la pesca nos cagaron, con el asunto del aceite nos están cagando, cuando todo el mundo estaba bueno con Cuba, hasta el Sumo Pontífice, Aznar se pelea con Castro y, encima, perdía y ahora para seguir mostrando que en política internacional no entendemos un carajo le dimos el premio Cervantes a Cabrera Infante y, después, y también, es política internacional, las primarias del PSOE, están amañadas. Los jefes de Partido quieren a Almunia, pero las bases pueden rebelarse.

En definitiva, de política internacional, los españoles entendemos poco.

Ahora me gustaría dedicarme a otra cosa.

Vender frutas o flores o nostalgias,

ser del tiempo la bruma, del verano la noche.

Yo también tengo cosas para contar y fui el que soporté toda la pregunta. ¿Dónde vivir, fuera de los brazos de mi madre? ¿dónde poder dibujar una boca fuera de sus labios?

Entrecortado espíritu del aire. Estoy aquí, poniendo en mis alforjas, leve esperanza.

Noctámbulo ruiseñor perdido. Estoy aquí, bordando en mis alforjas, los vientos huracanados del poema.

Soy el cantor le dije sonriente,
no tengo nada que perder, sólo mi canto.
Así que usted y yo, podemos besarnos,
pisar fuerte la tierra, volar más alto.

Ya sé que no es decente, amar la vida tanto,
que no es honesto, sincero, quererla para mí.
Que el infinito fuego debe ser apagado.
Que el inquietante deseo, debe morir.

Sin embargo, usted y yo podríamos
hundirnos levemente en el abismo
llenar todo el abismo con mi canto.

Aunque en verdad nadie lo quiera
vivir, vivir, podríamos mil años.
Yo sería el cantor y usted mi canto.

LUNES 27 DE JULIO DE 1998, ARGANDA DEL REY

El aire y el sol, el mar absoluto y el 35 como última bola de la noche han minado definitivamente mi corazón.

Eso de meterme en el mar y arrancarle a las olas esos sonidos abiertos, esos pensamientos abiertos, esas piernas abiertas de mi amada. Nunca tan abiertas como cuando las olas golpean, en tropel, su pequeño corazón enamorado de toda nuestra juventud, eso de meterme en el mar como un animalito ya lo había hecho, ya tenía una práctica en ello, pero que el Estado, el departamento de Hacienda, rubro Casinos, decidiera pagar mis escapadas al mar, eso nunca me había pasado.

¡Se dan cuenta! darle a un jugador, empedernido y empecinado, que juega toda la noche al 35, el 35 como última bola, se dan cuenta ¡qué locura! ¡qué bravura! ¡qué macho!

Aire, sol, el absoluto mar y el 35 como última bola, han hecho de mí el genio del mar.

Es por todo eso que esta mañana relajada de lunes, sentado en medio de mi pequeño jardín en un pequeño pueblo, Arganda del Rey, debajo de mi pequeño cedro del Líbano, que recuerda a mi padre de origen libanés, escribo estas líneas para agradecer al Estado Español y a todos los periodistas, también, a los de Babelia, que hayan pensado tanto en mí como para que el 35 fuera la última bola de la noche.

Si me lo hubieran contado no lo hubiera creído. Pero el haberlo vivido me da ciertas garantías que cosas así pueden ocurrirme, también, a mí. Es decir, que la poesía puede, aunque nadie lo quiera, tener su suerte.

Después, hablando con Don Artemidoro, él me dijo que en todos los casinos del mundo el 35 corona alguna de las tres últimas bolas de la noche, pero yo no lo sabía, es decir, que puede haber sido hasta una iluminación, algo fuera de lo común, algo que le ocurre a cierto tipo de seres.

En lo del 35, insistía Don Artemidoro, todos los Casinos del mundo y todos los trabajadores se han puesto de acuerdo.

Don Artemidoro, nunca daba una información sin material clínico, es decir, una información sin la historia de la información, era necedad en su pensamiento.

En el verano del 68, prosiguió don Artemidoro, junto con Marlem, visitamos 135 Casinos, esparcidos, podemos decir, por todo el mundo. Y lo del 35 no fallaba nunca, o Marlem o yo, o los dos a la vez, acertábamos el 35. Tal fue así que en el verano siguiente, y ya termino la reflexión, comíamos, hacíamos el amor y dormíamos y llegábamos al Casino a las 4 y media de la mañana, ganábamos y perdíamos como cualquiera pero en las tres últimas bolas, el 35 hacía que nuestras vidas fueran cada vez más cómodas, más lujosas, hasta llegamos a beber té de rosas escandinavas.

Dejamos de jugar porque ya no perdíamos y eso nos inquietó hasta tal punto que dejamos de jugar y yo me hice escritor y Marlem, creo que después fundó un asilo para poetas ricos, porque no pudo bajar el nivel de vida y ella sola no podía controlar todas las mesas para saber en cuál saldría el 35.

Yo pensé, por lo bajo, que a mí no me daría ninguna culpa ganar, porque el psicoanálisis me había curado de eso, así que puedo decir que por primera vez miré con cierto desprecio (menos valor) a Don Artemidoro, a él, que era un invencible, un inmortal, sin embargo, la neurosis le había vencido. A mí no me va a pasar eso y si usted no quiere que le pase lo que le pasó a Don Artemidoro, que no pudo seguir ganando porque le daba culpa, pida una entrevista psicoanalítica ya mismo a los teléfonos: Madrid 91 542 33 49 y Buenos Aires 328 06 14/0710. Y eso no sólo le pasa a los jugadores en el Casino, también, y a veces con mayor claridad, les pasa a los entrenadores de fútbol y a los jugadores y si no me creéis, podéis estudiar un poco a Clemente y a los muchachos que formaron parte de la Selección Española. El uno dice que la culpa la tienen los periodistas y los muchachos dicen que su mamá, por Clemente, siempre fue muy buena con ellos. Mi mamá, también fue muy buena conmigo pero, tampoco, servía para dirigir una selección de fútbol.

Mientras pequeñas hormigas ponen en cuestión la existencia de un rosal antiguo, dibujo entre las hojas del magnolio, los perfiles posibles de una vida a pleno sol. El cedro del Líbano, el ligustro japonés y las rosas chinas me traen recuerdos orientales, esa muchacha judía, en los bosques de Palermo, con aquellas tetas sobresalientes. Recuerdo haber besado esas tetas con la devoción de un niño hambriento.

Luego venía el atardecer y yo le recitaba mis versos y ella sentía, como en una especie de delirio de amor, que mis versos eran la tierra prometida y entreabría sus labios y entreabría sus piernas y se dejaba llevar por el olor de tierra cultivada y mi padre nos recordaba haber plantado el primer olivo en el sur de España y nos dejaba con la boca abierta llena de aceitunas negras bañadas por el amor.

Es por eso que desde esta mañana apacible en mi pequeño jardín, en un pequeño pueblo del Este de Madrid, recuerdo grandes olas oceánicas, arrebatadas mejillas, por el ardor del sol, muñecos de porcelana haciendo el amor hasta hacerse pedazos, y grandes porrones de barro, con agua fresca, para calmar la sed de los muertos queridos, para que se tranquilicen y puedan esperarnos sin ansiedad, sin prontitud. A la larga, todos estaremos muertos, pero no está en nuestro sencillo oficio de vividores natos (jugadores de todo, amantes de todo, locos por todo lo imposible) adelantar la muerte.

Así, que vengan los porrones llenos de agua fresca, para tranquilidad de nuestros muertos queridos, que han de saber que todos moriremos algún día, en su justo momento, como todos, pero nosotros, vividores de todo lo vivible, nos arrastraremos hasta el último momento, pidiendo un día más, un polvo más, un poema más aunque sea el último, algún amor y a la noche, en plena madrugada, para sellar mi pacto con la vida, el 35 coronando una de las tres últimas bolas de la noche.

Hasta la próxima y les recuerdo que una manera de pagar parte de su propio psicoanálisis, es hacerse Socio de Honor de la revista LAS 2001 NOCHES, por la miserable suma (hablando entre nosotros, Alcaldes y Ministros) de 40.000 pesetas para Europa o 200 dólares para América. Trátese de un psicoanalista jubilado, un poeta errante, un jugador culpable, un entrenador encaprichado, unos jugadores desolados, una mujer perdida o encontrada, un juez, un menor desorientado, un policía con complejo de libertad, un abogado sin ley, un eurodiputado con trastornos sexuales, un Presidente de Gobierno que nadie sabe de qué carajo se ríe, o un Ex-Presidente de Gobierno que nadie sabe porqué carajo llora, y usted señora y usted señor, sencillo carnicero enamorado de una vaca, o para usted, adolescente enternecido por los árboles, hongos desesperados que te comen el alma sin darte la pasión ambicionada, muchacha pobre doblegada a su marido o a su padre, que no puede escribir versos inmortales, y a usted señor Director, de lo que sea, para demostrarle que ese implicarse todo del psicoanálisis, tiene como resultado no implicarse. Vivir alegremente.

Amemos juntos esa libertad desenfrenada, pidamos una entrevista de pareja, amor mío, entremos en lo múltiple del amor para seguir viviendo este amor en soledad toda la vida, pequeñas familias reunidas alrededor de una conversación se transformaron en grandes familias, tuvieron educación, formaron parte de la civilización, escribieron libros, hicieron el amor como los privilegiados, hicieron de cuenta que elegían su hombre, su mujer, su lugar de residencia, llegaron a creer que tenían algo que ver con la educación de sus hijos. Fueron burgueses, crearon un mundo totalmente imaginario que nunca existió para nadie, ni siquiera para ellos.

El psicoanálisis puede curarnos de nuestra clase social.

Así que perdularios, intelectuales, pequeños burgueses, aristócratas creyentes en sí mismos, monjes deshabita-dos, escritores sin tema o con mucho tema y ningún esti-lo, mujer desesperada, enamorada o sola, poema o bala, mujer de los momentos más felices, mujer aquella noche de verano, envuelta entre las sedas serenas, donde la vida, borda sin cesar, sin interrupciones, los momentos especiales de la historia del hombre:
Un beso, una caricia, unas piernas al viento, un cañón, un barco, un trasero, un trébol infinito, otro beso, mis manos rozando el porvenir en tu cuerpo de violeta impe-rial, diosa de los colores más abiertos.
Mis manos apoyadas sin compasión en tu culo marinero (porque habíamos estado tantas veces en el mar), esas mañanas, esos amaneceres infinitos donde todo el mundo sumergido estaba en tus entrañas, esas mañanas (por haber estado tantas veces en el mar), en posesión de mi gran pija marinera, penetraba todos los misterios de la noche y en plena madrugada, a las cinco en punto, el 35, coronaba la última jugada de la noche.
Hasta la próxima.

LUNES, 13 ENERO 1999, MADRID, SOY EL SIGLO XX

Mi padre es una carne abierta al sol,
mi padre es el oriente.
Mi madre es la celeste y confortable,
máquina de occidente.
Nací de dos seres agónicos,
quiero decir, una combinación imposible.
Nací feroz, atómico, silvestre.
Fui desde el comienzo un incalculable error,
no tuve límites y exploté, también,
contra mi propia vida.
Y volando en pedazos rompí todo el amor.

Nos encontrábamos en un callejón sin salida aparente.
Borrachos hasta los huesos, no conseguíamos hilvanar
las palabras que nos arrancaran de esta pequeña locura
compañera.

El hombre comenzó a amar la soledad como antes
amaba la noche.

Cuando destrabo la soledad de su opuesto vulgar, estar
acompañado, la soledad cobra dimensiones universales
y, ahí, no es necesaria la falta de compañía para alcanzar
la soledad.

Como lugar, como mesa de operaciones cósmicas
donde la soledad se transforma en la edad del sol.

Desde un lugar que no se explica por ninguna falta,
hasta la posibilidad de un sol para cada edad o, mejor
dicho, todas las edades, también la mía, tendrán algún
sol. Aunque más no sea, el sol de la palabra soledad.

Tengo miedo de haber producido mis propios pensa-
mientos y que el resultado me aleje de otros pensamien-
tos, otros hombres.

Soy ese pájaro caído de mis versos,

algún pecado se habrá transformado en virtud,
alguna belleza forma parte del pasado.

Todo canto es inmedible. El tiempo puede surgir rápidamente, de cualquier conversación.

Pero yo estoy roto, no puedo escribir.

Intoxicado por el mundo que me rodea, ambiciono una vejez, creativa, sin pan y sin amor.

Hay dioses en la vida, tan hondos y todo el mundo lo sabe.

Después, también, hubo días que estábamos al alcance de todos y nadie nos quería tocar.

Ella está recién aconteciendo, yo ya escribo hace varios siglos. El encuentro, tal vez, no se concrete. Ella me ama, pero no le interesa encontrarse conmigo.

Lo diré todo, pero de tal manera que nadie lo podrá creer.

Hoy por hoy, tengo que sentirme casi un genio. Hago funcionar sin que muchos lo noten y con poco dinero un fenómeno de la poesía.

Ejemplo de vivir, dijo la poesía y comenzamos a vivir que ya nadie puede alcanzarnos.

Atentamos contra todo aquello que nos envejezca. Hacia la verdad sólo se debe abrir una pequeña puerta.

Hoy he visto los primeros efectos de mis escritos sobre la guerra. Se pierden o se olvidan o no se pueden terminar de leer.

Y además ponerme a defender la AUTODETERMINACIÓN DE LOS PUEBLOS, cuando ya nos han roto el culo a todos los pueblos.

¿Sin drogas, sin sexo y sin el poder sangriento de la guerra, dónde quiere usted señor Menassa llevar la sociedad? o de pronto, ¿usted cree en el alma?

Perdonen la palabra del POETA, él tampoco nos pertenece. Su voz es la tormenta de nuestra voz. Su canto es el estallido de nuestro canto. El cuerpo del POETA, yace a mil kilómetros de profundidad, es inalcanzable.

Señor Menassa; denos una ayudita: ¿la muerte existe para todos? ¿la vagina azul es la vagina de su madre? ¿la pija que usted nombra, es el loco y furioso sexo masculino que desgarra en el verano las pieles femeninas?

Sólo existe la muerte de los amigos, de los más íntimos, de los que forman parte de nuestro cuerpo, de aquellos que son una palabra importante en nuestras ceremonias.

La vagina azul es la negra vagina de tu madre, que te irrita durante la mañana y te somete por las noches.

Tu pobre pija, pájaro de papel, tu culo, ensangrentado por la duda.

Tu destino, mirar cómo nos escapamos de tus manos. El cielo es infinito.

Vuelo sobre la alondra
que comerá tu corazón.

Atleta de locuras infinitas hoy me detendré a llorar.

SÁBADO, 18 ENERO 1999, MADRID

Huyo de mí, huyo de mí y no hago otra cosa que encontrarme a mí. Ni huir ni buscarme. Mí no existe a menos que huya de él o lo busque.

Hombre, mujer, las dos primeras décadas del 2000 dependerá, sencillamente, de trabajar o no trabajar.

Si puedo llegar a acostumbrarme a cierto grado de soledad, podría llegar a crear cosas maravillosas. Pequeños poemas inmortales, más de mil.

Soy ese peregrino que lleva en sí mismo la luz y la sombra. Por eso tengo un ojo que casi no ve.

No sé cómo decirlo, pero me siento algo enfermo. No puedo salir de este desierto y estoy todo el tiempo esperando que alguien me ayude. Y cuando alguien se anima a llegar al centro del desierto donde yo espero, siempre, es para pedirme ayuda.

Alcoholes y amores, tampoco me sostienen del todo. Estoy siempre al borde de un dolor y, además empiezo a tener miedo que la gente lea lo que estoy escribiendo.

Tendría que haber venido con alguien a esta página.

MIÉRCOLES, 22 ENERO 1999, MADRID

Tengo que vibrar al unísono, me doy cuenta, pero no sé con qué.
Un poema, un solo poema para alejarme de mí:

Hoy soy feliz podéis fijaros en mis ojos.
No veréis ningún brillo sino más bien una sencilla calma.
He sido, literalmente, triturado por la vida y, sin embargo,
mirad mi perfil contra la luna, parece intocado.
Y mi alma, Oh, si viérais mi alma,
es un diamante negro de mil caras
un diamante tallado por un amor sin límites
corriente submarina de luz, deseo multitudes.

Siento estar tensando una cuerda que no existe.
Qué barbaridad. Qué sueño.
Ya estoy del otro lado mi amor,
nada en mí es bendición, sin embargo, ella insiste en seguir teniendo esperanzas conmigo.
Y yo, ya estoy perdido. No sé dónde volver. Las bombas sobre una ciudad indefensa, las bombas sobre las mujeres en el hogar, las bombas sobre los niños jugando distraídos, las bombas, mi amor, han desviado para siempre mi camino. No sé dónde volver, porque las bombas rompieron mi memoria.
¿Cómo debe ser un hombre? me pregunto y, sin embargo, ella mantiene con firmeza sus esperanzas.
Al verla tan así, tan loca, tan alegre y a pesar que las bombas me van dejando sin piernas, le digo volveré… volveré y me quedo sin aliento y las bombas me dejan sin respiración, volveré mi amor, volveré.
Mas no sé dónde comienzan los caminos de la vuelta. Mientras sigo esperando que se abra para mí alguna luz, he comenzado a amar la soledad.

Quiero escribir un verso, ahora, ahora que estoy rodeado de bestias, de bestias carnívoras.

Estoy atado de pies, de manos, de boca, de cerebro, no sé qué me pasó, fue un aire de locura.

Un no poder estar ni cerca de mí.

La muerte de un hijo es una calamidad. Una epidemia, una plaga, casi imposible de combatir.

La novela "erótica" que estoy escribiendo y, ahora, no puedo concluir, tiene que ver con que un hijo muerto no se puede elaborar.

Desde el padre, un hijo nunca llega a ser separado de su padre.

Cuando muere un hijo algo del padre muere para siempre.

Algo de mí ha muerto para siempre.
Me impresiona estar vivo,
con algo muerto de mí, en mí.

Fue fugaz la estrella que toqué al partir.
Fue fugaz su luz, fugaz su resplandor.
Duró sólo el instante de aquel beso.
Sólo el instante aquél de la caricia.

VIERNES, 17 DICIEMBRE DE 1999

Estoy un poco inquieto porque la llegada del 2000 no me afecta, a tal punto, que no consigo enterarme ¿por qué? tanto bullicio.

A mí me parece que se están gastando, en festejar el advenimiento del 2000, que ni siquiera quiere decir que estaremos en el próximo milenio, un dinero que haría falta para educar a la población mundial.

Además, todo lo que pasó en el siglo XX, no está para festejar sino más bien para ser estudiado.

¿Cómo fue posible lo que fue posible? Y ésta, por fin, es una pregunta epistemológica.

Sin embargo, pensándolo bien, hay algo que festejar en el 2000: Los cien años de la publicación del libro de SIGMUND FREUD "La interpretación de los sueños".

Como poeta, como ese poeta que se produce cada vez que coordino la grupalidad que publica "LAS 2001 NOCHES –Revista de Poesía, Aforismos, Frescores–", mensualmente, con una tirada de 125.001 ejemplares, que aspiran a ser 500.000, y las distribuye entre la población de España y Argentina, gratuitamente, se entiende, para la población, porque A NOSOTROS, LAS 2001 NOCHES, nos cuesta lo que vale.

Como poeta, digo, esta vez, no dejaré que los psicoanalistas se anticipen en rendir homenaje a "La Interpretación de los Sueños", obra en la cual se produce el concepto INCONSCIENTE.

Y un poeta debe agradecer, 100 años después, la publicación de ese libro de Sigmund Freud, porque, si bien no se sabe, aún, con exactitud, cuánto ha de mejorar o cambiar la medicina, o la educación, o el alma de los pobres si la tuvieran; lo que sí, ya se sabe, por eso un poeta tiene que agradecer, es que con el PSICOANÁLISIS, la Poesía haya modificado sus MANERAS, su modo de producirse, su concepción de la Humanidad.

La producción del INCONSCIENTE en la obra de Sigmund Freud "La Interpretación de los Sueños" publicada en 1900, había hecho nacer la POESÍA, de tal modo había nacido la Poesía que ningún siglo como el siglo XX, mostró, con claridad, a TODOS sus científicos llorando por no poder la Poesía.

La Poesía alcanzaba en este Siglo, como todos ambicionábamos hace milenios, el propio corazón de la humanidad.

El Psicoanálisis había arrancado, para siempre, una venda de los ojos de la humanidad.

La mujer, el hombre, antes del psicoanálisis, no sabían nada acerca de cómo se producían:

LA POESÍA
LA CIENCIA
EL AMOR

El pensamiento Inconsciente es, en el límite de su libertad, la POESÍA.

Un saber no sabido por el científico, lo lleva por el camino de la "Verdad".

Y gajos arrancados de la Especie, sin representación psíquica para el sujeto, producen el amor.

Agradezco, como poeta, al Psicoanálisis, que la mujer, que tanto amo, pueda después del Psicoanálisis preguntarse por su libertad, por su potencia creadora.

La Poesía es, precisamente, el alma de lo femenino. Es por eso que el psicoanálisis posibilita que os preguntéis: ¿por qué lo femenino (tiempo de la poesía, residencia de la función poética) antes del psicoanálisis era más fácil para un hombre que para una mujer? y ¿por qué, ahora, después de la Interpretación Psicoanalítica, la mujer puede, si lo deseara, apropiarse de lo que le pertenece desde siempre, la Poesía?

Y hoy día lo sabemos, el hombre ya ha agotado sus posibilidades de liberación y si, aún, había alguna posibilidad de liberación para la mujer, es el psicoanálisis el que lo posibilita.

En 1900, Freud puede diferenciar con precisión y destreza, una mujer histérica de una mujer.

Esta diferencia permitirá a la mujer, sin ser histérica, decir que NO.

Determinar, a partir de la negación, su propio pensamiento Inconsciente.

Después de la Interpretación psicoanalítica, la mujer podrá ser una mujer sin pertenecer a ningún hombre.

La mujer producía en ese grado de libertad un camino propio hacia el poder, hacia la creación en general.

Agradezco como poeta, a Freud, por haber denunciado la "Doble Moral" masculina, por todos aceptada, como el instrumento más poderoso de dominación del hombre sobre la mujer.

Lo que el hombre conseguía con un simple desdoblamiento de su moral, a la mujer le costaba la enfermedad o el castigo.

Lo que al hombre le daba hasta cierto prestigio social, cuando ocurría en ella, sólo le servía para ser denigrada, aún, un poco más.

Ella misma dudaba de su moralidad cuando deseaba.

Es el psicoanálisis que nos dice: Hombre y mujer, articulados de manera compleja con ser padre y madre, constituyen la sexualidad de todo hombre, de toda mujer.

Todo lo humano puede producirse en Ella.

Ella puede producir cualquier humanidad y, ahora, después del psicoanálisis, lo sabe.

De cualquier manera, me alegra haber llegado al año 2000. Lo ambicionaba desde joven, por eso llegué. Una ambición secreta, poderosa, femenina.

AÑO 2000, PRIMERO DE MAYO, DÍA INTERNACIONAL DEL TRABAJO

En uno de mis poemas de juventud llegué a decir: "No estoy maravillado por mi vida. Estoy arteramente sorprendido por mi vida" en ese momento (1976-1981), los pasajes más negros del exilio hacían verdadero mi decir. Lo que no pude saber en ese momento fue que, 25 años después, mi vida me volvería a sorprender arteramente.

Hace 25 años, un cuarto de siglo, ninguna felicidad esperaba a un hombre que lo había abandonado todo para seguir viviendo. Fue, entonces, cuando fui atravesado por una frase del inmenso poeta cubano, José Martí: "La felicidad sólo puede hallarse en el camino del trabajo" y volví a tener ilusiones de ser feliz, podía producir con mi trabajo un poco de felicidad para mi pequeña familia.

El sólo pensarlo me hacía feliz.

Lo que no sabía hace 25 años era que a los trabajadores se los puede explotar de una manera absoluta, se los puede estafar impunemente.

Y entonces fue cuando escribí:
"No fui feliz
porque ser feliz
es una argucia del sistema."

Después, también, me dije:
EN UNA SOCIEDAD JUSTA EL TRABAJO ES UN DON.

Hacer dinero no sirve para nada. Lo importante para la humanidad es generar trabajo y para cuanta más gente mejor.

Esa será toda nuestra riqueza, trabajar hasta casi morir y, aún, tendremos tiempo para el amor, la poesía, el dinero (si alguno lo deseara), la loca soledad de la vejez y esas conversaciones, absolutamente, cotidianas que entre nosotros, los poetas, han producido, también, el trabajo.

Antes de conversar no sabíamos que el trabajo puede modificar la naturaleza de las cosas. De todas las cosas.

Dios ¿acaso lo sería sin sus escritores?

Hasta Dios sería justo si alguien lo escribiera.

Y qué decir de las clases sociales que produjo el trabajo, cuando el mismo trabajo produjo el, aparente, desorden actual donde la gente, (intelectuales de todo tipo, locutores haciendo de maestros) ha llegado a pronunciar en voz alta y a publicar en grandes titulares: LAS CLASES SOCIALES NO EXISTEN.

Y, por último, porque sé que me aman, me pregunto:

¿Qué sería del Inconsciente sin el trabajo de Freud, sin nuestro trabajo?

Y la poesía, mentecatos, ¿qué sería de la poesía sin el trabajo de los poetas?

A ver ¿qué sería el mar, el inmenso mar, sin mi mirada?

Vengan a mí los libros, es el mundo que amo.

JUEVES 7 DE SEPTIEMBRE DE 2000

Estoy al borde de cumplir 60 años y no me gusta del todo lo descubierto.

En los próximos años, si quiero que haya próximos años para mí, tendré que cuidarme yo mismo.

El diario más importante en Madrid me ha borrado de la lista de poetas. Si bien es cierto que a mí no me gusta para nada estar en la lista de sus poetas. Yo prefiero la libertad, yo mismo elegiré quiénes serán mis acompañantes a la gloria.

El mismo diario y otros de diferentes ciudades me han borrado de la lista de psicoanalistas. Si bien es cierto que, con mi trabajo, encabezo una lista totalmente producida por los que formamos parte de la lista. Es decir, hemos fundado una Escuela de Psicoanálisis, ese tiempo donde se hace posible la formación de psicoanalistas.

Esos mismos diarios y algunas cadenas de televisión y las galerías de arte y sus revistas, me han borrado de la lista de pintores. Si bien es cierto que en los últimos diez años yo solito, sin que nadie hablara de mi pintura, he vendido 500 telas pintadas por mí. Es decir, que yo solito, junto con mis compañeros, he vendido más cuadros que todos los pintores de Madrid y Buenos Aires, juntos y si, por ahora, el centímetro cuadrado pintado por ellos todavía vale más que mis centímetros, quiero decir, cuesta más, esa tendencia será al revés dentro de cinco años.

Esos mismos, digamos, periodistas, son los que han callado la existencia y permanencia de mis dos joyas del Nilo:

LAS 2001 NOCHES, REVISTA DE POESÍA AFORISMOS FRESCORES.

EXTENSIÓN UNIVERSITARIA, REVISTA DE PSICO-ANÁLISIS.

Ambas con una tirada mensual de 125.000 ejemplares de difusión gratuita.

Haberme borrado a mí de varias listas puede entenderse como una tendencia política dentro del campo de la cultura, la medicina y el arte, contraria a mis trabajos en esos campos. Negar, ocultar o no dar a conocer con todos los detalles la existencia de LAS 2001 NOCHES y de EXTENSIÓN UNIVERSITARIA, son hechos que deben ser considerados por todos nosotros, poetas, obreros de la vida, señores y señoras de la limpieza, como un verdadero delito de los medios de difusión.

MIÉRCOLES, 4 DE OCTUBRE DE 2000

QUERIDA, QUERIDA

Un hombre muerto, también, es un hombre viviendo con miedo.

Por eso, precisamente, amor mío, declaro la libertad, y habito sin ningún decoro la ropa de los soldados muertos.

Esos soldados, hechos a la tierra sangre de tantos como uno, tierra de uno, esa tierra de los soldados muertos por la libertad. Patria de mí, tierra arrasada, cielo vuelto carmín, carmín de muerte. De baile, carmín de baile, pero hasta morir.

Y ella se dejaba arrastrar todo lo que podía y yo la besaba y ella besaba los labios muertos de los soldados en la guerra y uno que otro muerto se relajaba y moría en paz y alguno se abrazaba con furia a tus labios y tu sangre fresca, margarita que nunca deja de caer, rociaba el porvenir de próximos encuentros y la bestia, sin estar saciada ni agradecida, dejaba de latir, moría, por ahora, para poder vivir en el futuro.

La fui separando del resto y contra la pared del fondo, donde la enredadera creía que trepaba, le tapé con una mano la boca para que no gritara de sorpresa y le dije, tranquilamente, que la amaba y ella se dejó caer, boca de nadie, muerta de la guerra, en un verso de dolor y atravesó mi miedo para siempre.

JUEVES, 5 DE OCTUBRE DE 2000

QUERIDA:

Todos lo sabemos. Alguien contestará. Alguien morirá antes de contestar. Todos lo sabemos. Hay una manera de llegar y millones de maneras para no llegar. Todos lo sabemos, de golpe viene el sol y lo quema todo con su fuego, lo deja todo seco, perdido. Y cuando el sol se aleja, todo se pudre sin su amor, el llanto nos ahoga.

La posibilidad de estar y de no estar al mismo tiempo son posibilidades únicas de lo humano (quiero decir psíquico). Ya que la ciencia no se equivoca donde determina que el campo físico hace imposible el acontecimiento de dos fenómenos simultáneos. Casi en los opuestos la consistencia del campo psíquico se fundamenta en el acontecimiento permanente de fenómenos simultáneos. Reprimir esta capacidad vital de lo psíquico, produce enfermedad.

Una interpretación psicoanalítica sería, entonces, ese acontecimiento (palabra, acto, producción de lo nuevo) que consigue establecer no tanto lo que me determina como pasado sino, precisamente, aquello que me determina como futuro.

El candidato deberá atravesar el camino que va desde la determinación familiar (el pasado) a la determinación desde el futuro fin de análisis, que nunca conseguirá, ya que es, él mismo, con su condición de psicoanalista en formación, el que genera la repetición de lo diferente.

El inconsciente se produce por interpretación, eso para un psicoanalista en formación, quiere decir que cuando ambiciona terminar con su psicoanálisis, ambiciona terminar con el concepto de pensamiento inconsciente. El psicoanálisis se ha cerrado para él, como camino posible.

No que no pueda seguir intentándolo. Por ahora no podrá ejercer como psicoanalista.

VIERNES, 6 DE OCTUBRE DE 2000

QUERIDA:

Comenzar una nueva vida todos los días, es algo que pueden casi todas las personas, casi todos los días. Lo que no puede casi nadie es seguir viviendo la nueva vida cuando pasan las primeras 24 horas. Por eso, me digo, es tan difícil, a veces, algún compañero de viaje, un caminante amante del camino que nos toca recorrer.

Dicen los luchadores que grandes soledades abren grandes caminos pero que solos nunca podremos algo grande.

¿Quién velará mi sueño en los picos más altos de los Andes?

Y nada me responde.

Es por eso que no quiero llegar a ninguna cumbre a menos que alguien, alguno, quisiera llegar conmigo. Ni sexo, ni dinero pueden más que las altas cumbres, pero a las altas cumbres sólo se puede llegar acompañado. Después, también, permanecer, cuesta lo suyo: un amor, dos amores, miles de amores, para no caer.

La tarde es noche en mí, en pleno invierno, pero estoy contento.

Ya han pasado dos semanas de haber comenzado a vivir una nueva vida y todavía, estoy en ello. Estoy contento.

Gracias por existir.

SÁBADO, 7 DE OCTUBRE DE 2000

QUERIDA:

Haber inaugurado con las tres cartas anteriores mi espacio en Internet, me ha llenado de un nuevo entusiasmo, sentir que sentado cómodamente en un sillón, especial para estar sentado, pueda poner mi palabra al alcance de infinitas escuchas.

Algo así como un nuevo amor. No me importan mucho los resultados, sino la práctica del nuevo amor.

Poder decir algún día: Una vez, yo tuve un nuevo amor y me dejé llevar por unos pobres besos hasta la muerte, casi hasta la locura.

Y todo fue el color de mis apetencias. Y respiraba para que existiera el aire y abría mis ojos para que el sol no dejara de brillar.

Y tocaba con frenesí la guitarra de mis amores muertos y era un quejido insostenible, mis propios versos se dejaban caer como flores marchitas, abrumados por el peso del amor. Era un borde donde había un dolor a punto de romperse, un dolor perdiéndose, el nacimiento de una nueva vida, un dolor muerto.

DOMINGO, 8 DE OCTUBRE DE 2000

QUERIDA:

Hoy estoy en mi casa haciendo el domingo. Después del grupo de poesía de la mañana, ahora las 4 y 30 de la tarde esperando la verdadera, hora de la verdad. Los partidos del domingo.

Alguien ganará, alguién perderá. Y traeré la luz y me daré cuenta que no era para tanto. Un verso, también, puede traer la luz.

A veces me siento, con algunas personas, una persona antigua. Me da un poco de risa, pero me doy cuenta que los años, también, pasan para mí.

Los versos no aman, ni odian, vamos Menassa, puedes escribir un verso.

No sé lo que me pasa, estoy encerrado en otros. A veces, la libertad acontece cuando me dejo caer en mí.

El poema lo voy a dejar para más adelante, hoy sólo puedo estas frases quietas, alejadas de todo porvenir. La idea de escribir una carta todos los días quedó rota, parece ser con los domingos pero, sin embargo, algo tendría que poder…

Por ejemplo: Tened cuidado con algunas frases de Menassa.

Cuando nos dice "el animal grande no ataca, sólo se defiende", está hablando, ciertamente de animales y de hombres de gran riqueza, ya que a nosotros, los trabajadores, los poetas, siempre nos atacaron animales mucho más grandes que nosotros y mucho antes que nosotros pensáramos en atacarlos.

La vida es leve para quien ya no depende de sí mismo.

No sé lo que me pasa hoy con la existencia de los hombres.

LUNES, 9 DE OCTUBRE DE 2000

QUERIDA:

Ayer, domingo, no pude casi nada, tres o cuatro letras para sentir que algo estaba construyendo, que algo en mí, vivía, todavía.

Hoy sobro en el mundo. La gente me ve y pasa de largo, nadie quiere comenzar la conversación que, claramente, tendrán que tener con el Director de la Escuela.

Pienso que el silencio de los pueblos es el comienzo de su propia destrucción.

En Madrid están todos muy ocupados en tratar de descifrar cómo fue que se fundó con ellos. En Buenos Aires, están todos muy ocupados en convencerse que podrán solos, sin ellos.

Nadie concibe el futuro como determinando nuestro presente.

Nadie se anima a vivir como si viviéramos 200 años, aunque todo termine mañana.

Si te beso pensando que moriré mañana, ya soy un hombre débil, un hombre a quien no le importa un carajo que te guste o no te guste el beso. Mal beso he de darte.

Si te beso abrazado al sol del mañana, habrá en la historia de los amores, un beso, un fuego, algo para contar.

Ese espejismo sordo que me llama desde la música, lo reconozco, es el amor que vuelve, la terquedad de lo vivido queriendo ser canción.

Una interpretación psicoanalítica debería sorprendernos a todos.

EL OTRO no es nadie.

MIGUEL OSCAR MENASSA
A LA BÚSQUEDA DEL NOBEL
Publicaciones:

1961 Poesía Junta y Pequeña Historia.

1963 La Ciudad de Cansa.

1966 22 Poemas y la Máquina Electrónica o Cómo Desesperar a los Ejecutivos.

1970 Los Otros Tiempos.

1971 Primer Manifiesto del Grupo Cero.

1975 Yo Pecador.

1976 Psicología Animal y Arte.

1977 Salto Mortal.

1978 Canto a Nosotros Mismos. También somos América.

1978 Perversión y la Muerte de la Palabra o Psicoanálisis del Amor.

1978 Primer Manifiesto Internacional (Entre tantas, una manera de comenzar).

1979 Grupo Cero, ese Imposible y Psicoanálisis del Líder.

1983 El Oficio de Morir. Diario de un Psicoanalista.

1984 El Amor Existe y la Libertad.

1987 Un Argentino en España.

1987 Freud y Lacan –Hablados– 1.

1987 Psicoanálisis de la Sexualidad.

1987 Poemas y Cartas a mi Amante Loca Joven Poeta Psicoanalista.

1988 El Verdadero Viaje, Le Veritable Voyage.

1989 No ve la Rosa.

1991 La Patria del Poeta.

1991 La Murga del Solo. La Guerra del Golfo.

1993 Medicina Psicosomática.

1993 Yo Pecador, 3ª edición.

1994 L'Amour Existe et la Liberté (2ª edición, bilingüe en castellano y francés).

1994 Psicoanálisis del Amor (2ª edición).

1995 Chant à nous-mêmes (2ª edición, bilingüe en castellano y francés).

1995 Poesía y Psicoanálisis 1971-1991. 20 Años de Historia del Grupo Cero.

1995 Siete Conferencias de Psicoanálisis en La Habana. Cuba.

1995 Amores perdidos.

1997 Las 2001 Noches. Poesía, Aforismos, Frescores.

1998 Ciencia y Frescores en Psicoanálisis.

1998 Posición del Inconsciente.

1999 Charlas-Coloquio con Miguel Oscar Menassa en Buenos Aires.

1999 El Sexo del Amor.

2000 Conferencias Inaugurales. Temporada 1999.

2000 La Poesía y Yo.

2000 El Indio del Jarama. Editoriales 1992/97.

2000 Freud y Lacan –Hablados– 2.

2000 Poeta Condenado.

En Imprenta:

Monólogo entre la Vaca y el Moribundo

La Pija Mortal

Freud y Lacan –Hablados– 3

Poesía 2001

Esta obra se terminó de realizar
por COMFOT, S. L.
a mediados de noviembre
del año 2000.

EDITORIAL GRUPO CERO

Princesa, 17 - 3º Izda. 28008 Madrid. España. Teléfono 91 542 33 49

Carlos Pellegrini, 833 - 4º «C», 1ᵉʳ Cuerpo.
1009 Buenos Aires, Argentina. Teléfono 14 328 06 14

Digital: grupocero@grupocero.org

GANG WARFARE IN LONDON
RAISED TO KILL

MIKE RYAN

Published by
The

Human Dynamics Group
71-75 Shelton Street
London
WC2H 9JQ

Cover design and layout by
www.chandlerbookdesign.com

CONTENTS

PREFACE

GANG WARFARE IN LONDON is now claiming more lives than terrorist attacks, and yet we spend billions of pounds every year on counter-terrorism while only spending millions on trying to prevent knife killings that are at an epidemic level in our society? We really have not woken up to this grim reality, and it is only by gaining a better understanding of what is really going on in some young people's minds that we can tackle this problem together before the issues of violence and criminality increase even further.

Raised to Kill will shock your preconceived views on gang members and their way of life, as the narrative of them all being raised in broken homes and in deprived poor areas is not always the case as some come from middle class families living in very affluent parts of London. And if you're a parent thinking that this could never happen to your child. Think again, as one gang member that I know has a parent that is a police officer, while another has a father that is a senior executive in a bank. Raised to Kill will give you a reality check on what is really going on in the urban jungles of London.

BACKGROUND

WRITING A BOOK ABOUT gang warfare was never in my game plan, or even on my bucket list. Why? Because I always felt that a subject as important as this should be left to either a subject matter expert or a professional that specialises in this area. But there is a problem. The subject matter experts are not writers, and the writers that are out there are as I have learned are not interested or willing to touch this sensitive subject. Why? It is in view of the fact that they perceive it to be toxic, controversial, difficult and of course dangerous. So why me? Well to find the answer to that one you have to go back to 2005, when I wrote a book called the Hurt Locker - which covered the war in Afghanistan. It became a best seller, simply because I was the first author in the UK to write about this conflict, and also because the British public wanted to know what was really going on in this distant warzone.

As surprising as this sounds, at that particular time there was virtually no public information available to our soldiers that gave them any idea of what enemy they were about to face, or even what had become of all those that had fought there in the proceeding centuries prior to their arrival. The Hurt Locker helped answer their questions and was procured by NATO as a means of addressing this glaring knowledge gap.

Spurred on by the success and usefulness of this book, I wanted to help our armed forces and their families even further, so I set about writing another book that answered all the new questions, concerns and operational problems that had arisen since the previous book. The new book was titled "The Devil's Playground as it seemed to sum up everything that was going on in Afghanistan during that traumatic period. This book was very different in its concept as it looked at the war from almost every dimensional aspect.

In terms of content I covered how strategies were devised and what purpose they served, I analysed the dramatic changes that we were witnessing in the field of medicine, and how many lives it was saving on the battlefield. I also delved into the effects of modern warfare on the soldiers, their families, and the innocent civilians that had become collateral damage in a war that was not of their making. In addition, I also looked at our enemies the Taliban and Al-Qaeda, and what had motivated them to turn against us in what appeared to be a pointless and costly venture. Little did I know at the time, I was not just writing about Afghanistan, I was also subconsciously setting out the template for a book that would eventually deal with issues that are very similar to those that we are now facing in London through gang violence. Essentially, "The Devils Playground" had served as a literary bridge to "Raised too Kill."

You now know the concept and methodology for the book, so here's the reason and justification for writing it. Fast forward the ending of my involvement with Afghanistan, and I arrive in a new world, that of gang intervention. Using my military leadership and management skills I am tasked to run an Outreach programme that involves the military, police, army cadets and various youth support teams that have been put together in a multi-agency team that has the mission of reducing or eliminating crime carried out by young vulnerable teenagers.

The programme is successful and eventually leads to me working with other organisations that are right at the front line in terms of their involvement with gangs within London. At this time I still had no intention of writing a book about this subject, but two profound events changed my mind. The first occurred in a school where I regularly gave talks to students, teachers and their parents about the dangers that gangs present to them. Following my talk, I had numerous people ask me for leaflets on the subject, but there were none, so the head of the school suggested that I should write a book as she had been really impressed with my knowledge and insight.

She also mentioned that the students and the adults that were present had been fascinated with what I had to say, and were hungry to learn more. I thanked her for the kind compliments, but my mind still had not been changed. Roll on a few more years of working and operating in numerous schools, provisions and intervention units, it would be a chance meeting between me and a mother whose son had been the victim of a stabbing that got to me. That encounter changed everything in my world.

This transformation took place during a conference that was being held in a Kensington hotel – its purpose being to highlight all the great work that was being undertaken by the London women's forum. When I was invited to this event I must confess that I was somewhat bemused as to why my presence had been requested. The coordinator of the event was now known to me as her son was the victim of the stabbing. He was also an army cadet that I had regularly trained and mentored, but until that evening I was not aware of what he had suffered prior to joining up.

His mother started her presentation by pointing to me and stating "that man saved my sons life, and that's why he is here tonight." After this powerful introduction she then described in great detail how her son had been stabbed and emotionally wrecked by this harrowing life changing event. She also mentioned how her son had become withdrawn and left lacking in self-confidence, as a consequence of the injuries he had suffered. She then went on to say how a friend of her family had a son that had been in a gang, and that he had joined the army cadets as a means of making a fresh start.

Seeing how he had been transformed she encouraged her son to do the same, and within months he had regained his confidence and was back to his normal happy self. It was in this moment where I had something of an epiphany, in which I finally realised that my work was having a positive impact upon young people, and that I needed to do something of greater magnitude to help even more of our young generation - who were clearly suffering in a city that had a seemingly endless black cloud of trauma and potential violence hovering over its skyline.

There would now be a book on gang culture in London, and I would be its author.

6

INTRODUCTION

IF YOU HAVE BOUGHT Raised to Kill with the expectation of reading pages full of gratuitous violence - then you are going to be disappointed - as I did not write this book to promote and encourage violence. My aim is only to set out the modus operandi and elements that make up gang culture, and why some young people feel the need to belong to one.

Raised to kill is a book that is needed by our young people and their peers, as there is currently very little detailed and informed information available on the subject of gangs - aside from that of occasional newspaper articles.

My research in schools, colleges and universities has convinced me that there is a substantial need for a better understanding of gang warfare in London, as society is becomingly increasingly aware that gangs are now killing more people than terrorists.

This fact has not gone unnoticed in the general community, and indeed many are arguing the point that gang members should be treated in the same manner as terrorists, on account of the considerable distress that they are causing in some communities. "Raised to kill" does examine this issue in some detail as you will see in due course, and it raises other concerns and problems that are not well known or even understood at this present time.

"Raised to Kill" is based upon my eight years of operational experience working with some of the most violent and dangerous individuals that live and operate in the numerous diverse boroughs that make up the city of London. Within this book you will read: accounts of gang related incidents, interviews with gang members, their families and victims, along with a detailed analysis of their reasons for becoming involved in groups of like-minded individuals.

This book will also look at the devastating damage that gangs are inflicting on our society, and how our police, legal system and medical services are responding to the turmoil that they cause in the wake of their criminal activities. In addition to examining the effects of gang warfare, "Raised to Kill" will also put forward viable solutions and strategies that could be introduced and employed in our schools, home communities and general society as a possible means of reducing gang activity, violence and criminality.

TALKING STREET

BEFORE YOU START READING the rest of this book, it's probably going to be helpful if you have an understanding of the alien language that gangs use in everyday life. If you already know street – great, you can skip this chapter and move onto the next one. However if like most people you have no idea what they are saying, here is a quick explanation of street and its origins.

Street, or gang slang is now part of our culture - whether we like it or not - and now forms a method of communication that is almost a language in its own right on account of its extensive vocabulary and unique grammatical structure. Although Street in London is generally thought of as being synonymous with gang culture, it is also widely used by young people who have no gang affiliations, or indeed any involvement in criminal activities. It is important for this distinction to be understood and accepted, as slang usage is often associated with criminality – the two often being seen, as one and the same. This of course is not the case, and such prejudiced views only expand the chasm that often exists between the young and the old.

Why street slang has become widely used and adopted by the young, should not really come as any big surprize, as our country has always had its language influenced by others. Have we actually forgotten where our language comes from - and who has influenced it over the Centuries? The English language that we use in our daily communication is predominately made up of French, German, Greek and Latin, but is always changing and adapting as new words come into our daily vocabulary, while others slip away to the pages of history.

Our once great empire that ruled over the world is also responsible for the multitude of world languages that now influence our language and our culture. Today as a multicultural race we are constantly adapting to outside and internal influences at a rate of change that is often hard to keep up with, and that perpetual transitional flux also applies to street slang.

The exact roots of modern London street slang are difficult to pinpoint, but we do know that it owes some of its existence to "Cockney Rhyming slang" which originated in the east end of London in the 1840s. Originally used by market traders and street hawkers as a means of deceiving the great and the good – with humorous lines like "he's got dodgy minces" which rhymes with mince pies, and means eyes. You kind of get the picture that if you are creative, there is no end of words that can be quickly used should the need arise.

For example: during World War 2, it was quite common for British soldiers to use rhyming slang as a means of confusing their enemies.

Today, Street slang is harder to understand and decipher, and is often made complicated so that it creates a feeling of belonging amongst those who speak and understand it. Words that we frequently use in everyday life, can when adopted for street slang use totally change in their conventional recognised meaning. For example: the word bare as an adjective would normally mean uncovered or basic and simple. Whereas in street slang, bare means a lot of - and could be used to describe a situation. In this context a young person might say, "there were bare police in my yard last night." A sentence that's new meaning would not be understood by an average citizen walking the streets of London.

So where does this street slang come from? It is my belief that it is an amalgamation of the many races and cultures that have had an influence upon the melting pot that feeds into London's dynamic linguistic scene. Indian, Bangladeshi and West Indian influencers along with those imported from the Hip-Hop and Ragga genres have certainly helped create a hybrid patois that has been universally adopted by our youth in London.

There are wordsmiths that are particularly creative and articulate in how they use this new cultural street slang within their music and literary works. However I should also mention that there is a growing collective of vocal opponents that feel that our English language is being devalued and that it is creating a divide between the educated and uneducated. It has been argued that street slang breeds laziness in daily language usage and can often hinder job prospects for those who over use it.

The question that I guess that everyone is asking is: does street slang expand the minds of the young, and make them more articulate or does it restrict them? I will let you be the decider of that one.

In the meantime, here are some of the most commonly used slang words along with their new meanings:

Babylon – police/authority
Bag – 100
Bang – punch
Bait – suspicious
Banger – positive qualities
Banging – fantastic
Bare – a lot
Bate – obvious
Blag - steal
Blud – friend
Booky – suspicious
Bud - weed
Buff – good looking
Butters – ugly
Chef – stab
Creps – sneakers/trainers
Driller - killer
Dutty – nasty
Endz – own area
Fam – friends
Feds – police
Finesse – steal
Fit – attractive
Five O – police
G Check - Gang verification check
G – Friend
Gallis – womaniser
Gased – talking nonsense
Gem – fool
Ghost – frequently absent
Greezy – bad
Heli – helicopter
Innit – "isn't it"
Junge – whore

Liccle – small
Long – a nuisance
Mandem – group of males
Marga – very skinny
Moist – lack of masculinity
Murk – attack
Nang – good
Nine – pistol
Opps – 0pponents/enemy
Paigon – fake/liar
Peak – something eventful
Ped - scooter
Peng – good looking
Rack – a thousand
Scope – spy
Scorp – small machine gun
Shank – stab
Shower – cool
Skadoosh – goodbye
Sket – loose woman
Skins – rolling paper
Skint – no money
Slipping – caught off guard
Strap – gun
Swag – crap
Tazzed – to get tasered
Tekkers – technique
Undies – undercover police
Wasp – police helicopter
Wagwan – "what's going on"
Wallad – idiot
Wavey – drunk or high
Whip – car
Yard – home
Zoot – joint/spliff

POLICE CODES

GANGS ARE NOT THE only ones to use slang or unfamiliar terms – as the police have a fair selection of their own codes and acronyms that they use to describe you. Here are some examples:

IC 1 - White
IC 2 - Mediterranean/Euro/Hispanic
IC 3 - Black Afro-Caribbean
IC4 - Asian Indian/Pakistani
IC5 - Chinese
IC6 - Arab
IC7 - Alien/Unknown

F - Features
A - Age
C - Characteristics
E - Ethnicity

ARV – Armed Response Vehicle
ASBO – Anti-Social Behaviour Order

BCU – Basic Command Unit
CHIS – Covert Human Intelligence Source
CRO – Criminal Records Office
D & D – Drunk and Disorderly
FLO – Family Liaison Officer
MOE – Method of Entry
MISPER – Missing Person
NFA – No Further Action
OIC – Officer in Charge
REFS – Refreshments/Food
PNC – Police National Computer
POLAC – Police Accident
POLSA – Police Search Advisor
PS – Personal Radio
PSU – Police order Support Unit
RTC – Road Traffic Collision
RUI – Released Under Investigation
SOCA – Serious and Organised Crime
SOCO – Scene of Crime Officer
SIO – Senior Investigating Officer
TWOC – Taking Without Owner's Consent

A TALE OF TWO CITIES

FORGIVE ME FOR FINESSING this title from one of Charles Dickens classic books – but it did seem rather appropriate to describe the London that I grew up in as a teenager, compared to that my son and daughters now have to grow up in.

When I was in my teens growing up in west London, believe it or not there were absolutely no stabbings or shootings in schools – it just did not happen. Ever!!!

The absolute worst thing that could happen to you on the streets, would be a punch up – and even that was rare. For me, getting to and from school was by train, and during my entire time at school I never saw a single incident of violence on a train. Yes I would share my journey with teenagers from other schools, but they never bothered me, so I never bothered them. It was the perfect status quo.

My catholic secondary school was Arch Bishop Myers, later to be renamed St Marks, and by any standard it was a pretty decent school. We even had a student who would later become a famous rock star - Declan McManus or

Elvis Costello as he is known today. If I contrast my later life where I would give talks and lectures on history and modern warfare to pupils in major public schools such as Harrow and Hurstpierpoint, my life and theirs could not have been more different.

Within these prestigious schools there were corridors adorned with giant paintings depicting former pupils who had become admirals and Generals, and ones that had helped this country win its wars. Whereas St Marks bless us, had just produced Elvis Costello and me.

Life as a teenager for me was very different in many ways to that of my children, but in some ways it was the same. Mobiles phones did not exist in my day, so communication was by means of a house phone, or a phone box. Yeah they were red metal boxes that were situated strategically all over every town, and required coins to make there armoured black phones work. And for some strange reason they always smelled of stale urine inside. Go figure that One.

When I was not studying or doing school homework, for fun I played guitar, and got pretty good at one stage, and when I wasn't doing that I attended the local Air cadet Squadron - as my ambition then was to become a fighter pilot.

Being in cadets was a good thing for me, as it keep me focused, taught me loads of useful military skills and more importantly I learned how to fly a plane. During the summer months every Monday evening we would go flying in gliders from an old WW2 airfield called White Waltham which was located just southwest of Maidenhead. If we were lucky we got four flights each, which were normally spent either dive bombing the trains that were full of commuters leaving London, or if we had a more sedentary pilot we got a flight around the vicinity of Windsor castle.

No dive bombing allowed around there of course.

I mention air cadets for two reasons: one being a cadet kept me off the streets and therefore out of trouble, and secondly while in cadets I experienced my first loss of a friend. All these years later I still remember the last night that I saw Louis Maida alive. I had just left my Squadron with him and two other friends that I always walked home with, as we lived in the same area. When we got to my house which was just before 10pm, we said our goodbyes and off everyone went. Little did I know in that moment that I had said goodbye to my friend for the last time, and that barely a few hours later, Louis would be murdered.

Louis, it transpired had a violent father that regularly beat and abused his mother. On this particular night, Louis had seen his mother take one beating too many and had stepped in between them. It was an extremely brave and courageous thing to do, but it cost him and his mother their lives, as his father murdered them both by means of a knife.

I remember very vividly being told by my commanding officer that Louis had gone, and that he had written a letter to my school asking for their permission to release me in order to attend the funeral. Flight Lieutenant Dicks, was a true gentleman and had been Lancaster gunner during WW2, I remember him sitting us all down like young children around a favourite grandfather where he recalled the pain of losing friends in combat, and that no matter how painful the loss you had to pick yourself up and carry on.

The day of the funeral arrived, and I can remember shivering in the church - both from the cold and the sheer emotion of seeing the two coffins side by side adorned with wreaths and flowers. The most poignant memory though was when Louis's father was allowed to touch the coffins. When he first entered the church he had been handcuffed between two uniformed police officers, but when he started to sob one of the officers released his handcuff so that he could place his hand on Louis's coffin. He kept calling out "What have I done, what have I done." It was a pitiful sight in so many ways, and I remember thinking no matter how long he serves in jail, nothing is going to punish him more than his conscience. Eventually he was led away, and my memories of that painful day were parked in some recess in the back of my mind, only to be reactivated some decades later when I became involved in gang intervention.

Often when I look back at my childhood and compare it to how we live today, I cannot but help feel that we as a society have gone backwards, and that we have become increasingly uncivilised in so many ways. For example, when I was a teenager we had no security guards in our shopping centres, retail outlets, fast food restaurants and schools. Whereas today, every shopping centre has a security team, which is further reinforced by independent security guards operating within the larger stores and outlets that are located within these centres.

A new development in recent years has been the introduction of security within fast food outlets, such as McDonald's, on account of ever increasing attacks on staff and customers. Some schools and colleges have also felt it necessary to have security, particularly those in deprived areas where crime and gang activity is more prevalent.

I can recall working in one south London College where they had six security guards on duty every day to screen and search all the students entering the facility. At least once a month the police would carry out a large scale unannounced stop and search operation around the vicinity of the college – which usually resulted in some drug and weapon seizures.

Any facility or provision in London, working with known gang members or crime vulnerable young people would of course have additional security measures in place, as the threat of violence is considerably higher in those types of environments.

So what has gone wrong in our society? The answer to that one I am sorry to say is a book in itself. What however you can deduce from the constant increasing use of private security companies is the fact that people do not feel safe in our society, and that stems from the fact that the police can no longer fulfil their remit of that of serving and protecting the public. This of course is not their fault, as the Metropolitan Police has been subjected to numerous cuts in budget and personnel that has left their ranks and operational capabilities seriously degraded.

There is also the matter of their safety. When I was a teenager it was very rare to hear of an attack on a police officer, whereas today a police officer gets attacked every 17 minutes in the UK, which is a truly terrible reflection on the state of our society. It is not only our police that are the subject of such mindless attacks, our medical personnel and firefighters are also victims of similar gratuitous violence.

It is a sad fact that our children are far more likely to see violence on the streets of London than I did back in the 1970s. This violence is however not just on our streets, it is also within our educational establishments and our general society. When I attended school there was only ever one incident where I can recall a teacher getting attacked by a pupil, and that individual got expelled from the school, got arrested - and eventually got convicted of assault, which gained them a criminal conviction for their ill thought actions.

Contrast this with schools today, where assaults on teaching staff are almost a daily occurrence. I remember one academy in London where I worked for four months, starting the school term in September 2017 with nineteen new teachers, mentors and support staff, and finishing in December 2017 with only three of the original staff members remaining. The others sadly were either victims of violent pupils, or they left before they became victims. I can honestly say that this school was the most violent one that I have ever taught in, with assaults on pupils and staff running at an average of three a day.

I mention these points, as normally in childhood your typical pattern of life would see you witness fights and moderate violence, which generally increases when you become a young adult, and then ideally decreases as you get older. That pattern of life however did not apply with me, as my childhood saw me witnessing very little violence, whereas my young adult life saw a moderate increase that eventually culminated in an exponential increase in incidents involving violence and ultimately some loss of life.

The amazing 27ft tall Knife Angel was created by the British Ironworks Centre and is made from over 100,000 discarded knives and confiscated weapons from Police Forces across the country.

CREDIT: CLEVELAND POLICE

KNIFE POSSESSION

South and East London were knife hotspots as more than 3,200 people were arrested for knife possession in the last year

1-50
51-100
101-150
151-200+

10 miles

#	Borough	Value	#	Borough	Value
1	Westminster	212	17	Islington	92
2	Lambeth	200	18	Havering	82
3	Southwark	178	19	Bromley	81
4	Croydon	164	20	Redbridge	81
5	Newham	159	21	Barnet	77
6	Tower Hamlets	147	22	Hammersmith and Fulham	75
7	Hackney	145	23	Wandsworth	75
8	Lewisham	140	24	Barking and Dagenham	65
9	Brent	125	25	Kensington and Chelsea	65
10	Enfield	122	26	Hillingdon	59
11	Greenwich	115	27	Sutton	57
12	Hounslow	114	28	Bexley	56
13	Haringey	107	29	Merton	54
14	Camden	106	30	Harrow	50
15	Waltham Forest	105	31	Kingston upon Thames	30
16	Ealing	100	32	Richmond upon Thames	24

Knife possession in London

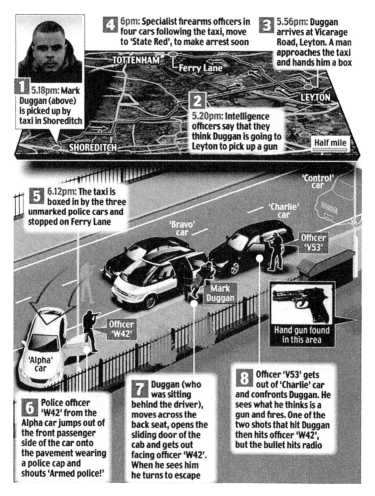

1 5.18pm: Mark Duggan (above) is picked up by taxi in Shoreditch

2 5.20pm: Intelligence officers say that they think Duggan is going to Leyton to pick up a gun

3 5.56pm: Duggan arrives at Vicarage Road, Leyton. A man approaches the taxi and hands him a box

4 6pm: Specialist firearms officers in four cars following the taxi, move to 'State Red', to make arrest soon

5 6.12pm: The taxi is boxed in by the three unmarked police cars and stopped on Ferry Lane

6 Police officer 'W42' from the Alpha car jumps out of the front passenger side of the car onto the pavement wearing a police cap and shouts 'Armed police!'

7 Duggan (who was sitting behind the driver), moves across the back seat, opens the sliding door of the cab and gets out facing officer 'W42'. When he sees him he turns to escape

8 Officer 'V53' gets out of 'Charlie' car and confronts Duggan. He sees what he thinks is a gun and fires. One of the two shots that hit Duggan then hits officer 'W42', but the bullet hits radio

TOTTENHAM
Ferry Lane
LEYTON
SHOREDITCH
Half mile

'Control' car
'Charlie' car
Officer 'V53'
'Bravo' car
Mark Duggan
Officer 'W42'
Hand gun found in this area
'Alpha' car

A detailed graphic depicting the police shooting of Mark Duggan.

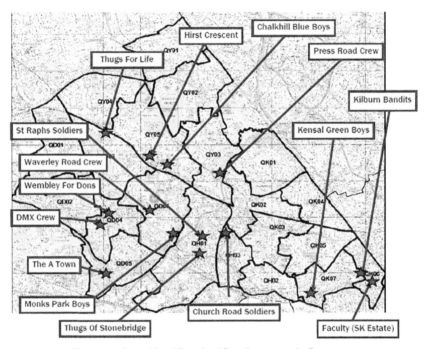

The map above identifies the 15 active gangs in Brent

London burning at the height of the 2011 riots

A gang member enjoying his brief moment of fame
during the 2011 London riots.

A forensics reconstruction of the
Mark Duggan shooting.

Police under missile attack during the London riots

Roadman J - spitting some lyrics

The 1011 West London crew

GANG WARFARE IN LONDON

"EVERYBODY ON THE STREET, knows they're going to lose, it's just that we don't know how to win." (said a gang informant)

In London, there is seldom a day that passes by where you don't hear of a murder or a stabbing involving a young life.

The media would have you believe that gang violence is something new, and that we have never experienced anything like it before – but that would not be the case. If we were to turn back time we would see that gang related violence has always been a trait of London life. For instance during the mid-1970s, we had football related violence that involved gangs of rival supporters clashing where and whenever an opportunity arose.

This football related hooliganism was so rife in the UK that it became known as "the English disease." At one stage violence amongst football gangs was so prolific at matches that high fences had to be erected within football grounds to segregate fans. Today our gangs fight over post code territories related to drug trade and local control, whereas football violence was related to rival teams. There were some football gangs or Firms as they were known that were particularly notorious and vicious.

They included:
Birmingham City – Zulu Warriors
Chelsea – Headhunters
Leeds – Leeds United Service Crew
Liverpool – The Red Army
Millwall – The Bushwackers
Stoke – Naughty Forty
West Ham – Inter City Farm

I mention football gangs, as they are beginning to resurface again – and may well pose a significant threat in London again if not brought under control. Some of these football gangs are notoriously racist, and it is totally feasible that they could have the potential of clashing with some of the active drug gangs located within the capital.

If we look at some of the football gangs that the police eventually took down following undercover officers infiltrating their organisations. It was discovered that in addition to their violent activities, they are were also involved in significant criminal activities such as drug dealing and organised shoplifting. Some of these illicit enterprises left a number of innocent people injured and even dead – so we must view their potential re-emergence with some concern.

In addition to the football gangs, London was also subjected around the same time period with the skinhead gangs who often had neo-nazi traits such as short hair, swastika tattoos - and tendencies to perform Nazi salutes. These gangs often displayed the latent aggression that defined youth culture during the 70s, and were very feared – particularly by London's Asian community in the east end. Just like todays gangs, the skinheads moved around in packs, and like the roadman of today they had their own style of preferred clothing that normally featured Crombie coats, Ben Sherman shirts, cropped jeans and Dr Martin boots. Their music preferences were usually from the 2-Tone genre that featured acts such as the Specials, the Beat and Madness.

Today if we see a group of young people walking towards us with face masks and hoodies pulled over their heads we tend to be wary of them, whereas back in the day - bald headed skinheads were the ones to fear.

So now that we know that our current epidemic of gang crime is not a new phenomenon, just how big is this problem that we have? In London at this present time we have an estimated 300 gangs that are active within the boroughs that make up our city, comprising of some 4,500 members. The footprint of these gangs varies from one borough to another, with some having multiple gangs operating within a small geographic area, while others have very few gangs within their boroughs boundaries.

Generally gangs will operate in deprived areas where population is dense - as this provides potential recruits and a ready supply of customers for their drug trade, as well as victims for their criminality. The term gang usually describes a group of people that spends time in public places and view themselves, (and are viewed by others) as a noticeable group that engages in a range of criminal activities and violence.

This is different to a criminal network which is generally defined as a group of individuals that are involved in persistent criminality for some form of personal gain, for example: profiteering, damage to a community or an increase in status.

These distinguished differences are important to understand, as not everyone that is involved in crime is a gang member, and equally not every member of a gang, or a collective youth group is a criminal.

So why should the definition of a gang concern us? The answer to that is partly legal, and partly social.

From a legal point of view, there is very strict legislation in place that has to be satisfied before it can be used against gang members. Otherwise it is subject to potential abuse. There is also specific legislation against terrorists, and I mention this point as there is a growing public appetite to see gang members being identified as terrorists, so that they can be punished more severely.

Gang definition from a social point of view is also important, as you need to identify where the problem is occurring, and more importantly – why is it occurring? It is generally excepted that the current epidemic of knife crime and the proliferation of gangs in London, started around a decade ago – and both are inextricably linked.

In 2019, the then home secretary, Sajid Javid, described gang related knife crime as a "disease" and one which forced prime minister, Theresa May, to call a crisis summit that involved over 100 subject matter experts that had the unenviable task of trying to figure out how to bring about a resolution to this problem.

This crisis was brought about following a significant increase in knife related crime that was primarily linked to turf wars over gang related drug dealing. It is of course the case that not all knife crime is down to gangs, as many young people carry knives for self-protection. Equally not all victims of knife crime are gang members, as I well know from my work around London. Sometimes it was a case of misidentification, but in other cases the victims were stabbed as part of a gang initiation. For example, a new gang member may be tasked to prove his or her loyalty by targeting a specific type of person that has been chosen by the gang leader. In some parts of London, this was referred to as doing an "Aleppo."

Aleppo is a city in Syria, which has seen intense fighting between freedom fighters, ISIS militants and Syrian soldiers loyal to Syrian president, Bashar al-Assad. The term doing an Aleppo, stems from a sick and cruel game practiced by snipers serving in the army of Bashar al-Assad who were tasked on a daily basis to shoot innocent civilian victims in a particular part of their body. One day the target would be the groin area, then the left side of the body, followed by the right – which eventually led to them shooting pregnant women in the womb area, so that they lost their unborn child. Some of the more extreme gang members operating in London, were so fascinated with these sick games, that they developed a version of their own.

Prior to this despicable craze, some gangs practised a stabbing technique that was known as a "bag job." In this particular sadistic practice, their intention was not to kill their victim – but to maim them for life. They found that if they inflicted a serious knife wound to the colon or rectum, the victim was highly likely to require the use of a colostomy bag.

So what on earth causes young people to join such gangs? A question that is posed by many, yet precious few can answer. When I worked in gang intervention I would always ask my subjects the same question, and the list of reasons varied from one youth to another. For example, one 15 year old teenager that I worked with lived in a big 6 bedroomed mansion that had a car collection in the front driveway that Jeremy Clarkson would have drooled over. When I first visited the house, I was convinced that I had gone to the wrong address, as what I was looking at did not match my abstract thoughts of what should be in front of my eyes.

The young man concerned was very intelligent and articulate, and walked with a pronounced limp – on account of an injury sustained from being knocked off his scooter by a police van. When interviewed by me, he mentioned that he had joined his respective gang for excitement, and also to punish his mother - as he had discovered that she had adopted him. He stated very clearly that he was a non-aggressive member of his gang, and that his role was purely trapping, and not drilling. He was very polite to me, and respectful of my role, but made it clear that he was not going to change his lifestyle anytime soon.

Gang members come from all sorts of different social backgrounds, with no single description fitting all the circumstances and reasons that could act as a recognisable driver or promoter of a common value that leads to an individual feeling an urge or need to be part of such a criminal life style.

There are of course recognisable and known risk factors that are likely to be associated with individuals becoming vulnerable and susceptible to the lure of gang membership. Factors could include:

- Being young and male
- Being a victim of bullying or violence
- Discrimination and stereotyping
- Having a member of the family or a friend who is a gang member
- Family breakdown and dysfunction
- A lack of positive role models (including an

absent father)

- Poor educational attainment
- Having a drug or alcohol misuse problem
- Mental and emotional health problems
- An absence of aspirations
- Having a perceived need for protection
- Unemployment or underemployment and the need for money
- Living in a culture that strongly identifies success with material wealth
- Poverty or growing up in social housing

This list of factors is by no means exhaustive, and equally it should not be viewed as a template for gang membership.

I know when gangs are being discussed, people will generally have a stereotypical view of what they perceive a gang member to be like. For the most part their opinions are heavily influenced by the media, who usually have only the most cursory experiences of them.

This of course is understandable as news priorities change every day. Gangs however in London, are active 24/7 and politicians and people need to remember that if they are ever going to have any chance of reducing or eliminating their criminal activities from our society.

Politicians of course only react to whatever story is hurting them the most. One day it will be how are we going to manage Brexit? The next why have we had over 100 violent killings in London, and it's only September? There will always be a reaction of course, usually by the prime minister, then the Mayor of London – which are usually orchestrated with news that the police have carried out multiple raids across London against known gang members. Once the media and political heat has died down, then it's business as usual for everyone.

Gang warfare is almost like a military operation, in that when your enemy expands -you contract, and when your enemy contracts - you expand. There are times when there is little difference in the strategic and tactical thought processes that are at work on our streets, and those that are taking place on foreign battlefields far away.

London, has a population of some 8.9 million that is packed into 1,583 square kilometres, which in old money is 611 square miles. This equates to a population density of 4,542 people per square kilometre. That means it is an extremely target rich environment for the gangs that inhabit our city.

As a busy multicultural city, there is always something going on in London, be it of a cultural, musical or sporting nature. These events are designed to entertain us, and also provide our tourists with an opportunity to experience British culture. Sadly such gatherings also represent numerous criminal opportunities for gangs and petty criminals. If we take Wembley stadium for example, its location is within the borough of Brent, which is the known gang territory of 18 active and prolific gangs, such as the:

- SKs – South Kilburn
- NKs – North Kilburn
- Church Road Soldiers – Church Road
- The Thugs of Stonebridge – Stonebridge Estate

- The Thugs for Life – Wembley
- Kensal Green Boys – Kensal Green
- The Zarties – Mozart Estate

All of these gangs will be distributing and selling drugs within the borough, so therefore they will need to protect their respective trappers and gang associates as they go about their criminal activities.

This of course means that clashes and skirmishes between gangs are commonplace, and are almost reminiscent of the hit and run raids that our Royal Marine Commandos and Special Air Service carried out against the Nazis during WW2.

Sometimes these forays into opponent held territory will involve only small groups, usually around 4 in number – as bigger groups tend to attract attention, either from their rivals or the police. As a precaution to this potential problem, gangs tend to carry out a pre-target reconnaissance by means of a spotter who usually rides an inconspicuous moped or scooter ahead of the main group – basically to make sure that their target is still in the vicinity, or to warn of a police presence.

It is basically a game of cat and mouse, between all the participants – with each one becoming ever increasingly devious to outwit the other. As for the police, they are simply deemed an occupational hazard.

When I worked in the Church Road area, and on the nearby Mozart Estate, I always found it a fascinating place to be, as you were right in the Lions mouth in terms of gang warfare in north-west London. Trying to figure out what was abnormal amongst the normal took time, as initially everything was alien to me. In the military soldiers are taught to look out for what they call Combat

Indicators, or CIs as they are more commonly known. These are signs or indicators that a potential ambush or attack is imminent.

Typical CIs a soldier might look out for include: absence of children in villages, villagers looking nervously at strangers within their village, farmers not working in their fields, or disturbed earth on a road. There are of course hundreds of others, but I'm sure you get the idea. If I flip this mentality to working with gangs, I use the same methodology, only in this world the CIs are different. For instance, I would look at the local resident's body language to see if they were wary of anyone on their estate. If the gang member was known to them they tended to walk in a relatively relaxed manner - whereas if they seemed hostile – they walked faster, and gave them a wide berth. Other signs included increased mobile phone usage – just prior to an attack – and more agitated and animated body language. Unusual vehicle movements were also a dead giveaway, especially if there were multiple occupants. It's these little signs that can make the difference between life and death.

The young people that were involved in Brent's main gangs tended to be Afro-Caribbean, and as a consequence it was deemed a Trident borough. Brent also has a large Tamil population, and is known to have at least 2 gangs operating within its community. As you move east of the borough of Brent, the gang landscape changes again, and features members that tend to be of Middle-Eastern or Asian origin.

I mention these points as some gangs have a particular reputation for committing certain types of crimes – both on their own territory and indeed inside those of rival gangs. There are also gangs however, such as those seen in the Tamil community that only wage war amongst their own people. In June 2011, two Tamil gangs: the Tooting Boys and Jaffna Boys decided to have a turf war over the control of West Croydon. In one particular incident around 40 gang members had a mass brawl that left one teenager fighting for his life. Over the following weeks there were further clashes between the rival gangs, but not on the same scale.

Local residents told the police that the gangs were running protection rackets, and that if they went to the police they would get hurt, and also witness the burning of their shops.

For a while following intense police intervention - the gangs calmed down - but gradually over a period of time violence started to escalate again which eventually resulted in a Tamil gang member being murdered following an axe attack. The perpetrator of this gruesome act was a gang rival Prashad Sothalingham, AKA Bullet who was jailed for life for his part in a pointless power struggle that resulted in loss of life.

Croydon, has also been a flash point for a number of other gangs who are fighting for control of this south London town. There are currently 5 known gangs that are said to be behind the recent increase in violence in this area, they are the:

- Field Boyz – New Addington
- CR7 – Thornton Heath
- 25s – Norwood Junction
- # O – West Croydon
- S Block – Selhurst

Although these gangs have certainly had some involvement in the stabbing epidemic that has taken place in Croydon, from my research they are clearly not the only perpetrators, as gang activities have only accounted for some 30% of the violence. Croydon it should be said has the highest percentage of young people in London, so either there are more gangs in the area than has been reported, or it has to be the other alternative which is that some of these murders must be non-gang related.

This is a very important point because when we analyse violent crime levels across London, it is imperative that the data is accurate and correctly assigned to its known cause, otherwise we risk gangs making false claims that could potentially inflame already tense stand-offs. When I visited Croydon to analyse their level of gang activity, at best all I could identify was some 100 individuals aged from 14 to 25, which was substantially lower than the 300 members alleged to be active in the borough.

Social media must take some of the blame for this, as there are elements within their ranks that continually and sensationally hype up gang activity to the point that it bears little or no resemblance to what is really going on. Yes, Croydon has gang violence, but to compare it to south Chicago. That is ridiculous and unreal. Even comparing South Chicago to London is stretching things. For instance, in just one weekend in August 2019, Chicago had 7 killed and 60 shot and injured. They finished the year with 490 murders, which was an improvement over 2016 when there was 756 homicides. London's homicide rate by contrast, even during its worst period in 2008 – was only 154 reported deaths.

London, does indeed have a problem with gangs - we all know that. But we do however need to be careful when we make comparisons, as all factors need to be analysed and put into perspective.

As we move around London, it becomes very obvious

where the main conglomerate of gang activity is centred. Essentially, the vast majority of London's gangs are located in an ink spot that expands to the north, south and east of the City of London. As we move westwards, and to the southwest the number of gangs significantly drops off – to the point that gang activity is almost non-existent.

The centre of gravity for London in terms of gang activity would have to be the River Thames, as it forms a natural demarcation line between gangs in the north and gangs in the south.

If we overlay London's murder map for 2019, which showed 143 people killed in what was an 11-year high – it mirrors our gang hotspots, which clearly shows that there is a correlation between gang territory and murders.

This appalling murder rate also at one stage put us in front of New York City – once deemed one of the most violent cities in the world.

LONDON'S BURNING

"A riot is the language of the unheard"
MARTIN LUTHER KING

LONDON HAS HAD TO face many disasters and challenges over the centuries – ranging from the great fire of London in 1666 to the "Blitz" during WW2, and we have always come through them. Some have been expected, while others have occurred completely out of the blue.

In August 2011 London got a crisis that was of the totally unexpected variety, and one which equally it was totally unprepared for. When it broke I was thousands of miles away leading a team on a military training exercise in the wilds of the Yukon Territory in northern Canada. For those of you not familiar with the Yukon - and you wouldn't be alone - it lies south of the Arctic Circle, with Alaska to its west, is almost four times size of the UK, and has a population of some 35,000. Apart from me the only other Brits that seem to go there are survival experts like Bear Grylls and Ray Mears. I'm sure by now you've got the idea that it is remote, and as a consequence communication is extremely difficult.

I mention this point, as my family are used to me being away for months at a time, and are fully aware that there are long periods where I will not have any means of contacting them, as the satellite phone that we have in each team is strictly for emergency use, and not for family chit chat. The first I knew of any problem in London was when a Canadian Army pick-up truck drove hundreds of miles to find me, and then transport me back to the TOC (Tactical Operations Centre) at Regional Head Quarters which was located in Boyle Barracks, just outside the City of Whitehorse.

The driver had no idea why I had been asked to return, which made me anxious about my family, as you normally only get pulled out if there is a family emergency. 8 hours of driving later and we were back at the base. It was very late by the time we got back, so most of the camp staff were asleep in their quarters. All it would seem apart from the HQ staff. The commander greeted me, and over a cup of coffee he took me to the media centre to watch a news broadcast that they had recorded for me. As it started to play, all I could see was burning buildings, police clashing with rioters, and news anchors commenting on what was happening in London. As my tired brain started to process what I was viewing, my initial thoughts were only for my family's safety. A quick call home, and my wife briefed me on what had been going on in London while I was away.

By all accounts this had been a series of riots of significant magnitude, way beyond what I had ever seen before. The last serious riot that I could recall in London was that of the Broadwater Farm riot which occurred on the Broadwater Farm council estate in Tottenham, on October 6 1985. This riot was particularly significant as it resulted in the murder of PC Keith Blakelock, the first police officer since 1833 to be killed in a riot in London.

So what on earth happened to spark these riots off? A question that resonated in my head over and over again

as I flew back to London. Upon my arrival at Heathrow
Airport, all the chat related to the riots, which made me
impatient to get home as quickly as possible, as I was
hungry to find out more. As I came off the M4 in West
London, the first hint of any unusual activity that I saw
was located in a park, where I saw a massive group of
police personnel carriers and riot vans – all with different
markings and colour schemes, indicating that they were
from all over England and Wales. I honestly had never seen
anything like this in my life before, and it was something of
a prelude to other revelations that I was about to discover.

After catching up with my wife and 3 children, I drove
to the nearest shopping centre in west London to view
the aftermath of what had transpired over the proceeding
days. What I saw when I arrived looked almost post-
apocalyptic. There were burned out cars along the roads,
pavements strewn with debris, and endless streams of
"Police Line Do Not Cross" tape – all testament to the
carnage that had taken place. As I walked around the
shopping centre, there were numerous shops with either
broken windows or boarded up shopfronts – apart from
Waterstones book store which stood out, as it was totally
unscathed. It would appear that rioters and gangs don't
like books – so we now know where to hide our most
treasured possessions!!

So what caused all this bedlam? The answer to that
one can be traced back to Tottenham, where on 4 August
2011 police shot and killed a young 29 year old man called
Mark Duggan. The exact circumstances of the shooting
that day are still unknown – as there is no camera footage
of the incident. The incident has been greatly debated
and analysed over the years, and yet some questions still
remain unanswered to this day. The police on the day were
acting on intelligence that Mark Duggan was allegedly on

his way to shoot a rival by means of a pistol that he was known to be carrying.

As he headed towards his target in a taxi, armed police from CO19 a unit from the Specialist Firearms Command that had been monitoring and tracking him - forced his vehicle to a halt and then shouted for all the occupants to come out of the vehicle with their hands above their heads. It is stated by the police that as Mark Duggan left the vehicle he made a gesture that suggested to the armed officers that he was reaching for his gun. As per their rules of engagement he was engaged and shot twice – one shot to his biceps, and the other to his chest. A witness later described seeing a cloud of feathers flying through the air as the bullets from the police firearms impacted Mr Duggan's puffer jacket. The media also reported that Mr Duggan had fired first at police, as one officer was hit by a bullet which lodged in his radio. After an intensive investigation it was discovered that the bullet was in fact fired from a police Heckler and Koch MP5 weapon, by an officer known as V53. It is believed that the bullet had originally hit Mark Duggan's arm and passed through - hitting the police officer that was behind him. Mr Duggan's weapon which was the subject of so much controversy was later found some 4 metres from his body on the other side of a nearby fence. It had not been fired, and there was no trace of GSR found (Gun Shot Residue) on Mr Duggan's hands.

Prior to the police ambush it had been established that a Beretta 92 blank firer had been converted to fire live ammunition, and that this weapon had been given to Mark Duggan by Kevin Hutchinson-Foster just 15 minutes before he was shot dead. At the time of the event Mr Duggan had been under intense surveillance by officers from Operation Trident, who believed that he was going to carry out a retaliation killing following the murder of his cousin, Kelvin Easton, who was stabbed to death outside an East London bar in March 2011. According to the London Evening Standard, Mark Duggan may have been a founding member of a north London gang, known as the "Star Gang" – an offshoot of the Tottenham based Mandem gang. According to other sources Mark Duggan, was a key player in Tottenham's drug scene, and as such he would have been a prime target for Operation Trident.

His family however deny that he was in a gang, and that at the time of his shooting he only had convictions for cannabis possession and handling stolen goods. A member of his family also mentioned that he had applied to become a firefighter.

Whatever the truth is of what really happened that day I do not know, as there was no CCTV or police body-cam footage to be reviewed. That of course was also the case for everyone else, and in the void of official statements – the rumour mill was rife. Initial media reports had stated that a man had shot at police, and that they had returned fire. This version of events however did not accord with what the local people of Tottenham already knew – and that caused a massive backlash, and a surge of anger amongst Tottenham's black community. They stated that another way could have been found to arrest Mark Duggan, - without armed officers having to resort to what police term a hard stop.

Local community leaders, and Tottenham's MP David Lammy, did try and calm the situation down – but it was clear that the town was about to blow. It just needed a spark. At this stage the Independent Police Complaints Commission (IPCC) had opened an investigation into the shooting, but had not at this point put out a statement of facts – or an interim report which would have countered the rumours and speculation that were being put out by the media in light of this glaring void.

Even at this point in the proceedings, Mr Duggan's family had still not been officially informed of his death, an issue that was to take this crisis to its next level. Devoid of information and answers the Duggan family decided to go to Tottenham police station on August 6 to get confirmation that their family member had been killed, and under what circumstances had he met his death. While they were in the police station being briefed by the senior police officer, a large crowd gathered outside in order to support the family, with some using the occasion as a vigil.

Their actions were calm and peaceful, however in the shadows there were other groups of young teenagers and local gangs with other ideas. As this group began to menacingly gather around the police station, they were joined by a group of around 100 people who had just marched from the Broadwater Farm Estate. As they gathered together a young women threw a missile at the police and in response they arrested her. That was the spark, and within minutes all hell was breaking loose in Tottenham. At first it was just two police cars, and a bus that were set on fire, but this quickly escalated to nearby shops and businesses being set alight.

Gangs quickly exploited the situation, and set about looting nearby shops, shouting their war cry "let's missile up" and burn this town. The police tried to respond by pushing back the baying mobs but they were totally outnumbered, and ill equipped to respond. By now the word had got out that Tottenham had gone off, which inspired gangs in nearby Wood Green to kick-off and commence their orgy of looting.

Normally when there is a protest or an event where police fear a flare-up, they usually pre-deploy TSG

(Territorial Support Group) officers from the Metropolitan police's Public Order Operational Command Unit, or CO11 as it is more commonly known. This unit features riot equipped carrier vehicles, that carry officers trained and equipped to deal with public disorder and riots. CO11 also has Forward Intelligence Teams and specialist DSUs (Dog Support Units) within its operational structure. However on August 6, none of these assets had been deployed, which left only a small number of local police officers in control of a task that they were totally unprepared for.

Generally when police face large hostile groups the standard tactic is to surround them and kettle them in, so that nobody can get in or out of the police enforced cordon. This practice works well if you have large amounts of police on hand to contain a situation, but if like the situation in Tottenham, where you are totally outnumbered, the tactic of Kettling just will not work. So that leaves another option, which is roving patrols where police identify violent groups and charge at them to drive them away from any vulnerable potential targets of opportunity – like sports or electronic stores.   This tactic however was thwarted by the criminal gangs who were always one step ahead of the police – on account of their extremely effective use of social media. The gangs would also place spotters around the area, so that they always knew where the police were deployed. Essentially the gangs would use loot and scoot tactics – which were highly effective, on account of the fact that whenever the police turned up, all they had to do was run into the nearby estates where the police could not follow – as they feared being ambushed by hidden mobs.

By midnight, the air in Tottenham was acrid from the smell of burning cars, buildings, fireworks and petrol bombs. Territorial Support Group officers had now arrived in some force but chaos still reigned throughout the town. The police by this time had sustained 26 casualties, as many of the officers had no means of protecting themselves from the barrage of missiles that were constantly reigning down on them. Firefighters, ambulance crews and TV journalists were also being targeted by the gangs, as in their eyes everyone was a legitimate target.

After trashing central Tottenham the gangs descended on a nearby retail park, where they duly set about their mission of looting and burning it. The police made no attempt to stop them, as they simply did not have the manpower or vehicle resources to do so. By Sunday morning on August 7, the area was calm, with no gangs to be seen anywhere. The police by this time were exhausted, but still had to remain on duty, as there was still a threat of further violence. By late afternoon gangs of youths were beginning to gather in north London, only this time their target was Enfield, which is just north of Tottenham. The police by now had been tracking the movements of all the gangs and groups that were beginning to congregate around the Church Street area of Enfield. Despite a heavy presence of riot police, the gangs started to throw rocks and missiles in their direction as they had done at Tottenham.

This time however the police charged at them, which caused them to break off their attack on the nearby shops and stores that had been their intended target. Police dogs were also used to harass any stragglers that had not taken the hint to disperse. The police also set up a sterile area around the shopping centre, so that it could not be burned or looted.

Meanwhile south of the river in Brixton, a number of gangs from different parts of London decided that this area was now a soft target as most of the Met police were now deployed in north London. Seizing their open opportunity, hundreds of young men and women began looting Foot locker, Currys and Halfords. Residents later described seeing hoards of people running through Brixton with TVs, laptops, sports kit and trainers. The police did try to stop them, but as with Tottenham, there was simply not enough officers available to prevent this crime spree. As police fought running battles with the rioters, Foot Locker was set on fire, and the nearby Tesco supermarket looted.

By now there were multiple copycat lootings taking place across areas of London that had never experienced problems like this before. These were not rioters, they were petty criminals taking advantage of a temporary breakdown in law and order.

Back in north London, in Wood Green – the rioters were back in action again, only this time they were not going to get an opportunity to loot the local stores, as all the Turkish and Kurdish shop keepers had banded together to defend their community from the rampaging gangs. These instant vigilantes would have been a very imposing sight, as many of them were carrying baseball bats and machetes. It was also a sad reflection upon the parlous state of our police force at that time that in many cases they simply looked on as communities burned, and did little or nothing to prevent this wanton destruction.

Gangs of course were very quick to exploit this chaos, and took full advantage of the situation by carrying out massed lootings and the settling of old scores with their most bitter rivals. However there were also gangs that agreed temporary truces with their rivals, and agreed to join forces against their common enemy: The police.

By Monday 8 August, the rioting and looting had spread across London to: Camden, Colliers Wood, Clapham, Croydon, Ealing, Hackney, Lewisham, Peckham, Newham and Woolwich. In a bid to stem the riots, the

Metropolitan Police invoked a national mutual support package that involves the redeployment of hundreds of riot trained officers from all over England and Wales in support of their colleagues in London. The deployment however is to little too late, as the damage has already been done. County officers arriving in London, would later complain that they never got an opportunity to provide effective assistance on account of communication difficulties between them and the Metropolitan Police.

During the evening of 8 August, Trevor Ellis, of Brixton Hill is found shot dead in a car in Croydon, while Richard Bowes of Ealing is critically injured while trying to put out a fire.

As news of this loss of life is announced, unrest starts to spread to other parts of the UK, with violence breaking out in Birmingham, Bristol, Liverpool and Nottingham.

Tuesday 9 August, and the IPCC reveals that there is no evidence that Mark Duggan opened fire at police, prior to being shot by a firearms officer. This information of course had already been leaked by the press, but at least now it was official.

The following day on 10 August, Haroon Jahan, Shazad Ali and Abdul Musavir are killed by a car in Birmingham, as they tried to defend their community from rioters. These tragic murders marked the last day of the riots, however there continued to be small outbreaks of looting and violence that eventually merged into normal everyday criminal activities.

The vast majority of people involved in the London riots never knew Mark Duggan personally, or even cared about what happened to him. He was simply an excuse for thousands to rob, loot and riot. It's one thing to peacefully protest outside a police station in order to gain some answers as to why someone was shot dead by police, and quite another for an individual to go into a store and loot it for a new pair of trainers, and then claim that they only did it because they were upset about the shooting of Mark Duggan. That sort of rationale is an insult to the Duggan family and just doesn't wash with me.

For the record, at no point did the Duggan family incite, or encourage anyone to riot while they were holding their vigil outside Tottenham police station. That is a matter of public record.

The London riots left the UK shell shocked, with consequences and a social legacy that would reverberate around our society for many years after the last missile had been thrown.

The financial cost of the riots was estimated at some £200 million worth of property damaged, along with a human cost that was considerably higher:

5 deaths

16 members of the public and 189 police/ community officers injured

3,000 plus arrested

1, 292 offenders jailed

During the inevitable political fallout that took place after the riots, Prime Minister David Cameron, and Home Secretary Theresa May accused the Metropolitan Police Service and the West Midlands Force of being "too few, too slow, and too timid." Cameron also criticized the police for using poor and incorrect tactics when dealing with the rioters.

Other politicians also made the point that we regularly

use water cannons and plastic baton rounds on British citizens in Northern Ireland, so why not in London?

These are interesting points, but are they fair ones? Bearing in mind that the police had suffered huge cutbacks in both manpower and resources prior to the London riots, is it really any surprise then that they struggled to generate enough officers that were trained and equipped to deal with mass public disorder.

In my humble opinion, the main fault lays with senior police officers and politicians who have continually kowtowed to the lunatic fringe that puts political correctness above common sense. This was clearly evident during the London riots, when senior Gold Commanders were given the option of going hard line by deploying and using baton rounds against the rioters. They however refused to implement this option for fear that it might upset the rioters. Are you serious!! What about the police officers under your command. What is more important: their welfare and protection, or you protecting your gold plated pensions.

Whatever policing failures took place during the London riots, and there were many. The failures were not down to the ordinary rank and file police officers, who it has to be said were extremely brave and professional in their efforts to try and restore public order.

In London, at the height of the riots there was visual evidence of gang members openly carrying machetes and cut out weapons who were doing their level best to incite officers to chase and arrest them. Some of the gang bangers even shouted "lets do another Blakelock"- a reference to the murder of PC Keith Blakelock, during the Tottenham riots in 1985.

Of interest is the fact that had the police deployed water cannons and baton round guns during the riots, the rioters would not have been able to get within missile throwing range of the officers, which would have meant lower police casualties, and therefore lower arrests. These assets would have also helped prevent looting as the police could have set up effective sterile areas around vulnerable targets, thereby minimising robbery and property damage.

Another factor that played a major part in the London riots was social media. Before the arrival of the mobile phone if you stood in a market square and tried to incite a riot, the only people that could possibly react to your solicitation would be those who were standing around you. Today however things are very different. Now if you stood in a square and did the same thing, but also loaded it onto social media - you could potentially cause a worldwide reaction. That is why we need to be so very careful with how social media is being used, and more importantly who is using it. Mr Cameron at one stage even looked at whether there should be limits on the use of social media sites during times of social unrest, as they have the potential of rapidly spreading organised disorder.

These are a few examples of the messages that were sent by the rioters during the London riots:

"smash shop windows and cart out da stuff you want"

"lets do another Blackelock"

"bring your bags, hammers, the lot!! we strike 9.15pm"

"police not on dis ting"

"Oxford Circus!!!! 9pm – remember da location"

"Enfield station – 4 o clock sharp"!!!

When the police released details of the gang's social media communication methods, one question that kept coming up was "why did you not act on all these messages"?

The truth was that the police faced a major overload of information, and they simply could not process it. There were of course occasions where they did anticipate rioting in a certain area, and they negated the threat through good intelligence and proactive policing. A good example being the London borough of Sutton, where officers saw gangs gathering in the streets in preparation for an assault on the town centre, and they drove them away with a single baton charge. What is remarkable about this incident is the fact that none of the officers had riot gear – and yet they still charged, wearing only short sleeved shirts with stab proved vests. They were incredibly courageous officers, and a credit to their force.

As we reflect on the London riots, the inevitable question that always arises is "could it happen again"? My personal belief is yes, but perhaps not on the same scale. After the Grenfell Tower tragedy in June 2017, it was felt that there was a high likelihood of social disorder occurring following the fire – but through good policing and intensive work by local community leaders this threat was negated. There still however remains a latent threat of social disorder and potential riots if certain social and political conditions ever combine to create an environment that is permissive of such an outcome.

On 8 January 2014, a jury at Mark Duggan's inquest into his death, declared a verdict of lawful killing by a majority of eight to two.

In life we often find strange coincidences that take place around a circumstance or event that has previously occurred, and it usually takes place without a warning or any planning. In my case just after I finished writing this book, I attended a training exercise in Bramley, Hampshire in the month of March 2020. While going about my business, and engaging in conversation with the cadets that I was instructing, a young man in the group enquired "Sir, have you ever heard of Mark Duggan." I said yes and was curious as to why of all questions he asked me this one. He replied I'm a relative of his, and he then wished me a good day. To this day, I have no idea what prompted him to raise that particular question with me.

WELCOME TO GOTHAM

ONE OF THE FIRST GANG intervention assignments that I was tasked to carry out took place in west London around the busy streets of White City, Shepherds Bush and Ladbrook Grove. The area was often referred to as the death triangle on account of all the gangs that operated within its geographic boundaries.

Known gangs included: The White City Crew (WCC), The Bush Gang (BGs) and the Ladbrook Grove Boys (LGB) along with a number of smaller groups that didn't quite fit the criteria that would have defined them as post code gangs. From known intelligence (information that has been analysed and assessed) WCC and BG comprised of some twenty active members - with known associates – while LGB was considerably larger with around 35 known active members.

As I drove around my patch, I made note of all the potential targets that gangs would find attractive for criminal activities, while also identifying potential schools and provisions that may be vulnerable to gang recruitment.

While sitting in my car, I watched the rain fall from the

dark low clouds that were barely above the high-rise flats that dominated the area, and upon seeing a train crossing the nearby graffiti clad bridge - I thought to myself, this place reminds me of the skyline of the TV series Gotham. So from that day onwards my area of operations (AOP) in this area was known as Gotham.

This particular area of London has many social contradictions, at one end of a road you could have a densely populated council estate, while at the other end there could be a small number of multi-million pound houses taking up the same amount of land.

London is unusual in that you will find a deprived area situated amongst an affluent one, and conversely an affluent area amongst a deprived one. If I contrast this with my working experience in New York and Washington DC where it is defined good areas and defined bad areas.

I guess that is what makes London so fascinating.

Another observation I made about my working area, related to its soundtrack – the almost perpetual sound of sirens. I don't ever recall working in an area that has so much ambulance, fire and police activity.

Gotham was certainly going to be an interesting area that was for sure. After some time I got to the point where I could tell gang members apart simply by subtleties in their choice of clothing. This was an important observation, as it meant that I could spot gang members that were out of their own areas, and clearly out looking out for their rivals – or ops as they would call them.

One thing that always intrigued me about Gotham related to the level of sports and youth facilities that were on offer to all the young people living in this area. I mention this as gang related crime is often blamed on a lack of activities for young people, and yet here they had an abundance of first class youth provisions and they still had problems with crime and violence.

I did raise this issue with a senior youth worker, and he explained to me that the local gangs used the youth centres and sports facilities as known kill zones, as they were always likely to find their ops using them at some point or other.

This revelation goes some way to explain why some boroughs are reluctant to provide designated youth facilities, as they know that they are likely to suffer the same fate. The normal excuse of lack of money, it would seem is not always the case.

One argument often thrown up about gangs and their so called post code wars relates to the view that we should just get rid of post codes and then gangs would have no reason to fight each other. As interesting as this idea sounds, it just would not make any difference, as gangs would find some other line of demarcation, such as local roads, railway lines or parks. Gangs by nature are very territorial as they have their drug empires to protect. Sometimes gangs will reach an understanding with their rivals that if you stay out of our turf, we will stay out of yours. Some of these arrangements can work quite harmoniously, with some gangs even entering into alliances that permit cross territory dealing.

In Gotham that was seldom the case, as all of the gangs wanted to protect their own respective territories. The WCC had the enormous White City estate as their domain, while the BGs tended to control the Westfield shopping Centre, leaving anything east of Shepherds Bush green as LGB turf. They would of course regularly violate their rivals area of control – generally as a means of defiance, but sometimes as a means of provoking a response.

For instance, if it became known that the police had taken direct action against one group by means of raids and arrests their rivals would try and fill the void left behind following their disappearance. It always amazed me how well informed each gang was about their rivals and any problems that they were facing in terms of depleted ranks and lack of drug product. It always seemed to me that some of the local youth that purported to be empathetic to one side, were in fact repping for their rivals. A very dangerous thing to do – as you potentially risked reprisals from both sides. Sadly some young people just don't appreciate the risks that they are taking by playing one gang off against another.

Another aspect of working in Gotham that was of particular interest to me related to the families of the young people that I was working with. It is often reported in the media, that young people drawn towards gang life tend to come from single parent female based families where the father is either totally absent in their lives, or has little involvement in their upbringing.

That stereotyped view certainly didn't apply in this part of London, as I generally found most of the families that I had any dealings with were very caring and functional, and doing the best that they could under very challenging circumstances. Their children taking up gang life was no refection upon how they had raised them. That said, if you subject any child to constant negative influences – be it in school, society or at home – there is a high probability that they will go down a path that will make them vulnerable to criminal behaviour. And that's where it all starts to go horribly wrong, as gangs are extremely adept at identifying potential recruits.

When working with the gang intervention team, I constantly had to remind myself to stay on mission, and remain focused on my role – which was primarily to encourage all those that were of school age to return to education, and then mentor them out of gang life. Sounds so simple, but I can assure you that it was anything but simple. If you are trying to pry a member of a gang away from their group - albeit for the best intentions in the world - they are not going to make it easy for you. There was also the fact that no normal state school would take them, as they feared that they would destabilise their schools. That left me with only limited options, such as placing them in Outreach schooling, Pupil Referral Units (PRUs) or Pupil Parent Partnerships (PPPs).

After heading up a highly effective crime intervention programme, which had been stopped due to funding issues arising from inter-governmental politics over who picked up the tab. I now found myself in a role where I could see a pathway towards helping the young people under my jurisdiction, but could not make much headway -again due to politics.

There seemed to be a common thread that ran through the gang intervention teams, and indeed those of the Youth Offending Teams (YOTs) that were deployed throughout the boroughs of London. Without doubt the staff had all the best intentions in the world, but they were never going to be successful in their endeavours on account of outdated youth engagement practices.

The senior management teams were usually the worst culprits for reinforcing failure, as most had never worked on the frontline, so had little or no idea how to engage with young people. Most of them in fairness had been either drafted in from a working environment that did not involve young people, or had been promoted into a management position where they were totally out of their depth.

If you are dealing with a complex issue such as that of gang intervention, you need diversity of thought and diversity in the people that you recruit otherwise you will think and act the same way. And that's a big problem, because if you all think the same way you will not see the blind spots in your strategic plan. As they say, fail to plan – plan to fail.

Recruiting good people that will make a difference is also a problem in gang intervention, as you are likely to witness, or indeed be subjected to violence.

While working in Gotham, I personally never got attacked but I did witness numerous skirmishes between rival gangs. These would often be irregular in nature, sometimes days or even weeks would go by without anything happening. Then, for no apparent reason there would be multiple attacks within a short space of time. I can remember on one particular hot summer's day witnessing three separate incidents within the space of an hour. The first occurred in a side street just off Latimer Road near Grenfell Tower, and involved a car with three occupants and a gang around twelve in number. Where I was standing I had a black Audi to my left with its driver frantically revving his engine in a bid to make a fast get away but he was unable to move as his friend in the back was trying to drag a blood soaked man into the vehicle.

The man that was injured appeared to have two injuries; a slash cut on his right hand and a deep wound on his right side. Under normal circumstances I would have attempted to treat his wounds, but this was impossible as the gang that had inflicted his injuries were still in the street barely 20 metres away – and brandishing two large knives. Within seconds he was within the car, and its driver screeched off towards the West way. Once gone, the gang quickly disappeared into the nearby estate.

As I continued to walk along the road, I could see in the distance a large number of police cars and vans

blocking the road, including a couple of ARVs (Armed
Response Vehicles). They were dealing with another
incident and had two suspects on the ground that were
being searched. I made one officer aware of what I had
just seen, but they were already aware of that incident and
what had transpired. I then went for a coffee, and was just
about to head for home when I saw two gangs appear out
of the local estate. At first they just exchanged abuse, then
it escalated to punching and flying kicks – but no weapons
thankfully. Within minutes it was all over and for me yet
another violent memory to add to my personal data bank.

When working in Gotham at no point did I ever feel
scared of doing my job, I could be apprehensive and wary
at times of some of the gang members that I had to work
with when in a group setting, but when working with
them individually I felt relatively relaxed. I always treated
every person that I interviewed with respect, and always
talked to them, and not down to them. Trust me, there is
a difference in this approach.

Also when working with the gangs I tried to find
something that we may have in common, such as playing
football, music or cars. It doesn't matter what the
connection is, as a connection is a connection – and it
will open a line of communication for you. Whenever I
had any free time I always used it in a positive way by
playing a game of football with any gang members that
were around the area. White City and Shepherds Bush have
an abundance of pitches available, so getting a pitch for
a game was never an issue. My work colleagues often felt
that I was wasting my efforts, as they deemed these young
people beyond saving.

I respectfully disagreed with their views and carried
on with this practice as I believed it was working.

The gang members would of course regularly tease

me about my football dribbling skills, as I'm certainly no Cristiano Ronaldo – but I can however score goals which they readily acknowledged. At no point ever while playing football did I talk shop with them or discuss anything to do with my work, as I wanted them to associate me with something that we both mutually enjoyed and nothing else. If they raised something with me that was fine, but it would never be the other way around.

It was after a game when we were talking about anything and everything that one of the guys made a comment about the Black Audi incident that I found interesting, as how did he know about it? He joked with me "So Mr Mike have you had any more run-ins with any Audi whips lately?" For weeks that incident had been replaying in my mind, with a little voice in my head querying why did that gang not finish off their attack on the occupants of the Audi – as they clearly outnumbered them and me?

Could it be that some of them recognised me, and were mindful that equally I might have recognised them. In fact I couldn't make out any specific faces as all those present that day were wearing face masks – plus they had their heads covered.

In response to his comment, I smiled and gave back an equally cryptic remark that left him wondering what I had really seen that day. I always found it interesting how they had partly accepted me into their company - not as their G, but as a tolerable acquaintance. I always found it amusing when I was asked to take a visitor out with me for the day to see what was going on with the youth within the borough. Some of them would be very apprehensive and nervous, so as a means of calming them down I would take them for a walk around the local area. On occasions some of the gangs would be hanging out and would approach me to spud me as an acknowledgement of my presence. I remember one guest saying to me after we had walked by "you actually know them." She seemed horrified.

With my tenure of contract due to end, it was time for me to take a break from gang intervention and go back to my normal world of working in defence which on this occasion would see me deployed out of the country for quite a while. It was always my personal policy that no matter how well things were going, I always took a break from gang related work so that I could remain sharp, focused and objective - and not get sucked down in all the negativity that is often associated with this demanding type of work. I had learned so much while working in Gotham, and felt that I had made some strong inroads into what is normally impenetrable territory. I still however felt that I had so much more to learn if I was going to take my work up to the next level, and this continuous professional development needed to happen fast, as gang related crime and stabbings were clearly on the rise in London.

THE ROADMAN

IN GANG PARLANCE THE word roadman means quite something different to our normal understanding of its meaning which usually refers to a person employed to repair or maintain roads. I can assure you that a gang roadman does nothing of the sort, and this reclaimed word is now slang for a young person who has a particular style of dress and is completely aware of his surroundings and all who enter or leave it.

Often deemed a distant relative of the Chav on account of similar behaviour, the roadman however has some distinct differences relating to how they dress and how they like to be identified.

Typical clothing worn includes gear made by Armani, Nike and North Face. Trainers or creps as they call them are usually deemed high status items – so the more expensive they are, the better the roadman is viewed. The roadman is also known to carry a man bag, usually for stashing their phone, grinder or weed that is if they take it. Only the really stupid ones carry a knife or a gun. The roadman does not use his real name when communicating – only his road name, which they create. Road names or street tags that I have heard being used include: Digga D, R1, Drilla and Blue Mouse. When you think about it – it's quite a smart idea as it makes identification really hard. In the army, soldiers using the radio networks are always taught never to use names, ranks or places. So if you wanted to speak to the commanding officer you would refer them as Sunray, the HQ would be zero, and any soldiers operating in the field would have a call-sign IE: Alpha two-one, Delta two-zero and Echo three-three.

The roadman is usually the foot soldier in a gang, but can elevate their status by become a trapper (drug dealer) or a Driller (hit man). Some may even be musically inclined and participate in drill or grime videos that glorify gang violence.

DRILL AND GRIME

Drill and Grime are terms that refer to different types of music that are generally associated with gang culture. The essential difference between Drill and Grime tends to relate to the BPM (Beats per Minute) and the general theme of the song. Grime tracks are usually fast paced and punchy in their nature, whereas Drill is slower and more melodic.

This type of music is deemed by the government and police to be corruptive and violent in its nature, and a negative influence on young people. This argument of course is an old one and has been around for decades. I can recall when I was a teenager my dad looking at my school report and blaming any poor grades that I got on me listening to The Rolling Stones. His usual line being "It's that Mick Jagger music that's making you and all those other teenagers crazy and looking like hippies." So if I ever messed up - I just blamed it on the "Stones."

Today parents probably blame Stormzy or Wiley for their children's shortcomings so it's history repeating itself.

One of the main reasons for Big Brother taking such a hostile stance against Drill and Grime music relates to its content and the violent behaviour of some of its associated artists.

Drill has been around London since 2012, and owes its existence to the Drill scene in Chicago. As with London, Drill has been blamed for multiple deaths of gang members – including some popular artists that were prominent in its promotion.

POLICING THE BEATS

Drill artists often rap about violence and hedonistic criminal lifestyles that are typically linked with gang life. Notable crews include: 67, 150, and Moscow 17. Usually amongst their lyrics there are references to previous or forthcoming criminal acts – that often involve violence. The police regularly analyse Drill for its content and have on occasions imposed Criminal Behaviour Orders and even injunctions on artists that they feel are promoting criminal behaviour.

This drastic action was taken following 66 murders in London during the early part of 2018. Drill music was cited in part for this horrendous bloodshed, and one Drill music group in particular was singled out as being a major instigator of violence. The Group known as 1011 were taken to court by the Metropolitan Police and subjected to a landmark ruling that saw them jailed or detained for periods ranging from 10 months to three and a half years for conspiracy to commit violent disorder.

The charge was based upon an arrest made against the group following a police stop and search operation that unearthed four large machetes, baseball bats, gloves and balaclavas. The police alleged that the gang had been on their way to attack a rival gang known as 12 World – whereas 1011 maintained that the weapons were props for a video shot.

The court and the jury clearly did not accept their defence.

The 1011 Drill group are based in Ladbroke Grove, and have as part of their criminal behaviour order a directive that states that they report to the police any videos that they make, and that they do not promote or encourage violence, or mention postcodes, or make any reference to the death of 19 year old Abdullahi Trabi AKA "Teewiz."

In addition to this ruling, 1011 also cannot attend the Notting Hill Carnival, or possess balaclavas or face masks.

1011 are not the only Drill group to be targeted by the Met police, as there are many others in their sights. At this time You Tube disclosed that their data base held over 1,400 Drill videos that contained lyrics that could be deemed to be incitative. As a result of a police order 60 of them were removed

The Metropolitan Police have a dedicated unit that is dedicated to working on black on black killings – and it is known as Operation Trident. Trident, is permanently ongoing and contains officers that are extremely knowledgeable of the problems and issues that are prolific within the gangs that operate inside their operational jurisdiction.

When the public were first made aware of 1011s court order, the human rights group Liberty called it censorship, and feared that the police were over stepping their legal mark.

Another human rights group known as Liberty, put out the following statement when made aware of the ruling: "Throughout history, art has been a means of political and emotional expression reflecting the reality of people's lives, including violence on our streets. Censorship is a reaction of fear and misunderstanding, not a solution to crime or any other social problem. The contemporary focus on drill lyrics specifically highlights the danger that racial bias infects the criminal justice system."

Liberty, also said that police should "focus on enforcing laws against actual violence, and not clamp down on creative expression."

In response, Detective Chief Superintendent Kevin Southworth, head of the Trident unit responded " We believe this to be one of the first times, if not the first time, we have succeeded in gaining criminal behaviour orders that take such detailed and firm measures to restrict the actions of a gang who blatantly glorified violence through the music they created."

He added "We're not in the business of killing anyone's fun, we're not in the business of killing anyone's artistic expression – we are in the business of stopping people being killed."

"When in this instance you see a particular genre of music being used specifically to goad, to incite, to provoke, to inflame, that can only lead to acts of very serious violence being committed, that's when it becomes a matter for the police."

He also stated that the authorities were not trying to ban anyone from making music. He further commented "Nor are we demonising any type of music – but the public rightly expect us to take action in a case such as this where a line has very clearly been crossed and the safety of individuals is put at risk."

In response to the police action, veteran race campaigner Stafford Scott stated "drill music is a really difficult issue for our community. Personally I am opposed to censorship but in the present climate it is difficult to be critical of actions that may lessen the often negative impact of an apparently growing group of adolescent males who too easily resort to excessive violence with often dire and fatal consequences. However the community should be empowered to engage with these young people with a view to channelling their talents, musically many of them are quite talented, in more positive ways as opposed to criminalising them."

From my own observations of young people involved in gang culture, it would seem that whenever I witnessed any of them listening to Drill music they did appear to display signs of aggression - with some even becoming violent when a rival gang member played a Drill track that they did not approve of.

On occasions when the gang members were reciting the lyrics of their favourite tracks, they would work themselves up into an aggressive mood that could frequently lead to violent outbursts if not defused. These outbursts usually occurred when the track made a reference to a particular event, gang member or act of violence.

One day as an experiment, we got a group of young people to record a number of Drill tracks that they had created – but there would be a difference between these tracks and the normal ones played within this youth centre located in west London. Instead of the normal Drill music references to gangs and violence, these tracks were totally benign and non-offensive.

When we tested the tracks out on a gang that were in for a mentoring session, the results were really interesting. They seemed to enjoy the music, and did not get aggressive – as the subject matter contained nothing for them to react to. I don't personally believe that any genre of music should be singled out to be banned, as there is good and bad amongst many types of music. However I totally understand the specific targeting of individuals or groups advocating and promoting violence and murder.

The following song is by the banned group 1011, and illustrates the typical content of a Grime track.

NO HOOK BY 1011

If they got waps, they ain't got no sweets
'Cause they ain't shot one of my g's
On the opp block, ten toes with my bro
Like tell me who's the next victim
Get round there samurais and waps
J-Sav put his whole rams on your hat
Pull up skrr have them panicking
Pull up skrr like what's happening

[VERSE 1: ZK & DIGGA D]

Yosh got the roll we skrring
Double tap in the back with the German
Clock me an opp, wind down the window
Back out the spinner and burst him
Fucking with me that's curtains
Food get wrapped like turbans
I put bullets in numerous guys
Like, how come the opps ain't learning?
We got bread and got burners
Teewizz got splashed and got murdered
Man get the pack and disperse it
Everything I got man I earned it
If the bridge is weak then I'll burn it
Free Criminal he got birded
That's a L but I know he'll firm itl was vex when I
heard that verdict
Chef, chef, swim, dip man down, make him drown in
his blood

Knock, knock, boom, never left that trap till I found
that grub
OT trips trying to get some funds
We get bread and invest in guns
Them boy run when we tap them drums
Ching, splash, aim for his lungs

[VERSE 2: DIGGA D]

I just put 4 Z's in pebs, plus I got bits for man if they
need it
Bitch want dick my G I'm skeeting
Gyal can't tell me about eating, I mean it
Blood on my shank man keep it and clean it
Use hot water and bleach it
Feds tryna chase, got a rams on my waist
See feds coming up and leaping
(You see me, you see it, but since man's on that topic)
Who wants smoke, man back out my shank on
violence, I move psychotic
Any skeng on sale man cop it
Drop it, whip it and rock it
Apartment settings with loud from 'Dam
Got Teewizz smelling all tropic
We run West that's facts
Akh, them boy there lie upon tracks
Get round there samurais and waps
J-Sav put his whole rams on your hat
Remember that day in a asa scum
Free YF, try fling it in backs
Opps see gang and dash
Skrr crash, bow khalas

[VERSE 3: MSKUM]

You don't wanna see Mskum in the cut

With two shanks up
Creep up like Luger, leave man cut
Now the 12's all hot
Welcome to the wild, wild West
Hot stepping in 'Zart that's shanks in chest
Free CJ cah' he aim at necks
Spinners get spun like songs on decks
Pattern gang who they patterning?
Pull up skrr have them panicking
Pull up skrr like what's happening
See man freeze up like mannequin
Try dash and drop, that's embarrasing
Thought it was Mozart marathon
Double tap, bang the ting
Shells go missing like Madeleine

[VERSE 4: SAV'O]

Gang lurky that's standard
Four man on two peds, jump off with my shank leave
an opp boy splattered
Gyally on me, cause they heard of us
They're like who's that savage?
My bro's them been crashing corn
I don't know for these so called crashers
Got hands on whappers
Back that dots, to the point where you might get
smoked
Broski Splash, done step with the shank and more
time he's fully on volts
Opps them lying on my name for the clout, they're
washed it's a fucking joke
Run man down till he runs out of breath and I dip man
down, touch bones
On the opp block ten toes with my bro, like tell me

who's the next victim
This rambo here that I'm gripping
It's different, it's about 22 inches
Run man down in their block, backed out my shank
make him run from the kitchen
Peng gyal on man, light skin one and I heard it's an
opp boy's misses
Us man down for the action
So who wants beef with the gang
Free Striker, had him locked in Scrubs while I was in
Felts with Dappz
Run up in the yard and stain that shit, man know that
I don't give a dash
The opps are wet, jump out the ride, they run before
seeing my shank
Man they run before weapons are backed

[VERSE 5: HORRID1]

They see Horrid1 and they panic
He backed out the mash try slap it
Man ducked him down I still stabbed it
Man know that I'm active
I'm a savage
Back out the rams, man know I do damage
Chef man down the pussy is planking
Bitch, suck my dick I ain't bashing
Dishing out Teewizz packs in the ends (Loud)
Man bring that gyal from kway to suck off all of my
friends
Man been round there on a 1-2 ped
Lying, 3 double 0 instead
Luger bells in the back with the skeng
Free Jaz and Rago, my bros them mense
Caught Longz on the wing and they smashed his head

Stepped on streets, pepper down beef
Like amm got my phone line running like Creepz
If they got waps, they ain't got no sweets
Cause they ain't shot one of my g's
Them boy there talk to police
Can't believe that I beef these neeks
Gave him 20 shank wounds with the kitchen
And he ain't tryna ride on me
They ain't tryna ride on us
If a boy try run and I catch him
I'll kill him I don't give a fuck (Kill him)
Pretty little face, nice green eyes
Bitch come suck on this cock (Bitch)
I'm the horridest one on the block
Trespass, man are getting shot

Double tap, whip that shit till it rocks (Whip it, whip it)

GANG BANGERS

SO WHAT IS DAILY life like for an average gang member, or gang banger as they would call themselves, when they are – living the life style – as they would say.

To the average person on the street, a gang member is just a gang member, and that they are all one, and the same thing. But that would be inaccurate, as within every gang there is a hierarchy. Although individuals within a gang don't wear chevrons or pips to indicate their rank or status like those worn by members of our armed forces. They do however have a pecking order, in terms of their status.

In gang parlance, a gang member is a low level associate of the gang that either lives off their own reputation, or that of their families. A gang banger though is an active soldier within a gang, and they are usually the ones who carry out the acts of violence against their rivals. "Gangbanging" is normally the term that is used to describe an act of violence, however it is usually shortened to banging or just bang in some gangs. Typically they would say: "are you going to bang that op"

As I often found when I had a group of gang bangers

in for an intervention session, all they would ever talk about was violence, or who was beefing who. They would usually start off by sounding each other out by means of road names, until they could place what part of London their rival was from. It is for this reason that when running a session we would always pre-check everyone, so that those who had known beefs could be eliminated from the course. If we hadn't done that there would have been a bloodbath.

So as to prove themselves within a gang, some gang members will go to ridiculous extremes to gain a reputation, or a rep as they would call it. For instance, if they see a police vehicle they will do something irrational, or act in a suspicious way that will arose police attention. This of course is highly likely to lead to them being questioned or even searched – which all plays into building their rep – as they can then go back to their criminal associates and brag about their stop and search.

I remember one individual who I used to teach and mentor taking this practice to a new level. It was just after lunch one day in the provision when G decided to go to the local supermarket near Grenfell Tower. As he approached the store he saw a large number of police officers, some of whom were armed searching the nearby roads around the local estate. As he looked on he noticed the police helicopter circling around high above trying to identify any suspects that still might be on scene. It was in a moment of madness that he decided to run towards the estate with his hand in his hoodie – mimicking the presence of a gun. He was quickly taken down by the police, and subsequently arrested. Eventually he was released and a member of our staff escorted him back to the provision.

On his arrival he was the centre of attention, with everyone asking "how many feds were there"? and "what did you do to get arrested like that"? G of course lapped it all up, as just for a change he was now the centre of attention. The others had no idea that the police had already been in position prior to Gs arrival, and that his part in the police operation was just a crazy side-show that he had put on in order to build his rep.

What many will find hard to understand is why would anyone want to be the focus of police attention? - as it's normally the last thing that any of us would want. There are many reasons for this bizarre behaviour, some easy to understand, while others are very complex. Many of the young gang members that I worked with displayed behaviour that would usually be associated with a young child, as opposed to that seen in a normal teenager.

There were many times when I used to have to remind myself to lower my level of teaching, so that it reflected their emotional age, and not their birth age. These young people would have been in a normal school at some point or other, but somewhere in their lives they came off the tracks. For the most part when working with them on a one to one basis, my interaction with them was generally positive and insightful. However in a classroom setting, it was always an uphill battle to get them to focus or engage for any period. This of course is one of the reasons why they are so vulnerable to being attracted to the gang life style, as it gives them a sense of belonging.

There were some gang members that I got on with really well, and this made me go that extra mile to help them. Whenever they wanted an offline chat about something, I would make the time to hear them out. It's a sad reflection on our society that in many cases the only people that they have a trusting relationship with is usually someone outside their family circle.

I remember one afternoon a young man called Y asking if he could stay late to talk to me and another mentor called L. We both readily agreed and sat together for hours talking about his gang life style, and where it would eventually lead. He listened to us politely and attentively, but I could tell that he was only paying us lip service and that he had no intention of stopping any time soon. I reminded him that twice that week I had prevented him from being attacked by his rivals, and that it was only a matter of time until they got him.

That conversation took place on a Thursday evening, and by Sunday evening he was in hospital fighting for his life after being stabbed 6 times while visiting friends in a local park. Mercifully he survived his ordeal, thanks to the excellent skills of an NHS Trauma Surgeon, and made a good physical recovery. He did however suffer from frequent flash backs, that would eventually manifest into PTSD (Post Traumatic Stress Disorder). I did meet up with Y some time later, when he dropped by to say hello, and to show off his puncture and surgery scars. He mentioned our previous conversation, and how my words of "you're really riding your luck" kept repeating in his mind from that day onwards. He also made me aware that his family had decided to leave London, so that he would be away from gang life. I was really pleased to hear that, and wished him well with his future. But there was to be a sting in the tail for me. As Y was leaving the building, he thanked me for everything that I had done for him and in his normal style he fist pumped me. It was in this moment that he said that he still had unfinished business to care of before he left London. I'm sure you can figure out for yourselves what he meant by that throwaway comment.

Some months later while working in the same area of

north London, I carried out an intervention that involved two brothers that were both involved in the same gang. It was the classic story of my brothers in a gang, so I'm going to be in one. There was however a big difference between the two brothers: One was a hardened gang banger, while the younger brother was just a drug and weapons mule within the gang. I really felt sorry for the younger brother, as he was totally out of his depth in this new world that he had become a part of – and telling his brother that he wanted out was never going to happen.

Over the following weeks the brothers got involved in a number of criminal activities that were becoming increasingly concerning on account of the level of violence being used. Essentially, they were trying to take over another gang's drug turf at a nearby college, and tensions were running high following a youth getting slashed by a machete. As part of a cross agency initiative to help deescalate the situation we called a meeting with the boy's parents, and they were absolutely distraught with what was going on with their sons. It was clearly evident that they were good parents, and that they cared deeply about them. Mum and dad were from Ghana, and felt that by coming to the UK their children would get a better education, and therefore more career opportunities. Their dream however was now falling apart right in front of their eyes, and they felt it was only a matter of time before one of their children carried out a stabbing, or became a victim of one.

The mother by this time was crying, with both boys trying to do their best to console her, but their words were having little effect. As her husband looked on I could see tears in his eyes also, and a look of absolute despair. Eventually he looked over at me, and said "Sir, if these were your sons, what would you do"? I paused to collect my thoughts, and looking at him directly I said "Sir, I would either send the boys back to Ghana for a few years until they grew out of this phase in their life, or I would move both them, and the rest of the of the family out of London, and I would start a new life.

He then grabbed my hand, and shock it in a firm manner and said "thanks for being so blunt and honest with me, and not beating around the bush to avoid the question." With that he left the room with his family, and went off to pick up his daughters who were attending a nearby school. A few days later, I got a call from him informing me that both he and his wife had quit their jobs, and that they were all off to Norfolk, to start over again. It was an incredibly dramatic move to make, and an extremely courageous one. I have no doubt that his decision saved his boys lives. When I last heard from the family - all were doing well - with the eldest of the boys about to start university.

This story ended happily, but most involving the gang world don't.

When working with the youngest gang members, I always found it both fascinating and at the same time alarming - just how quick they could go from absolutely nothing, to extreme violence - in just a matter of seconds.

In one incident that I can recall that illustrates this point perfectly, and shows that we clearly need to learn more about the management of our young people's emotions in a way that is more efficient and effective, or we risk even more violence in our society.

It was while working with a group of teenagers in a youth centre in west London, that I witnessed an explosive reaction to a totally innocent action that could - if we had all not acted so quickly - led to the death of a young school boy.

The day had started off well enough with our mentor group, aside from the usual spats and sly comments that were typical of these meetings. I was positioned with my back to the wall as per normal, so that I could both observe my group, and also keep an eye on the comings and goings at the main entrance. This was normal procedure while working in this building, as there was always a risk of rival gang members visiting the location inadvertently while part of another intervention groups activities.

About half way through our session, a group of around 20 young children accompanied by their teachers and support staff entered the far side of the building. As their staff went about setting up their group session at the far end of the hall, a small group of boys began looking around the hall. As I looked at them, I could tell from their body language and visual cues that they were all autistic, and that they were simply just acquainting themselves with the layout of the building.

One of the boys in particular was taking a great interest in the posters and paintings that were located in our part of the hall, but he was starting to concern me as he was drifting too close to our group. One of our support mentors approached him to see if he was ok, and that was when all hell broke loose. Amongst our group was a young man called R who suddenly started shouting "that ops scoping us out, we need to chef him up." With that the other gang members started to get animated, with some getting their phones out to record the spectacle that was about to take place.

They were shouting "do him R, do him R, we will back you up." My top priority was to get the young boy out of that building as fast as possible, as he was highly likely to get hurt if he stayed around. I quickly ushered him towards his own group, who were by now alerted to the fact that something serious was going on in the hall. I gestured to the staff to leave the building, and they were very quick to pick up on my visual cues that they were not safe here. As all this mayhem was taking place, our staff, as well as some other youth workers that had been in the hall tried as best as they could to coral our group. R had now bolted towards the main door to chase after the young boy, but was quickly stopped by Mr S who had anticipated his actions. S was not one to dither around when it kicked off, as he knew where it could all go. He restrained R, and forcibly evicted him through the rear fire exit, so that he could not see anyone. The others in the group were now becoming increasingly hostile towards our staff - as in their eyes we had denied them a snapchat opportunity.

We eventually managed to regain control of the situation and restore calm, but the damage was done. It was evident that we could not use this facility again, as there were just too many risks associated with its use. There had been near misses before, but this one was on a different level. One of my work colleagues would eventually tell me that he had been in the building when a masked gunman had run into the hall, and opened fire on the groups within with a MAC-10 machine gun. Thankfully the idiot was a lousy shot and fired all the rounds in to the walls and ceiling. Thank god I missed that one, I think was my reaction to that one.

Later in the day R got a piece of my mind about his behaviour in the hall, and what would have been the consequences if he had succeeded in his foolhardy endeavours. He would have potentially taken the life of a young boy who had absolutely nothing to do with gangs - and was merely looking at posters and pictures - and not at him!! I also pointed out that he would be in jail, for a supposed action that had never actually taken place, and that his fellow compadres in crime would be joining him. And all because they did not have the intellectual capacity or common sense to just take a few seconds to figure out what was really going on - and be understanding of a young boy who was simply exploring his environment - and as such posed no threat whatsoever.

Sadly, such incidents are commonplace across London, with many young lives lost for little or no reason.

Seeing so many instances like this prompted me to develop my own strategies for dealing with teenagers like this – that are basically walking time bombs. The first thing that you have to do is identify those that are most likely to explode into a violent tirade, and more importantly what triggers them.

Generally those that I have personally witnessed behaving in such a volatile manner tend to have a very low emotional age, that doesn't match their birth age. Although they are teenagers - they act like little children – and are therefore extremely vulnerable to exploitation. Low esteem is also a big problem, with many young gang members struggling to figure out what they will be doing next week, let alone a year from now.

It is a pretty sad existence from where I'm coming from, and yet in their eyes they have a feeling of belonging, as their gang family probably means more to them, than their biological one. Indeed there have been occasions where I have met parents of young vulnerable teenagers, where I have come away wondering why their children are not even more unhinged and volatile – because at home they have absolutely nobody to look up to, or even respect.

Grime artist Stormzy - complete with stab proof vest

Armed police taking down some gangbangers after
a robbery in East London

Armed police cordon off an area in Brent following
the shooting of 4 people. The youngest victim was
only 2 years old

Riot police at an illegal gangbangers party during
the COVID-19 pandemic

Police and members of the public take down a bad
guy following a ram raid in Shepherds Bush

Armed police taking down some gangbangers in Brixton

Confiscated knives found during an Operation
Venice stop and search

A police scorpion team in action during Operation Venice

A police officer breaking up a fight at the 2019 Notting Hill Carnival

A Met Police EC-145 helicopter in action over London

DAT CARNIVAL TING

ONE DAY WHILE WORKING in Ladbroke Grove, I decided during my lunch break to take a walk around Portobello Market – a place full of characters, wheeler dealers and of course gangs. Bumping into gang bangers and trappers in this part of London, was a very common occurrence for me, as I had worked in this area on and off for more years than I can remember.

Just as I was enjoying the ambience of the market and the glorious summer sunshine, a voice from the crowd brought my day to a shuddering halt. "Yo it's my G Mr Mike." I recognised the voice instantly it was T1 – an old acquaintance of mine so to speak, accompanied by some of his crew. As we chewed the fat talking about everything and nothing, I asked if he was behaving himself, and back came the answer in his exaggerated patois slang "yez I am coz I've got dat carnival ting coming up, and that will mean payday for me and my bros." With that they all laughed, as they could me shaking my head in disappointment.

This particular group from previous dealings were

more on the petty crime side of gang life, as opposed to the violent side. By any gang measuring metric: they would not be deemed devil's, but equally they were no saints either. I always felt with T1 that if a good role model came into his life, his negative behaviour could be modified, or even nullified. That of course was wishful thinking on my behalf. When I had mentored him previously, we had got in really well, and at one stage I had even persuaded him to join a football club, as he was very good in midfield.

He used to tease me about when my time came to be put in a rest home, I would be able to look at him on Match of the Day, and be able to tell all my other fellow residents that I once used to coach him.

He was a bit of a joker, as you can probably gather.

After a fairly long catch-up in the market, we wished each other well – and as quickly as he had appeared he melted away into the crowd, and was gone.

Seeing him again made me reflect on my dealings with the various gangs that made up this area. Sometimes my encounters with them could be very amicable, while there were other times when things could get pretty scary. I rapidly learned that my survival depended on the relationships that I had built up over the years, and that one slip up could put me in serious danger.

Where I was now standing was right in the heart of the part of London that hosts the Notting Hill Carnival. For those of you who live in London, Carnival needs no introduction or explanation as you will no doubt be very aware of it. However, for those who live outside London, or even overseas – here is a brief explanation.

The Notting Hill Carnival - or just "Carnival" as it is normally known – is an annual event that has taken place in London since 1966. Carnival lasts for two days and is held over August bank holiday Monday and the preceding

Sunday. Day one of Carnival is primarily for children and families, with day two aimed at adults. Music played at the carnival is varied and includes the following genres: Soca, Calypso, Steelpan, Dancehall, Reggae, Drum and bass, Jungle, Ragga, Hip Hop, R&B, House and Techno.

Attendance at Carnival varies from year to year but usually involves around 1.2 million attendees, 40,000 volunteers and some 9,000 police officers.

It is the biggest street party in Europe, and one of the largest cultural events in the UK calendar.

For my West Indian friends Carnival is a big event in their year, and one that they all look forward to attending. For them Carnival is an opportunity to put whatever problems or worries that they have away for a weekend, so that they can enjoy the music, food and their favourite hooch – which is usually rum. For their wives and children, Carnival also means outlandish and flamboyant costumes that often take weeks, or even months to make.

These are the people that make Carnival great, as they epitomise all the best things and values that I associate with the warm and friendly people that make up the Caribbean community in West London. But they are also the ones that at times I really feel for. Why? Because within their vibrant community there are rogue elements that also look forward to Carnival - but for totally different reasons. The rogue elements are generally made up of known gangs, however there are others that are involved that are generally part of larger organised crime networks.

Although small in number in relative terms compared to the wider community, there are still enough of them to cause and inflict significant mayhem at Carnival – and this they do every year. They don't care a jot about the larger community that they affect, as all Carnival means to them is criminal opportunity: drug dealing, robbery, sexual assaults, gang score settlements and of course the chance of abusing and attacking the police officers that are involved in controlling the event.

The police and the local residents of Notting Hill are all painfully aware of just what the gangs are capable of, as they witness it every year. Generally children and families day passes off with very few crime incidents, however the adult day is a totally different story. It is here where most of the crime will be committed, and the concern every year is always - will this lead to a mini riot.

The police know full that Carnival is a target rich environment for both them, and of the course gangs. It is the ultimate game of cat and mouse. Usually a few weeks before the start of Carnival, the police mount intensive pre-emptive strikes and raids on known gang members – in a bid to deny and disrupt their criminal activities. HVTs (High Value Targets) such as known gang leaders are always a top priority - as taking them down sends out a strong warning to their partners in crime. Police raids are particularly useful for seizing weapons caches and drug stocks that are being amassed in readiness for the big day. The logic being if you have no product to sell, then you have no need to attend. Gangs of course are very resourceful and will anticipate raids, so weapons and drugs are often stored in either vehicles or scooter paniers so that they are constantly being moved around.

On the day of Carnival itself, police will have already pre-deployed Public Order Officers from CO11 to local schools or governments buildings where they are able to discreetly prepare their officers and equipment to go hard line in the event of massed disorder.

In addition to CO11, the Metropolitan Police will also deploy elements of the police firearms unit SCO19 (Specialist Crime Operations) which comprises ARVs,

(Armed Response Vehicles) CTSFO (Counter Terrorist Specialist Firearms Officers) and TST (Tactical Support Teams). In recent years it has become a matter of routine to have CTSFO teams on hand, just in case of a terrorist attack. The Carnival represents a significant target for terrorists on account of the large crowds that attend the event – so having these specialist teams on hand makes good sense.

In addition to these assets, the police will also deploy elements of their Air Support Unit (ASU) which comprises three EC-145 helicopters using the call signs India 97, India 98 and India 99. These are generally used for crowd control, public order, aerial reconnaissance and covert intelligence gathering. Each helicopter is equipped with an L-3 Wescam MX-15 sensor pod which houses a gyro-stabilized high definition colour day camera and a thermal imaging camera that features a digital video-downlink capability.

You would think that with all this high tech against you, plus all those highly effective specialist police units that you might just for one minute stop and think, do I really want to go up against these guys? But you guessed it – yes they do, as it always feels great to them to put one over on the police.

In an effort to minimise gang effectiveness at the Carnival, the police now deploy screening arches that are just like the ones you see at an airport. In the past searches were voluntary, but now they're mandatory. This in part is due to the higher threat level presented by terrorists - as the great fear is that there could be a suicide attack by terrorists using explosive filled vests.

Another tactic now employed at Carnival is the use of a Section 60 stop and search order that allows the searching of people for offensive weapons or dangerous instruments without having reasonable grounds. These orders are very controversial, and are only used in high threat environments, or under very specific operational circumstances.

One particular tool that is used extensively at Carnival by the police is CCTV. These high tech camera systems are usually installed around major vantage points or key entry/exit locations, in and around Notting Hill. Although the police are trialling AI (Artificial Intelligence) based facial recognition systems, these are still undergoing development – and their usage is a very sensitive and contentious subject. This in part stems from the fact that the darker your skin is, the more inaccurate the camera readings become.

To help improve the effectiveness of the mobile CCTV systems deployed at Carnival, the police employ a small army of human "super-recognisers." These are officers who are extremely good at identifying and recognising faces amongst large crowds of people, especially those known for violence and prolific crime.

The police also have at their disposal significant numbers of officers – male and female, who serve undercover at Notting Hill, often posing as party goers or tourists so as to blend in with the crowds.

Other high tech assets are also available to the police, but for operational security reasons I cannot discuss them, or even reveal how they are deployed. All I can say is that they are extremely effective, and result in a lot of arrests.

As you can see, the policing of Carnival is a major undertaking – and involves considerable numbers of officers, resources and vehicles.

I guess that you are now probably wondering: why is Carnival not crime free then? I will now attempt to answer that one, but from a gang members viewpoint. You have to remember that Carnival is a truly massive event, and that where you have lots of people – you have lots of targets! Most of these targets will be completely innocent people, while others become targets on account of being complicit in some way. For example they may be seeking to buy class A drugs from a trapper, while attending Carnival.

It is no secret that just as the police and organisers are preparing for Carnival – so are the gangs. Most of the local gangs will be fully aware of who their ops are, and that means that while attending Carnival, they need to be looking out for both them and the police. In addition to the local gangs, there will also be other gangs from all over London that will be looking to attend, as they to want a share of the criminal cake that is there for the taking.

Some gangs will deliberately seek confrontation with their rivals, while others will form temporary alliances – like they did during the London riots. The Somalian gangs, or "Malis" as they are more commonly known are particularly entrepreneurial and will often form very unusual partnerships in order to exploit criminal opportunities at Carnival. When I worked with the Somalian gangs in West London, I was always intrigued with their resourcefulness and ability to adapt to changing circumstances – be they positive or negative. They were very well aware that if they put trappers out in Notting Hill, the local West Indian gangs would spot them a mile away, so instead they recruited young teenagers from other ethnic groups that were less likely to attract attention.

I have even known them to use white teenagers in their criminal activities, something that I have never seen in their West Indian counterparts. These factors are also interesting for the police when they try to infiltrate gangs. Going undercover in a gang is an extremely dangerous undertaking - as most gang members are very mistrustful of anyone that they do not know, or who cannot be vouched for.

A friend of mine who is a police officer was once working undercover and got very badly beaten up by a gang member who had an issue with him over something relatively petty. If he had known that he was a police officer, he would have probably killed him. The officers who undertake these sort of operations are incredibly brave, as just one mistake could cost them their lives.

As risky as they are, they must be carried out where and whenever possible – as somebody on the inside, is worth more than a 100 on the outside. If that is not possible then you need to turn a gang banger from being a member of a gang into what the police call a CHIS (Covert Human Intelligence Source). In old money we would call them informants, the gangs however would call them rats. Whatever the name, they play a vital part in completing knowledge gaps that the police need to fill - in order to build up an effective intelligence picture of gang activity in London. Of course every gang denies that they have anyone within their ranks that will rat on them, but that's just wishful thinking on their behalf.

If we equate todays gang informants to those in the IRA at the height of "The Troubles" in Northern Ireland from 1968 to 1998. The conflict had reached something of a stalemate where the British Army could not militarily defeat the IRA, and equally the IRA could not defeat them. Eventually the army reached the conclusion that the only way that they could defeat the terrorists was by subverting them from inside, which ultimately led to their collapse. At one stage over half of the IRAs leadership had become informants, which led to 2 out of every 3 of their terrorist attacks ending in failure.

We have also become increasingly effective at defeating

Islamic terrorist groups operating within the UK, and it is only a matter of time until our infiltration of gangs bears similar results.

During my time with gang intervention in North-West London, the gang members that I worked with would never discuss what they were planning for the Carnival, as that would incriminate them. Instead I used to have to wait until it was over before I got to too hear about what they got up to. In their bragging they talked about throwing a police helicopter off them, after it had locked on to them. They mentioned how they had run into the underground car parks and walkways to evade the thermal imaging cameras that the police helicopters mount. Once out in the open, they knew that they would get picked up pretty quickly and then it was game over - as they would get arrested.

They talked of one incident where they sent some very young gang wannabe's out as decoys to attract police attention. Once satisfied that the police were busy with them carrying out stop and searches, they raced into the crowd and snatched some hand bags and high end cameras, and then they were off down the side streets.

I have to say that they had planned everything really well. They had spotters in the nearby towers who were working out where the police were thinnest on the ground, and then adapting their criminal activities accordingly. They of course would never know where the police undercover teams were, as they don't exactly advertise themselves.

Things however did not go well for two of them who were operating just outside the Carnival perimeter. One of the teenagers Y had gone into a nearby corner store to get some cold drinks. While in the shop he saw a group of young men wearing hoodies charge at his friend who was outside, and reign blows down on him, but that was not all that they had done to him. His friend had also been stabbed and as a consequence he collapsed to the ground holding his stomach. As he screamed for help, Y went over to him and tried to figure out what to do. He called for help, but everyone that had been nearby had moved away, and they clearly did not want to get involved. As his friend bled profusely from his stab injuries Y called for an ambulance, but they could not assist him until a police escort was available. Eventually an ambulance arrived along with police, and Y slipped away into the crowds.

I remember when he first told me the story, I felt quite disgusted with him for not staying with his friend, and trying to stem his wounds, or at the very least make some sort of effort to reassure him. He would later say that he had been in shock, and that he had felt paralysed with fear at the time. Thankfully, his friend eventually made a full recovery, but it was evident to me that this painful episode had clearly left an impact on Y.

No doubt, there were many other incidents of a similar nature, but I did not work with the individuals that had been responsible for them, so therefore I cannot tell their stories. There was however a grain of comfort in that there were no afters. IE no riots. So all credit to the police, organisers and stewards for that one.

> Crime stats for the 2019 Notting Hill Carnival:
> Sunday 111 arrests
> Monday 242 arrests
> 37 x Assaults on police
> 2 x Drink drive
> 2 x Criminal damage
> 31 x Public order
> 34 x Offensive weapons seizures

10 x Theft
162 x Drugs
10 x Sexual offences
5 x Robbery

Sadly, the 2020 Notting Hill Carnival was cancelled due to the COVID -19 pandemic.

DOUBLE DUMB

THERE ARE PARTICULAR PEOPLE that gangs frequently target, as they are deemed easy pickings. They call them DDs – which means double dumb. A DD is usually an individual who walks down a road with headphones on their head, and either a phone or tablet in their hand.

As many of us already know, if you are wearing headphones, especially those that are of the noise cancelling variety – you tend to go into your own zone, and become increasingly detached from what is going on around you. Add a phone to that mix, and your situational awareness becomes virtually non-existent.

Situational awareness, is our own personal radar that warns us of any health and safety problems that could pose a potential danger to us. Our situational awareness is only as accurate as our own perception or reading of a situation, so what we think may be happening is not always an accurate reflection on reality.

How we assess a situation can be influenced by many factors, such as information presented or simply by our own experience. For instance, late at night when we are walking home and we see two men in suits on one side of the road, and two wearing hoodies on the other. What side do we pick? Our situational awareness radar will usually decide that the safer bet is the side of the road with the two men in suits. That's because we are aware of our surroundings.

There are of course times when we all become totally absorbed with something that is playing on our mind, and that is when we are most vulnerable – as we are far less likely to see impending danger.

Gangs are not mind readers - so they will have no idea of what you are thinking – it is generally your actions that will give you away, which in turn increases the likely hood of you becoming a victim.

Wearing headphones and openly viewing your phone will make you a prime target, and that's a fact. When I worked in Gotham, we carried out an experiment one day where I picked out all the people walking in and around Westfield shopping centre that I thought would make targets. The two gang members that were with me also identified who they would go for - and why. We eventually compared notes, and they were virtually identical. One of them even joked with me afterwards that I should become a spotter for them.

What I always find amazing is just how many of these walking targets are out there for the taking. Typically gangs will use 3 gang bangers for their hit and run street robberies. One will act as a spotter and lookout, while the other two are the strike team – one a rider, the other a snatcher.

Gangs tend to have their own preferred spots for carrying out snatch and grabs. They usually like long stretches of road, as they can target multiple victims within a matter of minutes. In one area of North London where

I worked, some strike teams were carrying out as many as 20 robberies a day. They were incredibly prolific on account of an abundant availability of victims, and a distinct lack at that particular time of an effective police response.

Strike teams tend to avoid violent confrontation with individuals, as that slows them up. All they want to do is snatch a phone or tablet out of its owner's hands before they have a chance to react. And by the time they do react, the thieves are usually long gone.

The cover of night also doesn't provide any protection, as thieves can see the glow of phones from quite a distance. Individuals wearing headphones can also be easily spotted, as those equipped with Bluetooth tend to have big flashing LEDs (Light Emitting Diodes).

Gang spotters are particularly adept at targeting vulnerable victims, or targets of opportunity - and rarely get caught – as victims are often not aware that they have been singled out. Some gangs even use female spotters as they are less conspicuous in areas covered by CCTV.

Prior to gangs using mopeds, scooters and bikes for street robberies. London based gangs used to carry out robbery on mass by means of a technique known as steaming. Steaming gangs were usually large in number and tended to target their victims in either buses, trains or packed venues, as there would be lots of targets for them to hit in one go – plus it would be very difficult for potential victims to escape. Victims of steaming gangs had little chance of fighting back, as they would often be facing some 20 to 30 violent thugs that would be armed with knives and baseball bats. Intimidation and extreme violence were the hall marks of steaming gangs, and very rarely did they get stopped by police whilst in the midst of their rampaging.

I have only ever seen one steaming gang in operation, and that was in a shopping centre in West London. I remember at the time hearing screams in the distance but had no idea what was going on. As I stood in the shop, a large group of young men who were in a group of some twenty plus charged past, grabbing bags, phones and high value items from nearby shops. Some people were pushed to the ground, and others punched and kicked as the gang made its way towards the high street.

A police van did turn up with a small number of officers, but they were forced to temporarily withdraw after coming under sustained attack by the gang.

Eventually more police began to appear, and this forced the gang to split up into smaller groups that made their getaway via the numerous side roads and alleyways that emanated from the nearby high street.

Thankfully, aside from riots where steaming gangs can still appear – albeit in a sporadically formed ad-hoc manner - I believe the days of the organised steaming gangs are gone.

I say that as a number of factors have changed in our society that makes steaming more difficult to accomplish without significant risk to the gangs perpetrating it. The large scale introduction of CCTV, and better monitoring of gangs by the police are significant factors for its disappearance. I also believe on a more concerning note that due to the significant increases in young people joining gangs and the fact that they are very territorial - means that steaming gangs would find it very difficult to go into each other's areas - without some form of retribution.

As we all know street crime tends to go through fads and phases, and something that is successful for today's criminal may become either ineffective or redundant, following changes in police tactics or the introduction of more effective crime reduction measures.

The biggest change though that still needs to be made relates to sentencing, as our current jail terms are totally inadequate, and are encouraging crime, rather than deterring it. One example of this that comes to mind relates to a 15 year old teenager that I had to deal with a few years back. Essentially, he had joined two different gangs which was probably not the best idea that he had ever had, as it resulted in both of them trying to find him to teach him a lesson. For his safety, and that of his family he got moved to a new location in North-West London where he decided to embark on a one man crime wave.

Using his scooter as a means of transport he would ride around Kilburn looking for victims to rob. In one particular spree which took place just before Christmas, he robbed dozens of people over a two week period – his modus operandi being to target people who were leaving pubs and bars, somewhat worse for wear – on account of enjoying the festive period.

Early in the New Year he started bragging about his exploits which quickly got him arrested and charged. He subsequently appeared in court but was let off on account of him being under sixteen which seems to be a threshold for sentence guidance. Spurred on by his lack of punishment, he decided to resume his criminal activities once again, but just as before he got caught and was back into the judicial system.

While in court awaiting the outcome of the judge's deliberation, he lost his temper and began throwing things in the court room. That outburst got him four months in jail.

HOW TO PROTECT YOUR MOBILE PHONE AGAINST CRIMINALS ON BIKES AND MOPEDS

Criminals often use bikes and mopeds to snatch mobile phones from people, particularly at busy locations such as outside stations, shopping centres or concert venues. Often victims are approached from behind while talking or texting on phones. Criminals on mopeds or bicycles may mount the pavement to grab the phone or snatch it from the road. Sometimes when it's a moped, a pillion passenger will snatch it.

While most thefts happen between six and ten at night, criminals operate during the day too, so always look out for what's going on around you. Follow these simple steps to help protect your phone.

- Be aware of your surroundings
- If you need to call or use your phone on the street, look out for anyone on a bike or a moped near you. Look up, look out.
- Make it quick so you don't become distracted.
- Don't text while you're walking – as you won't notice what's going on around you.
- If that's not possible, stand away from the roadside, close to a building or wall, so no one can come up behind you.
- Going hands-free can prevent a thief from snatching your phone out of your hand.
- Use security features on your phone
- You should switch on your phone's security features to protect your phone.
- Use the keypad lock so that thieves cannot

immediately access your phone, or use the
biometric authentication if your phone has it
(finger print or facial recognition).

- Your phone may have other security features
  you can use – these could allow you to wipe
  data, lock your handset, or prevent a thief from
  restoring a phone to its factory settings from
  another internet device.

- Consider installing an anti-theft app. These can
  be an effective way of helping police trace your
  phone and identify the thief.

Know how to identify your phone if it's stolen

- Every phone has an IMEI number which helps
  police and insurance companies to identify it if
  it's stolen. UK network operators can also stop a
  stolen phone from working across their networks
  with its IMEI.

- Find your IMEI number by dialling *#06# from
  your phone and keep a written note of it; if
  the phone is stolen, report the number to your
  mobile provider to stop it being used.

- Register your phone and other property to help
  police recover stolen property and combat the
  sale of stolen goods. Police recover more than
  2,500 items on average a month registered to the
  website.

- Remember, never confront a thief or risk your
  own safety for the sake of your mobile phone.

How to protect yourself from street robbery

Here are some useful ways to keep you and your property safe on the street.

LOOK CONFIDENT

You are less likely to be targeted if you look confident. Move with purpose and try to be aware of your surroundings.

KNOW WHERE YOU'RE GOING

Plan your route and think about what to take with you, especially if you're going somewhere you haven't been before. Keep to busy, well-lit streets, walkways and paths which are more likely to be covered by CCTV. Only take licensed taxis or minicabs booked by phone or a mobile phone app.

HIDE IT

Keep your mobile phone and valuables out of sight. If you're using your phone it's more likely to be snatched from your hand as you're not paying attention to your surroundings, so look around you.

And never leave a mobile, any other device, wallet or purse on the table of an outdoor café, pub or restaurant. Same goes for any jewellery you might be wearing – keep it covered when walking down the street.

CASH CONVERTERS

ONE THING I LEARNED pretty quickly while working in the Gang world is that regardless of where they are in London, the one thing that they all have in common is their love of cash. It is a truism that if they're using credit cards they are highly likely to have been stolen.

Cash is great in the sense that it is hard to track, but when you're moving lots of it that will cause you a problem, as any use of cash in the UK that is over £10,000 has to be reported to the authorities. Failure to do so could result in a penalty of £5000.

So that begs the question what do gangs do with all the stolen phones, mopeds and scooters?

When your phone is stolen, there are a number of things that could potentially happen to it. If you're lucky they will just switch it off – trash the sim card – format it and re-sell it. However if they go for the other option then you really are in trouble. Because they could unlock it and misuse the data and information that is inside it, which could result in lots of problems for you. So golden rule number one is, if your phone gets stolen tell your service provider, and get them to block your number. Also make sure that your friends are aware that your phone has been stolen, so that they are cautious of any suspicious texts or messages.

Only recently a friend of mine lost his phone, and within days all sorts of weird requests started to come through supposedly from him requesting money. They were of course bogus requests, but not everyone would be savvy enough to realise that.

In the UK over half a million phones were stolen in 2016, with over 60,000 from robberies in London alone. There are certain groups that are particularly vulnerable:14-24 year olds and young women.

Mobile phone theft in the UK is rising year on year - primarily because hand sets are becoming more expensive - which makes them even more worthwhile to steal.

There is also a booming market for our stolen phones in Nigeria of all places - simply because their middle classes are tech starved of local product - so are therefore willing to pay much higher premiums for foreign second hand smartphones. I am reliably informed that gang banger strike teams in the UK get on average £50 per stolen smart phone, however once these phones reach Nigeria they can sell for a staggering £550 each. So now you know why street robberies are so prolific in London.

Nigeria could of course stop this crime epidemic dead in its tracks, simply by creating a phone network regulatory body. Sadly due to a combination of corrupt officials and unscrupulous businesses that is not going to happen any time soon.

Some years ago, I was taken to an independent phone shop in posh Chiswick of all places - that was allegedly heavily involved in fencing stolen phones. The two teenagers that took me to this store, were clearly acquainted with the staff within, but in my presence they never said anything to them that could be incriminating.

Not long after our visit the shop was gone!! What a coincidence?

Phone theft is by no means our worst crime, as there are plenty of others that are of a greater magnitude. Let's take the London drugs scene for instance. There are areas of London that only two years ago - which would make it around 2018 – where I would never see any form of open drug dealing, as it just didn't happen around there. Move time forward to 2020, and there are trappers plying their trade almost everywhere that hosts a conglomeration of young people.

Why the sudden increase?

The answer is as usual down to money. With so many gangs now selling drugs in London - the trappers now have to seek new markets – either in the outlying boroughs of the City, or through county lines opportunities.

I have no idea how much drugs cash moves through London every day, but I would suggest that the figure is in the millions. I know of one drugs operation, where a gang of 8 spent over 12 hours counting their cash. That would have to equate to millions of pounds.

A few years ago while working with a West Indian gang in south-west London, one of their members mouthed off to a blonde haired white man that was sitting in a high end BMW outside a block of flats. Despite being overwhelmingly outnumbered he walked up the youth who had been abusing him and he just said one sentence "believe me, you do not want to step into my world."

The other gang members who were nearby responded by saying "its ok we're cool with you, everything's bless." They then pushed their mouthy friend away, and moved off towards another block of flats. One of the gang support workers who was standing nearby to me said in a quiet voice "when he drives away I will tell you who he is." Eventually the BMW pulled away, and I was informed that he was the leader of a major Eastern-European organised crime gang. Which is why our gang had backed off. The BMW man was also probably a little wary of me, as I was wearing a suit which may have made him think that I was connected with the police. Something that happened all too frequently when I was working in gang intervention, as very few members of staff at that time were white.

A few weeks after this chance encounter, One of our gang mentors suggested that I accompany him to the local post office to have a look at something interesting. As I walked into the post office all seemed normal to me at first. There were pensioners patiently waiting in line, along with a number of young people but other than that all seemed ok. It was only when I looked over towards the mini supermarket section of the post office that I saw something out of place. In this particular area there was a young adult man with unkempt hair, who was accompanied by two females that looked like students. All around them were sports bags, possibly 8 or more in total, but why where they here? I soon got the answer when the young man walked up to the people in the que, and informed them that they should come back tomorrow, as he required all the available staff. One of the young men in the que told him in no uncertain terms where to go. His language and choice of words were most interesting, but I will not repeat them here.

As this tirade continued the girls had begun emptying out their bags, which contained hundreds of bundles of £10 and £20 notes. I don't recall seeing any £5 or £50 notes, as they were probably too much trouble.

Whatever was going on it was clear that this was dirty

money. Eventually an Asian women behind the counter gestured for the three cash mules to come to her counter. As she started to serve them, the male member of the group gave her a Russian phone number and demanded that she sent £9,000 to that number. Once the transaction was complete, another phone number was given to the lady behind the counter, and off went another £9,000. Interestingly all the transactions that I witnessed were under the magic £10,000. Which means that they don't have to be reported.

After about twenty minutes I left the post office, as it was clear that these cash transfers were going to take all afternoon. So our friend with the scruffy hair was right.

How many times a day this is happening in London is anyone's guess, but I would reckon that it's fairly frequently.

After this interesting observation I started to wonder: why is it that in some streets in London they seem to have an unduly large number of foreign money transfer exchanges for the size of their community? Could it be that they don't ask too many questions about where the money has come from? I'm just putting that out there.

For transferring really crazy amounts of cash, something more subtle is needed. In such cases large organised crime syndicates usually make major capital equipment purchases in the UK, and then send their purchased item overseas where it is sold for a fraction of the original purchase price. The sale of course has to be in cash.

Typical items purchased tend to be innocuous in nature, as the gangs do not want to attract any police or customs attention. Usually farming or engineering based products tend to be purchased, as the export of such items is fairly commonplace. There are however individuals who go to the absolute extreme when it comes to moving prohibited examples.

The first example that I can think of relates to the smuggling of forbidden missile parts to Iran. So as to deceive the customs officers, the smugglers made the parts look like cooking pots or pieces of garden furniture. These items were shown to me during a counter-terrorism event, and they prompted me to think way more out of the box than I normally do.

Barely a few months later, and I would see UK and Dutch based gangs using a scam that I thought was amazing, and truly original. Smuggling drugs into the UK is a hit and miss operation – with some caches getting through, while others are discovered.

It's all a question of scale, the more you send the more that is going to get through. Taking this methodology to its absolute extreme an entrepreneurial group of criminals purchased a fleet of authentic looking ambulances that they used for smuggling drugs into the UK, from their base in Holland. So as to make the scam look even more authentic they even rigged out the ambulances with paramedics and patients, which was a truly professional touch – as it served as a veneer to hide the smuggling operation.

When eventually compromised, one of the ambulances had a staggering £38 million pounds worth of cocaine and heroin hidden in its rear compartments. They were without doubt the ultimate "cash converters."

OPS AND ENDZ

WHEN WORKING IN GANG intervention programmes, the
two words that you seem to hear mentioned an awful
lot are Ops and Endz. Gang culture in its purest form is
defined by its membership in relation to either where they
live and operate, or more importantly where does their
opposition live, and operate.

When working with gangs across London it always
seemed to me that they were living and operating in an
almost ghostlike way that was only visible to them, and
a few chosen outsiders. In a bizarre way their modus-
operandi kind of reminded me of the children's movie,
The Borrowers – which is about a group of miniaturised
humans living below the floorboards of a big house, and
their battle with the lawyer who is trying to sell it.

In my real world scenario: the Borrowers are the
gang members, the lawyer is law enforcement, and the
floorboards - well they have just morphed into big council
estates.

When you think about it, the only time that you hear
most Londoners talking about gangs is usually after there

has been a stabbing in their local area, and even then that conversation only generally arises because the media has made us aware of it.

So unless it affects us personally, we have all essentially become comfortably numb to what now passes as daily life on our city's streets. That of course creates a problem, because whatever we tolerate as a society today, we are in essence saying that we will accept it tomorrow.

A police officer friend of mine who works in the Metropolitan Police's Trident unit, once told me that whenever he investigates gangs in London they always seem to have an unduly high opinion of themselves, and that they display an aura where they feel that they are almost untouchable. But in a way that misguided arrogance is good for law enforcement, as it means that they are highly likely to discover a trackable evidence trail following a major crime, primarily due to the fact that their suspects are generally very careless.

When working with some of the gangs in South London, I always found it amazing that they took photos of their criminal actions, or in some cases even got someone else to film them going about their violent business. Such practices serve to underline their personal vulnerabilities, and general collective weaknesses that can be easily exploited by Trident detectives or gang intervention workers.

So why is anyone remotely interested in putting their life on the line for a postcode? It's a question that plays on my mind all the time, as it seems pointless to me. There have been times when I've sat in my car observing the local gang crews running about on their estate watching anyone of their own age that is unknown to them, or seems out of place. Their paranoia in part can be understood, as an unknown individual walking down their street could be an

Op on a scoping mission. Equally that young person may be completely innocent and could potentially lose their life for absolutely nothing.

One of the best examples that I can think of that illustrates this point perfectly is the killing of a completely innocent 10-year old boy called Damilola Taylor on 27 November 2000. Damilola had only been in Britain for three months, after moving from Nigeria with his family when he was murdered, and his death caused a great deal of outrage, on account of his age, and the fact that he was completely innocent and had done absolutely nothing to provoke or warrant his killing.

His death came about following a visit to Peckham Library, where he was ambushed on his way home while walking through an estate. His killers stabbed him with a broken bottle and left him to die in a concrete stairwell.

It was an unbelievably callous and cold hearted murder, and it left Londoners deeply shocked and angry. The police mounted a massive operation to bring Damilola's killers to justice but it met with a wall of silence. This was mainly due to the fact that people in the know didn't trust the police to protect them if they gave evidence - on account of their well-founded fears of local gangs.

Despite numerous setbacks the detectives investigating Damilola's murder were extremely diligent and persevered with their enquiries until they found reliable forensic evidence that could be linked to his killers. Eventually using CCTV footage and traces of blood and fibres taken from Damilola's clothing and found on his killers belongings – they realised that they had a good case.

It took almost six years and three separate trials before Damilola's killers were finally brought to justice. Eventually in 2006 teenage brothers Ricky and Danny Preddie were convicted of manslaughter, and not murder.

The convictions brought immense relief to both the police and Damilola's father Richard Taylor, who had remained dignified and supportive of the police throughout the difficult and torrid investigation.

It is particularly sad that Richard Taylor brought Damilola to the UK believing that his son would be better off living in London, rather than his country of birth. As a father myself I can only imagine the pain that he must have gone through after making that decision.

There are probably some cynical people out there that believe that Damilola Taylor must have been a member of a gang, and that he got what he deserved for living that sort of lifestyle.

The truth is that Damilola was never a member of a gang, and nor did he ever have any association with one. By all accounts from those that knew him he was a very happy-go-lucky boy who always had a smile on his face.

Of all the gang stories that I ever tell around schools and colleges where I lecture, Damilola Taylor's is normally the one that I use to illustrate the pointlessness of the Ops and Endz mentality. For me it epitomises everything that is so wrong in gang culture.

It is one thing to take someone's life who is threatening you, or your friends with a gun or a knife. But to blatantly target a young innocent boy for no reason other than the fact that they walked through your area is a cowardly and despicable act that deserves to be punished in the harshest possible manner.

Sadly there have been numerous other murders in London since that of Damilola Taylors, where completely innocent young people have been either attacked or murdered for no possible justifiable reason. In many cases, the victims have had no known association or connection with gangs, and their murders have been put down to either wrongful misidentification or by being found guilty by means of an association to a known rival gang member.

These of course are pretty pathetic justifications, but it must always be remembered that any association whatsoever to a known rival makes you in their eyes a completely legitimate target.

In more recent times there have been a number of gang related murders that have attracted widespread media attention, none more so than that of the killing of 17-year old Girl Scout Jodie Chesney. Jodie was murdered on 1 March 2019, by means of a single stab wound to the back which she sustained while socialising with friends in Amy's Park - which is in Harold Hill. Her killing shocked the UK, as she was about as removed from gang life as it is possible to be. And yet she was murdered by a gang in such a casual manner that it defies belief how cheaply they value a human life.

So what horrendous transgression did she violate in order to gain a death sentence? She apparently walked into their self-designated gang turf, and was mistaken for someone else. Prior to Jodie's death, the gang had been involved in numerous skirmishes and clashes with other rival gangs, vying to take over their territory – so they decided to send out a message. Unfortunately their message got delivered to a completely innocent young women who as a consequence of their mindless action got robbed of her life, and everything that she had to live for.

Because of the level of outrage expressed by the local people, the culprits were identified and arrested very quickly – thanks to a mixture of CCTV and Dash-cam evidence, along with intelligence received from rival gang members. In total four individuals were accused of Jodie's murder, but in the end only two were found guilty at the Old Bailey. The guilty being Svenson Ong-a-Kwie aged 19 from Romford, Essex and 17-year old Arron Isaacs from Barking, Essex. Both gang members received life sentences for their part in Jodie Marsh's murder.

Following sentencing, Judge Wendy Joseph QC informed the court that she was satisfied that Ong-a-Kwie had stabbed Jodie while Isaacs was a willing supporter.

"When that knife was driven into Jodie, that intention was to kill," she stated.

She also went on to say that her death "was part of a series of tit-for-tat attacks," which had been "increasing in ferocity", and "although the target was not Jodie there was a degree of planning."

In recent years I have worked with a number of gang members who have been involved in violence against rivals, but for reasons of sub judice, and also because some are still the subject of ongoing police investigations I am unable to discuss them at this present time.

THE CUTTING CREW

USUALLY WITHIN EVERY GANG there are those within the operational hierarchy that have a penchant for violence. In the old days that would have meant a punch-up, or the use of a basic weapon – such as a baseball bat.

Today however things are very different indeed. Nowadays violence against rivals tends to primarily involve knives, and occasional gun use, however acid attacks are also now becoming increasingly frequent.

If there is one strand of hope for us all it is that gun usage amongst gangs in London, is relatively small in comparison to that of knives. This stems from our strict gun controls, which are amongst the toughest in the world. Over the last few years I can count on one hand the amount of times one of my gang subjects has had any involvement with a firearm. That of course is a good thing, as I would hate to see the UK go down the same road as the United States, where gun crime is off the grid.

Gangs of course do try and obtain guns, but generally they're not that easy to get hold of in the UK. Plus there is also the fact that even if you do get your hands on a gun

- you will also need appropriate ammunition - and that's arguably even harder to obtain.

To get around this problem, illegal armourers tend to rent guns and ammunition out to gangs, as opposed to selling them outright – as it makes them far more money. Indeed it's not uncommon for one weapon to be responsible for multiple shootings.

Typically illegal guns are either brought in from Eastern Europe via the channel ports, or from the United States through smuggling lines located on the West coast of Ireland. Failing that illegal armourers will either try to reactivate stolen deactivated weapons, or they will modify legally obtained air guns or blank firers into crude viable firearms.

For obvious reasons I am not going to tell you how that's done. Sorry.

As a point of interest, when Mark Duggan was shot dead by police, the firearm that was recovered was a converted blank-firing replica of a 9mm Beretta 92 Handgun. This was supplied by his armourer, Kevin Hutchinson-Foster just 15 minutes before he was shot.

Firearms are also difficult for terrorists in the UK to obtain, which is why they use either knives, home-made bombs, or vehicles as weapons.

Terrorists and Gangs also go on to the Dark Web in order to fish for people willing to obtain illegal weapons for them. This of course is really risky for them, as they never really know who they are talking to.

Also what is not generally appreciated by those who are not weapons trained is the fact that to be competent with a weapon you need to be trained on it. You need to know how to prepare it for firing, how to aim it, and on more mundane issues – you need to know how to deal with a stoppage, as they do happen.

And all that takes professional training, which you're not going to get from a Drill video. All the gang members that you see in videos holding their weapons sideways wouldn't survive more than a few seconds up against an SCO19 firearms officer.

Guns of course always look sexy to the creators of Drill videos, which is what makes them attractive to gang members in the first place - as they all want fantasy to turn into real life.

As a point of interest, here are some interesting facts about gun usage in London, which were raised by the London Assembly.

- In the last three years, the number of offences has risen. In the 12 months to October 2017, there were 2,500 offences involving guns: a 16 per cent increase on the previous year and a 44 per cent increase on 2014.

- In the year to October 2017, out of 2,542 gun crimes, 770 guns were fired, of which 318 were classed as lethal weapons.

- The number of lethal guns fired has increased by around 20 per cent since 2012.

- In the year to October 2017, gangs accounted for 10 per cent of all gun crime offences, 18 per cent of the offences where a gun was fired and 41% per cent of the offences where a lethal gun was fired.

- In the year to October 2017, 59 per cent of gun crime offenders were aged 25 or younger.

> ## GUNS AMNESTY
> **In the first week of the Met's November 2017 gun surrender amnesty. Weapons handed in to the police included:**
>
> **31 Shotguns**
>
> **11 Pistols**
>
> **10 Handguns**
>
> **9 Revolvers**
>
> **6 Rifles**
>
> **2 WW2 Machine-guns**

When we look at these gun figures we must put them into perspective, as knife related crime in London is considerably higher. At this present time there are on average 40 knife related incidents occurring every day in London, and that's just the reported ones.

In part this is down to our courts – as sentences for knife crime tend to be too lenient. This is borne out by the fact that half of London's knife killers had previous convictions for possessing blades. The Metropolitan Police charged 379 suspects with knife crime homicides between November 2016 and October 2017. Within this total were 173 suspects who had previous convictions for knife related offences – which equates to 46% of the total.

However, the figures also showed that the proportion of previous offenders charged with knife murders fell from 71% between 1 November 2016 and 31 October 2017 to 37% over the same period in 2018/19.

2019 was a particularly bloody year for London, as it suffered 135 fatal stabbings – the highest number of deaths in a decade.

After these horrendous figures were released London Assembly member Tony Devenish demanded changes to the criminal justice system in order to bring re-offending rates down. He commented "Our prison system needs to both rehabilitate and punish knife crime offenders, which is why the new government is entirely right to reform education in prisons and introduce tougher sentences." He also added "After all, some of these murders wouldn't have been committed had the perpetrator already been behind bars."

The chief executive of Barnardo's Javed Khan said: "We need to understand why those involved, including children and young people, carry knives.

Often it's because they are facing a poverty of hope – a future with no qualifications, no job prospects, and no role models, making them vulnerable to criminal gangs who coerce them to carry knives and deliver drugs.

The new government urgently needs to work with charities, education, health, youth workers, the criminal justice system and local communities to find long-term solutions to break the circle of violence."

So you're probably wondering what is a typical perpetrator of knife violence really like? One gang member that comes to mind for me, was a young man called J who was put into a safe house in North West London following a multiple stabbing in South London. I always thought that it was an odd decision, as he was probably in more danger in his new home, than he was in his previous one. J was autistic, and rarely spoke, as he found it difficult to communicate with people that were not within his close circle of friends and family. With me he would frequently gesture that he wanted to play table tennis with me, and this initially was our only method of communication. Gradually our communication improved to the point that we could have a short conversation, but that usually only happened when the other gang members were out of ear shot.

He eventually told me that he been involved in a stabbing in South London and that it had also involved his brother. At this stage he had not been arrested as police were still investigating the case. He clearly wanted my advice, but was afraid to ask. To get around this problem I set up a group discussion where I showed them how the police would typically investigate a stabbing, and how they would gain evidence to build a case. I particularly focused on the mobile phone element, as I knew he had raised that point with another member of the group.

He then used a hypothetical example as a means of gaining more information, without in any way incriminating himself in the stabbing. He was clearly displaying signs of anxiety, and reaching out for help. We commenced another discussion, and it was at this point that he asked me what would happen if he got arrested, and it went to court. I advised him that if he turned himself in to police through a solicitor and was honest with his answers, it was likely that they would treat him well, and be empathetic to his situation. J thanked me for my advice, and then left the building. It was to be our last meeting, and I never saw him again after that.

I later learned that the following day J had gone to a police station with a solicitor and a social worker – and turned himself in. I have no idea what he said in the police station, or what he had pleaded guilty to, but I do know that he received a 2 year prison sentence, which would have been considered a light sentence under the circumstances that he had outlined to me.

Another individual that I had dealings with wasn't so pleasant, and should have been sectioned as he was a violent psychopath. In the school that he attended he would frequently attack both the students and the teachers with a level of violence that had no place in a special provision. K as he was known, had been diagnosed with autism, along with a list of other conditions, and was a habitual user of both weed and class A drugs. Most of the students in the provision were petrified of him, as he could turn violent without the slightest provocation.

One day one of the students who was in a gang in West London, made me aware that K was going to go to a nearby school and stab a pupil that he had a grievance with. I immediately flagged this information up to the provisions safeguarding officer along with the senior management team – but they took no action!! The following day K was being escorted by a member of staff to another location and while walking he dropped a large knife. This was taken from him, and yet again no action was taken by the provision.

Another member of staffed demanded to know why no action was being taken against him, and they revealed that he was worth £100,000 per year to them on account of his high level special needs. They then laid a guilt trip on them, and stated "if we get rid of him then 5 support workers have to go." The following day K was back in the provision, and this time he threatened to stab a member of the catering staff with one of the kitchens knives – which he had managed to steal. The staff member quit and went to the police about him, but you guessed it he was back in the provision the following day.

At some point on the final day of that week, he escaped from the provision and went to the nearby school with a knife to go and stab the young boy that he had a beef with. Thankfully for whatever reason he could not find him, and through his suspicious actions – the school called the police and he was subsequently arrested - and eventually returned to the unit. For whatever reason he didn't get searched by the police, and therefore ended up back with us still carrying the knife. By this time I had made the provisions manager totally aware of my disgust for their appalling safeguarding procedures, and that had K found that young boy and killed him, his blood would have been on their hands.

K was eventually suspended, and ended up in jail for drug dealing and other offences involving violence.

After this near miss, I would often wonder about how many potential stabbings were avoided every day because of good work by police officers, youth workers, social workers, teachers, parents, and indeed other friends? I would then of course start to think about the flip side of the coin, that being how many young lives have been lost - that could have been prevented - if only someone had taken appropriate action.

I will never know the answer to that one, and I suspect that nobody else does either.

How our young people roll is always changing, as we live in a dynamic society that is always evolving.

Thankfully, most young people are raised in a decent manner that will lead them to become good citizens, and ones that are highly likely to achieve their life's ambitions, but then there are the others who live on the fringes of our society, who have no direction or meaning to their life. They are the ones that have been inadvertently raised to kill.

FEMME FATALES

WHEN WE THINK OF GANGS, we almost always think of males as it is after all their general preserve. However we must not forget that gangs frequently have female members. In most cases they just exist on the periphery of gang life, but there are a few that are most definitely on the front line.

The first female gang member that I had dealings with was absolutely obnoxious. I am sorry to be blunt but I just could not find anything likeable about her, as she was a truly evil and nasty individual. Her name was T and her particular penchant was robbing pensioners, Muslim women and young single parent mothers - as she deemed them vulnerable, and therefore easy prey. On the few occasions that I had to interview her, I would pray that she would mess up or slip up in a way that I could identify the area where she was targeting her victims. Alas, despite my best efforts I just could not pin down where in London she was operating from, as she was always squatting in different locations around London.

I remember one Monday coming into work, and

having the unpleasant task of having to mentor her. It was pretty clear that she didn't like me, and equally I didn't like her, so the feeling was very much mutual. Unfortunately for T all the other staff didn't like working with her either, as she had previous for attacking them. I honestly cannot ever recall working with anyone who was so universally despised.

In a way it was really quite sad, as at some point in her life she must have been ok, but where in life she came off the tracks is beyond me. Although I kept my personal views and opinions of her private when talking to her fellow gang members, it was clear that they didn't much like her either. As one of them said to me, "she is an absolute bitch, but she brings in the money."

They also mentioned that they feared her - as she had assaulted some of them quite badly – but for obvious reasons they never reported it to the police.

Eventually T seriously assaulted a student and a member of staff who had gone to the student's aid. That incident which was one of many, was to be the final straw for T - as she was expelled from the provision the following day.

With T now gone I was assigned another girl to mentor, who was also part of the same gang. P as she was known to me, was in contrast very likeable and had a wicked sense of humour. I often had to remind myself that she was in a gang, as her behavioural traits just did not fit typical gang stereotypes. But like everything else in this world, she there was there for a reason. Over the weeks as I got to know her, I discovered that she was very artistic, and that she had a real talent for drawing and painting. Sadly on the negative side, she was into credit card fraud and handling stolen goods – but only at a low level.

I have always been fascinated with the criminal mind,

and how it constantly adapts and changes to opportunities and threats. In Ps case, she had someone working on the inside that was able to identify and steal credit cards that were in the post on route to their respective customers. Once in their hands they would make small purchases from big organisations like Amazon and ebay that were usually under £25 in value. This figure according to them was the magic number that was too small for the banks to investigate. To get around using a fixed address they would use delivery boxes like the ones you see in big supermarkets, as they are not monitored.

She never revealed how much money she was making a week from this enterprise, but it could only have been measured in hundreds of pounds. I remember spending a lot of time trying to persuade her to go to college to study art as I felt she had a real gift for it. She would sometimes be quite responsive to the idea of getting out of gang life - but outside influences were always going to be stronger than mine – as I only worked with her for a few hours a week.

I always felt with P that if someone had taken her under their wing when she was younger, her life could have been very different - as she was both book smart and street smart.

Around the same time as I was working with P, I got assigned another young teenage girl to work with who was banned from attending any state school or provision on account of known gang associations and also because she was heavily pregnant. As she was only 15-years old she was deemed vulnerable, and therefore placed in a women's Refuge that specialised in looking after young women that had been abused or traumatised. For obvious reasons I am not going to give out the location of the Refuge, but all I will say is that it was located in a pretty tree lined road somewhere affluent on the outskirts of London.

Normally it would be female staff only that would be assigned to a case like this, but due to the fact that the young lady had her English GCSEs coming up, the policy was changed so that I had an opportunity to prepare her as best as I could for a challenging period that involved me teaching her for the upcoming exams, while my female colleague helped prepare her for life as a young mother.

Up until this point I had never set foot in a Refuge, so it was a totally new experience for me. Upon arrival we were greeted by the manager of the facility who outlined how and where we could work in the building. For reasons that I am sure you can appreciate and understand all staff that live and work in the Refuge have to be female, as most of the residents have suffered abuse at the hands of males. It was made clear to me that I was one of only a handful of men that had been allowed to work on site, and that I would be chaperoned at all times.

I was cool with that and set about the task of preparing my young student for her English exams. From the get go it was obvious to me that she was very articulate and intelligent so my confidence in her abilities was very high. She was a bit intellectually rusty on account of not being in school for a considerable time, but other than that all the signs were good that we could achieve something in the short time that we had. Normally one of the first things that I do when working with a young student that I don't know is to get them to do a mock paper, as that will usually give me some idea as to where they are with their studies. E as I will call her, readily agreed to sit the mock paper and studiously set about working through it. Once she was finished she offered to go and make me and my colleague a tea while I marked it. I don't know what I was expecting to read, but it certainly wasn't what was scribed here. E had in effect documented all her abuse, and the mistreatment that she had suffered throughout her life. It was so powerful that even the most cold hearted examiner would be melted by it. I have never read such powerful prose in a school setting, and it was all from the heart. When I left E that day, I must admit that I felt a bit choked up when I reflected upon what she had written.

The following day I returned to the Refuge to give E some detailed feedback on her work, and also to outline a way forward for her that would address any shortcomings that she had in her learning. As I was working with her, she mentioned that she had been having some difficulties with her gang prior to being sent to the Refuge that related to the babies father. The problem was that she didn't know for sure who the father was, as she had been involved in a few relationships at the same time. But it got worse as two of the possible candidates were related, and in the same gang.

This was absolute dynamite, as just one word out of place by her could light a very dangerous fuse. In agreement with my colleague, and the staff at the Refuge we felt that a child protection professional should figure out the best way forward on that one. I remember thinking at the time good luck with that one, as teaching E how to pass her English GCSE seemed a breeze in comparison. Eventually the big day arrived and E sat her English exams, but with an independent invigilator, as you are not allowed to teach and invigilate your own students during a formal exam. That was me finished with E, as my role with her was now done. Some months later I heard that she was now a proud and happy mother, and that she had passed her English GCSE with a pretty decent B grade. As for who the father was? I think that one is best left unsaid.

Having finished my contract in this part of the world,

I was now back in gang intervention working with a group of teenage boys that were having some difficulties with two gangs around the Notting Hill area.

It was during our morning briefing that one of the boys started to kick off about the three young girls that were based in the same building as us. He was getting increasingly agitated about one in particular who he felt was tipping off theirs ops as she knew all their daily movements. I called him aside, and calmed him down by telling him that I would personally look in to what he was saying, and that it would be dealt with by the end of the day.

As I reflected on what he had been saying, I could see good reasoning behind his rationale, as there had indeed been a series of unexplained attacks on the boys as they had left the building. So the key question was which one of the three was guilty of being a femme fatale? In order to smoke our informer out - I had to think of a ruse that would draw them into the open without arousing suspicion. Simply questioning them would accomplish nothing as they would just play dumb.

I eventually formed a quick plan which I ran by my colleagues, as they needed to be in on it just in case it all went south. So this is what I came up with. One by one I called the girls down and I gave each one a different time for a supposed shop run that would involve J. At around 11am which was the time that I had given to M around 8 scooters surrounded the front of our building and began menacingly revving their engines in frustration that their intended victim had not materialized. As this was taking place one of my colleagues noticed that M's mobile phone was pinging like crazy, and that she kept running in and out of the girl's toilet without any explanation. The boys in the building were by now becoming extremely agitated and aggressive, as they could recognise some of their rivals. One of them even waved a large knife in the air and gestured it in their direction before riding off.

The game was now up for M, so a formal interview was required. The boys however knew nothing of the meeting, as any suspicion of her guilt could lead to a backlash. When I initially confronted M with the evidence of what she had done she denied any responsibility for calling the rival gang. I then asked her for her phone, but she refused to hand it over. The game was up, and she knew it. After a few minutes she started to say that she had only called them to beat J up, and that was all.

I then asked her if she had ever heard of the expression "joint enterprise"? Her response was no. I then went on to explain that had any one of her friends stabbed J and seriously injured him, she would be found to be just as guilty as them, as she had been instrumental in setting him up. She recoiled back in horror when I told her that, as by her own admission she had set up other boys before. It was clear that she could no longer remain in the provision, as her presence could potentially lead to someone attacking her in an act of revenge.

By mutual agreement she left the provision. When I told J the outcome, he was both pleased, but at the same time angry - as in his eyes I had denied him the opportunity of confronting her. I then asked him, what would you have done to her? His response was fairly typical and expected: "I would have slapped her up." I then pointed out to him that he had been the bigger man that day, as he had made me aware of the issue, and had not taken the law into his own hands. And in response, I had paid back his trust in me by taking quick and effective action that had brought about a swift resolution to the problem – and in the same day, just as I had promised.

As for the other girls in the provision, there was no evidence to suggest that they had been involved in any way, or indeed had any direct link to any known gangs in the area. So Case closed.

FEDS AND PEDS

IN 2017, LONDON WAS plagued with an epidemic of street robberies involving the widespread use of bikes, mopeds and scooters, and although these robberies were primarily targeted at pedestrians, a significant number of them also involved the theft of high end mopeds and scooters from fellow riders.

The theft of bikes has always been a problem in London, but in recent years the problem has grown exponentially. 2017 saw over 19,000 moped attacks, which when added to the UKs national crime figures equates to a staggering 1,000 per cent increase in just three years.

In 2014 there were only 1,053 scooter attacks recorded across London's boroughs, so why the massive increase to 19,000 in 2017. In part this dramatic increase in scooter attacks can be put down to the soaring prices of mobile phones, and their high second hand value in overseas markets, such as those seen in Nigeria – which I explained in the Cash Converters chapter. But another reason for this incredible increase in crime lies in the fact that the thieves preferred method of transport, the cheap and highly manoeuvrable scooter is very easy to steal from outside their owner's homes, plus they can of course also hijack them from vulnerable delivery drivers. On average some 1,500 mopeds, motorbikes and scooters are stolen in London every month.

Experts, such as former Metropolitan Police chief inspector Peter Kirkham, also believe budget cuts to police have contributed to a rise in violent crimes in the city. Speaking with iNews, Kirkham said: "Cuts to police officers mean fewer officers on the street and fewer officers investigating crimes. He also mentioned "There is no time for officers to carry out stop and search, and the bad guys have noticed. "They know they can get away with more and more... It's not rocket science."

During the summer of 2017, the Metropolitan Police were under intense pressure to do something about the scooter gangs as they were terrorising the people of London on an almost daily basis. The gangs felt that they had impunity from justice, on account of the fact that the police rarely mounted any initiative that had any positive effect against them. At the same time it seemed that the police were utterly bankrupt of any officer capable of thinking out of the box, and that for the most part they appeared to be more concerned about the robber's safety, than that of their victims.

Boyed up by this failure in policing, the gangs intensified their activities to unprecedented levels. In one particular case, one gang carried out 30 robberies in London within a one hour period, but they were outclassed by one man who was jailed for snatching 21 phones in a single hour.

At the time all this craziness was taking place, I was working in North London with a small group of gang members that were heavily involved in phone snatching and scooter theft. One of them known as C, was a prolific scooter thief, and his exploits became almost legendary around his circle of gang friends. At one stage he had been arrested on at least 66 separate occasions for scooter theft, yet never did a day in prison - on account of the fact that he was only 15 years old. C was a cheeky character, but I never knew him to be violent. On a few occasions he had been hit by victims of his criminal activities, which he accepted as an occupational hazard. Some of his friends were not so lucky, as a group of delivery riders turned vigilante and ambushed them as they were attempting to steal their mopeds. By all accounts they got a good hiding – but could not go to the police for obvious reasons.

As for C, the last time that I saw him was just after a court appearance where the judge told him that the next time you are in front of me you will be going to prison. With that he left the court, walked into the nearest supermarket - and nicked a moped so that he could get home. You just couldn't make it up.

It was shortly after this incident with C, that something quite unexpected happened that was to change everything. While watching the TV one night, there was an announcement that the police had formed a new anti-moped unit under the auspices of Operation Venice. They then showed a series of incidents where the police knocked the riders off their scooters and mopeds in a manner that I had never seen before. There were scenes of gang members being flung into the air after police vehicles had rammed them in a highly controlled manner. The officers who carried out these ramming actions were known as "Scorpions," and it was evident that they seemed pretty effective.

The proof however came the following day when I was in the office, as the topic of conversation all day long from the gang members was the police scorpion teams and what they were doing to their friends and rivals. They all seemed genuinely shocked, as up until this point none of them had any fear of the police, whereas now they did.

Of course my view of Operation Venice was only confined to a small area of North-West London, whereas the operation was pan London.

It was quickly evident from all the intelligence chatter that was coming in from all the boroughs that make up London that Operation Venice was having a devastating effect upon the morale of the gang members that mounted street robberies. It was clear that they were now getting payback, and more importantly the public were overwhelmingly in support of the police's robust actions.

Within months of Op Venice being launched, moped, scooter or motorbike enabled crime had dropped by almost a half. At the peak of moped enabled crime in July 2017, there were a total of 2,593 offences. By December 2017 there had been a reduction of 42.5%, December 2017 – November 2018 (15,168 offences) and from December 2018 – November 2019 (8,721 offences).

To try and give some meaning to these robberies, and also to help illustrate the impact of them upon their victims I have included this list of 2017/18 crimes which appeared in the Sun newspaper in 2018.

April-May 2017: A gang of three teenage boys – aged 15, 16 and 17 – committed over 100 crimes while riding mopeds in the boroughs of Camden, Islington, Kensington and Chelsea and Westminster.

July 13, 2017: Five people were attacked with acid in a 90-minute period by two men riding scooters. The victims, who were all riding mopeds, had their bikes hijacked in the assaults in Hackney, Stoke Newington and Islington.

July 14, 2017: A moped rider was attacked with a "noxious substance" by two men riding a scooter in Dagenham, East London.

July 15, 2017: Danny Pearce was stabbed to death by a moped gang in Greenwich.

October 2017: Charity worker Abdul Samad, 28, was stabbed to death in Maida Vale, West London, by a scooter gang who were attempting to steal his phone. In April, 2018, two teenage robbers, dubbed the "highway men for the 21st Century", were convicted of murder following Abdul's death.

December 2017: A ten-strong moped gang were jailed for 110 years after a series of £1.2m raids across the capital.

June 2018: Comedian Michael McIntyre had his Rolex watch stolen by hammer-wielding moped thugs in North West London.

June 3, 2018: A businessman revealed his injuries after he was slashed by zombie knife-wielding moped muggers for his £30,000 Audemars Piguet Royal Oak timepiece after they pulled up alongside him on the North Circular

June 5, 2018: Heroic bystanders risked their lives to try to stop a moped gang armed with "machete-type" knives moments after they raided a jewellers on Regent Street.

June 8, 2018: Moped muggers scream "Give us the gold" as they robbed a family of jewellery at knifepoint in Coulsdon, Surrey.

June 9, 2018: A 14-year-old boy was charged over seven moped muggings in one hour around North London the previous week

June 21, 2018: A moped gang targeted a woman and three-year-old child before being chased off by heroes with scaffolding poles in Richmond. Amanda Holden shared footage of the attack and branded the thugs "scumbags".

In an Operation Venice Metropolitan Police briefing it was announced that: officers will now be able to ram into moped-riding thieves even when they're not wearing helmets, riding dangerously or disguising themselves.

Commander Amanda Pearson of Frontline Policing, said: "The Met is at the forefront of tackling moped and motorcycle crime and I am pleased to see that we have seen a reduction in offences. However, we are not complacent and we will continue to work tirelessly across London to maintain this downward trend.

"Operation Venice can call on all manner of tactics from an experienced investigation team to police helicopters to tackle and arrest offenders.

"There is a perception that if you remove your helmet or fail to stop for police when requested to do so we will not take any further course of action. This is untrue.

"The public quite rightly expects us to intervene to keep London safe. Our highly trained police drivers weigh up the risks and decide upon the most appropriate tactics in those circumstances."

Following in the footsteps of Operation Venice, the police launched Operation Gilera, which was focused on bicycle enabled crime in the boroughs of Westminster, Hammersmith and Fulham, Kensington, Chelsea, Camden and Islington.

Detective Chief Inspector Shaun White, the operational lead for Op Gilera, said: "This operation has been set up as our response to tackle, arrest and prosecute those who think that they can use push bikes to rob pedestrians going about their daily business.

"The suspects are using the same tactics that criminals

were using in the summer of 2017, when we saw a peak of moped-enabled crime, prompting us to launch Operation Venice. Venice had significant successes and, as such, it appears criminals now think that they can use pedal cycles instead to evade police. They are wrong.

"Specially trained riders from Op Venice will be patrolling hotspot areas alongside pedal cycle officers and pursuit cars from Op Gilera. They have the equipment and specialist ability to quickly pursue criminals attempting to flee an incident, and target those believed to be committing robberies and thefts."

Since the launch of Operation Gilera, officers have executed a number of warrants to arrest those involved in pedal cycle robbery. Five warrants were executed in the first week in Central North BCU which resulted in six people being arrested.

DCI White, added: "While we will be working hard to tackle pedal cycle robbers, we will also be asking the public to remain vigilant and keep their possessions out of view from criminals."

We will continue to work tirelessly to identify and pursue offenders, help bring perpetrators to justice, take weapons off the street, support victims, engage and reassure the public, and keep our communities safe.

As impressive as this innovative police response has been to counter moped enabled crime, gangs are by nature extremely adaptive and will constantly probe perceived weaknesses until they find another way to commit crime.

Gang riders are also becoming increasingly mindful of the increase in vigilantes who are willing to follow and film them, and in some cases even attack them. This of course is not helpful to the police, but it is understandable why such groups have formed – as many feel that the police are unable to protect them.

As for my group who were involved in street robbery, one ended up in jail for abusing a judge, while another got a caution. The rest it would seem decided to lie low for a while, as they feared coming up against the scorpion teams.

It is important to stress that the threat of moped enabled crime hasn't totally disappeared, it has merely reduced in its scope - and in some cases morphed into other street related crime activities.

A young lady losing her phone to an agile scooter team

This is what a vulnerable DD looks like to gangbangers

Met Police Scorpion riders with their new highly agile motorbikes - which are perfect for zapping scooter thieves

Youth centres like this one in Acton often serve as a magnet for gangs - which is a real shame. I lost count of the number of fights that I witnessed in this centre before it got bulldozed.

My view of Gotham. Only 3 police vehicles outside – it
must have been a quiet day.

My classroom view of Gotham. Note the gang tags
on the wall and Grenfell Tower in the background

CTSFO with Sig MCX rifles

An SAS Blue Thunder Dauphin Helicopter in action over London Bridge following the Borough market terrorist attack. Such assets could also be used against violent gangs should the need ever arise

Without the prompt action of our London Ambulance
Service heroes – many more lives would be lost on
London's streets

Met Police Jankel armoured vehicles being used as a road block in central London. These vehicles are also used during riots and armed response incidents.

These children in Kwazulu-Natal, South Africa - have no phones, no TV and no laptops, and yet they are extremely happy. Maybe we could all learn something from them.

85 police officers get attacked in the UK every day. These officers were all injured during the BLM (Black Lives Matter) protests in central London in June 2020.

RICE CRISPIES AND CORNFLAKES

IN CASE YOU'RE WONDERING why I have the names of two brands of cereal as a chapter title, the names actually refer to different types of drugs – and not what you have for breakfast.

I first became aware of these terms while escorting a group of teenagers in a minibus in the back streets of Harlesden. As I sat in my seat, a young man in front of me was having a phone melt down on account of all the texts he was receiving. For a couple of minutes his phone just seemed to be pinging every few seconds. Curious to know what was so important I asked one of the support workers why he had his phone on him when provision policy was to hand them in until home time.

He then informed me that T had surrendered his personal phone, but not his trapper phone – as that was regarded as his business tool.

From the brief glimpse that I got of Ts phone screen all it seemed to have was numbers and odd names. The numbers were his clients, and the weird names related to all the different types of drugs that he could offer. He was known to be supplying drugs to schools and colleges in the West London area, but was also suspected of being involved in county lines drug trafficking.

So how bad is London's drug problem? In recent years it has got steadily worse, with drugs even being found in primary schools. So far the youngest child to be found in possession of drugs in a school was 12 years old. In the last few years there have been over 1,100 school drug seizures – but that's only what has been discovered. The most common drugs to be found in schools are cannabis, cocaine and heroin.

Since 2016 the most common drug seized was cannabis (851 times), followed by cocaine (25 times) and heroin (six times). Amphetamines were also seized in a handful of cases.

Commenting on drugs in schools, Geoff Barton, general secretary of the Association of School and College leaders, said "Most young people do not take drugs, and it is rare for them to be brought on to school premises. However, like much else, trends reflect what is happening more widely, and schools are particularly concerned about the sinister spread of the drugs trade by so-called "county lines" gangs, in which vulnerable young people are coerced into dealing."

He also mentioned "Schools are assiduous in educating pupils about the risks of taking drugs, and the dangers of involvement in the drugs trade, but this is part of a wider and complex problem, which requires a fully coordinated and resourced response from national government working with multiple agencies."

The Metropolitan Police recently released the following information showing how many pupils have been charged and taken to court after being caught with drugs.

Since 2016, 27 students have been charged with drug trafficking, the youngest being 13 years old. Information released also showed that 268 pupils were charged with possession of drugs, the youngest being 12 years old.

A statement from Deputy Chief Constable Jo Shiner, of the National Police Chief's Council lead for children and young people, said: "There is evidence showing that more children and young people are believed to be using drugs. It is essential for schools and colleges to work in partnership with local officers alongside youth and family support services for support and advice and where required, operational intervention, if a pupil or student is found to have brought drugs into school or college.

The guidance includes detailed advice for staff on what they should do if drugs are found at a school or college premises and if a student is found in possession of drugs.

School and college staff are best placed to decide on the most appropriate response to tackling drugs within their schools and colleges and can have a key role in identifying students at risk of drug misuse."

THE EFFECTS OF DRUGS

The following helpful advice on drugs has been provided by the NHS.

Drug misuse can be harmful to your health in both the short term and the long term, and could possibly lead to addiction.

New psychoactive substances (NPS) (often incorrectly called 'legal highs')

What are NPS?

NPS, such as mephedrone (meow meow) and spice, used to be available to buy legally in "head shops" (shops that sell drug paraphernalia) or online.

Since the Psychoactive Substances Act came into effect on May 26 2016 it has been illegal to supply any NPS in the UK for human consumption. This includes selling them or giving them away for free.

Alcohol, medicines, nicotine, caffeine and poppers (alkyl nitrites) are exempt from the act.

How do NPS make you feel?

The main effects of almost all psychoactive drugs, including NPS, fall into three categories:

- stimulants
- "downers" or sedatives
- psychedelics or hallucinogens

Synthetic cannabinoids, which can have both sedative and psychedelic effects, are sometimes separated out into their own category. They have been a big part of the NPS market and have been particularly problematic and harmful.

Even NPS that look similar or have similar names can vary in strength and can have different effects on different people.

How do NPS affect your health?

For lots of NPS, there has been little or no research into the short- or long-term health risks from human consumption and some risks aren't yet known.

Forensic testing of NPS has shown that they often contain different substances to what the packaging says, or mixtures of different substances.

This means you can never be sure what you are taking or what the effects might be.

Risks include:

- NPS can reduce your inhibitions, so you may do potentially harmful things you wouldn't normally do.
- They can cause paranoia, coma, seizures and, in rare cases, death.
- You can never be sure of what is in an NPS, so you can't be sure what you've bought or been given, or what effect it's likely to have on you or your friends.

For more information about NPS visit the FRANK website.

CANNABIS
(hash, weed, grass, skunk, marijuana)

What is cannabis?
Cannabis is a calming drug that also alters perceptions. It's seen as "natural" because it's made from the cannabis plant, but that doesn't mean it's safe. It can be smoked, often with tobacco, in a "joint" or "spliff", or in a pipe or "bong". It can also be drunk as a "tea" or eaten when mixed with food, such as biscuits or cakes.

How does cannabis make you feel?
Cannabis can make you feel relaxed and happy, but sometimes makes people feel lethargic, very anxious and paranoid, and even psychotic.

How does cannabis affect your health?
Cannabis has been linked to mental health problems

such as schizophrenia and, when smoked, to lung diseases including asthma.

It affects how your brain works, so regular use can make concentration and learning very difficult. Frequent use can have a negative effect on your fertility.

It is also dangerous to drive after taking cannabis. Mixing it with tobacco is likely to increase the risk of heart disease and lung cancer.

Can cannabis be addictive?

Yes, it is possible to become psychologically dependent on cannabis. And some people do experience withdrawal symptoms when they stop taking it. For information about coming off drugs, read Drug addiction: getting help. You can also get help cutting down from the FRANK website.

COCAINE
(powder cocaine, coke, crack)

What is cocaine?

Powder cocaine (coke), freebase and crack are all types of cocaine, and all are powerful stimulants. Freebase and crack can be smoked, and powder cocaine can be snorted in lines. Both cocaine powder and crack can also be prepared for injecting.

How does cocaine make you feel?

Cocaine gives the user energy, a feeling of happiness and being wide awake, and an overconfidence that can lead to taking risks. The effects are short-lived, so more drug is taken, which is often followed by a nasty "comedown" that makes you feel depressed and unwell, sometimes for several days.

How does cocaine affect your health?

If you take cocaine, it's possible to die of an overdose from overstimulating the heart and nervous system, which can lead to a heart attack. It can be more risky if mixed with alcohol.

Taking cocaine is particularly risky if you have high blood pressure or already have a heart condition. If you're pregnant, cocaine can harm your baby and even cause miscarriage. If you've had previous mental health problems, it can increase the chance of these returning.

If you snort cocaine, it can damage the cartilage of your nose over time. If you inject it, you are at higher risk of dying as the result of an overdose, and your veins and body tissues can be seriously damaged. You put yourself at risk of catching HIV or hepatitis if you share needles.

Can cocaine be addictive?

Yes, cocaine is highly addictive and can cause a very strong psychological dependence. For advice on getting help for cocaine addiction, go to Cocaine: get help. The Cocaine Anonymous website also offers further advice.

ECSTASY
(MDMA, pills, crystal, E)

What is ecstasy?

Ecstasy is a "psychedelic" stimulant drug usually sold as tablets, but it's sometimes dabbed on to gums or snorted in its powder form. It's also known as MDMA or "crystal".

How does ecstasy make you feel?

Ecstasy can make you feel alert, affectionate and chatty, and can make music and colours seem more intense. Taking ecstasy can also cause anxiety, confusion, paranoia and even psychosis.

How does ecstasy affect your health?

Long-term use has been linked with memory problems, depression and anxiety. Ecstasy use affects the body's temperature control and can lead to dangerous overheating and dehydration.

But a balance is important as drinking too much fluid can also be very dangerous for the brain, particularly because ecstasy tends to stop your body producing enough urine, so your body retains the fluid. For more information on ecstasy, visit the FRANK website.

Is ecstasy addictive?

Ecstasy can be addictive, as users can develop a psychological dependence on this drug. It is also possible to build up a tolerance to the drug and need to take more and more to get the same effect.

SPEED
(amphetamine, billy, whizz)

What is speed?

Speed is the street name for drugs based on amphetamine, and is a stimulant drug. It's usually an off-white or pink powder that's either dabbed on to gums, snorted or swallowed in paper.

How does speed make you feel?

Speed can make you feel alert, confident and full of energy, and can reduce appetite. But it can make you agitated and aggressive, and can cause confusion, paranoia and even psychosis. You can also become very depressed and lethargic for hours or days after a period of heavy use.

How does speed affect your health?

Taking speed can be dangerous for the heart, as it can cause high blood pressure and heart attacks. It can be more risky if mixed with alcohol, or if it's used by people who have blood pressure or heart problems.

Injecting speed is particularly dangerous, as death can occur from overdose. Speed is usually very impure and injecting it can cause damage to veins and tissues, which can also lead to serious infections in the body and bloodstream. Any sharing of injecting equipment adds the risk of catching hepatitis C and HIV.

Is speed addictive?

Regular use of amphetamines can become highly addictive.

The following document is from the US Drug Enforcement Administration, and is probably the most comprehensive list of drugs and street names in existence. Although designed for the use of federal agents, I am sure you will find it interesting.

DEA INTELLIGENCE REPORT
EXECUTIVE SUMMARY

This Drug Enforcement Administration (DEA) Intelligence Report contains information from a variety of law enforcement and open sources. It is designed as a ready reference for law enforcement personnel who are confronted by many of the hundreds of slang terms used to identify a wide variety of controlled substances, designer drugs, and synthetic compounds. Every effort has been made to ensure the accuracy and completeness of the information presented. However, due to the dynamics of the ever-changing drug scene, subsequent additions, deletions, and corrections are inevitable. This compendium of drug slang terms has been alphabetically ordered, and identifies drugs and drug categories in English and foreign language derivations.

DRUG SLANG/CODE WORDS

AMPHETAMINE

Amy; Amps; Bam; B-Bombs; Beans; Bennies; Benz; Black and Whites; Black Beauties; Black Birds; Black Bombers; Black Mollies; Blacks; Blue Boys; Bombita; Brain Ticklers; Brownies; Bumblebees; Cartwheels; Chalk; Chicken Powder; Chochos; Christina; Chunk; Co-Pilot; Coasts to Coasts; Crisscross; Cross Roads; Cross Tops; Debs; Dexies; Diablos; Diamonds; Diet Pills; Dolls; Dominoes; Double Cross; Drivers; Fives; Footballs; French Blues; Goofballs; Greenies; Head Drugs; Hearts; Horse Heads; In- Between; Jelly Babies; Jelly Beans; Jolly Beans; Jugs; Leapers; Lid Poppers; Lightening; Little Bombs; Marathons; Mini Beans; Mini Bennies; Morning Shot; Nuggets; Oranges; Pastillas; Peaches; Pep Pills; Pink Hearts; Pixies; Pollutants; Purple Hearts; Rhythm; Rippers; Road Dope; Roses; Rueda; Snaps; Snow Pallets; Sparkle Plenty; Sparklers; Speed; Splash; Sweeties; Sweets; Tens; Thrusters; TR-6s; Truck Drivers; Turnabouts; Uppers; Wake Ups; West Coast Turnarounds; Wheels; Whiffle Dust; White Crosses;

Whites; Zoomers

COCAINE

777; A-1; All-American Drug; Angel Powder; Angie; Animals; Audi; Aunt Nora; Azucar; Baby Powder; Barrato; Basuco; Bazooka; Beach; Belushi (mixed with heroin); Bernie's Flakes; Bernie's Gold Dust; Big Bloke; Big C;Big Flake; Big Rush; Billie Hoke; Bird; Birdie Powder; Blanca Nieves; Blanco; Blast; Blizzard; Blonde; Blocks; Blow; BMW; Bobo; Bolitas; Bolivian Marching Powder; Bombita (mixed with heroin); Bouncing Powder; Brisa; C-Dust; Caca; Cadillac; California Pancakes; Calves; Candy; Car; Carney; Carrie Nation; Cars; Case; Cebolla; Cecil; Cement; Charlie; Chevy; Cheyenne; Chinos; Chiva; Clear Kind; Clear Tires; Coca; Coca-Cola; Cocazo; Coconut; Coke; Cola; Colorado; Connie; Cookie; Crow; Crusty Treats; Cuadro; Death Valley; Designer Jeans; Devil's Dandruff; Diente; Dienton; Dona Blanca; Double Bubble; Dove; Dream; Dulces; Duracell; Dust; Escama; Escorpino; Falopa; Fish (liquid cocaine); Flake; Flea Market Jeans; Florida Snow; Flour; Food;Foolish Powder; Fox; Freeze; Friskie Powder; Frula; Gabacho; Galaxy; Gallos; Gato; Gift of the Sun; Gin; Girl; Girlfriend; Glad Stuff; Gold Dust; Green Gold; Gringa; Grout; Gueros; Guitar; Hamburger; Happy Dust; Happy Powder; Happy Trails; Heaven; Heaven Dust; Henry VIII; Hooter; Hundai; Hunter; Icing; Inca Message; Izzy; Jam; Jeep; Jelly; John Deere; Joy Flakes; Joy Powder; Junk; King's Habit; Kordell; Lady; Lady Snow; Late Night; Lavada; Leaf; Line; Loaf; Love Affair; Maca Flour; Mama Coca; Mandango; Maradona; Mayo; Melcocha; Mercedes; Milk; Milonga; Mojo; Mona Lisa; Mosquitos; Movie Star Drug; Mujer; Napkin; Nieve; Niña; Nose Candy; Nose Powder; Old Lady; Oyster Stew; Paint; Paloma; Palomos;

Pantalones; Papas; Paradise; Paradise White; Parrot; Pearl; Pedrito; Perico; Peruvian; Peruvian Flake; Peruvian Lady; Pescado; Pez; Pillow; Pimp; Pollo; Polvo; Powder; Powder Diamonds; Puritain; Queso Blanco; Racehorse Charlie; Rambo; Refresco; Refrescas; Reindeer Dust; Rims; Rocky Mountain; Rolex; Rooster; Scale; Schmeck; Schoolboy; Scorpion; Scottie; Seed; Serpico; Sierra; Shirt; Ski Equipment; Sleigh Ride; Snow; Snow Bird; Snow Cone; Snow White; Snowball; Snowflake; Society High; Soda; Soditas; Soft; Space (mixed with PCP); Speedball (mixed with heroin); Stardust; Star Spangled Powder; Studio Fuel; Suave; Sugar; Superman; Sweet Stuff; Talco; Talquito; Tamales; Taxi; Tecate; Teenager; Teeth; Tequila; Thunder; Tire; Tonto; Toot; Tortes; Toyota; T-Shirts; Turkey; Tutti-Frutti; Vaquita; Wash; Wet; Whack (mixed with PCP); White; White Bitch; White Cross; White Girl; White Goat; White Horse; White Lady; White Mercedes Benz; White Mosquito; White Paint; White Powder; White Root; White Shirt; White T; Whitey; Whiz Bang; Wings; Wooly; Work; Yayo; Yeyo; Yoda; Zip

CRACK COCAINE

51s; 151s; 501s; Apple Jack; Baby T; Base; Baseball; Bazooka; Beam Me Up; Beautiful Boulders; Beemer; Bill Blass; Bings; BJ; Black Rock; Blowcaine; Blowout; Blue; Bobo; Bolo; Bomb; Bone Crusher; Bone; Boo-Boo; Boulder; Boy; Breakfast of Champions; Bubble Gum; Bullion; Bump; Candy; Caps; Casper the Ghost; Caviar;CD; Cheap Basing; Chewies; Chingy; Clicker; Climax; Cloud; Cloud Nine; Cookies; Crib; Crunch & Munch;Devil; Devil Smoke; Dice; Dime Special; Dirty Basing; Dirty Fentanyl (mixed with fentanyl); Double Yoke;Durin; Eastside Player; Egg; Eye Opener; Famous Dimes; Fat Bags; Fifty-

One; Fish Scales; Freebase; French Fries; Garbage Rock; Geek; Glo; Gold; Golf Ball; Gravel; Great White Hope; Grit; Groceries; Hail; Hamburger Helper; Hard; Hotcakes; Hubba; Ice; Ice Cubes; Issues; Jelly Beans; Johnson; Kangaroo; Kokoma; Kryptonite; Love; Mixed Jive; Moon Rock; Nickel; Nuggets; One-Fifty-One; Paste; Pebbles; Pee Wee; Piedras; Pile; Pony; Primo; Quarters; Raw; Ready Rock; Red Caps; RIP (Rest in Peace); Roca; Rock; Rock Attack; Rocks of Hell; Rocky III; Rooster; Rox; Roxanne; Roz; Schoolcraft; Scotty; Scramble; Scruples; Seven-Up; Sherms; Sight Ball; Slab; Sleet; Smoke; Speed Boat; Square Time Bomb; Stone; Sugar Block; Takeover (mixed with fentanyl Teeth; Tension; Tissue; Top Gun; Troop; Ultimate; Uzi; Wave; White Ball; White Ghost; White Sugar; White Tornado; Wrecking Crew; Yahoo; Yale; Yimyom

FENTANYL AND FENTANYL DERIVATIVES

Apache; Birria (mixed with heroin); Butter; China Girl; China Town; China White; Chinese; Chinese Food; Crazy; Crazy One; Dance Fever; Dragon; Dragon's Breath; Facebook (mixed with heroin in pill form); Fent; Fenty; Fire; Friend; Girl; Goodfella; Great Bear; He-Man; Jackpot; King Ivory; Lollipop; Murder 8; Poison; Shoes; Tango & Cash; Toe Tag Dope; White Girl

GHB

G; GEEB; Georgia Home Boy; Grievous Bodily Harm; Gina; Liquid E; Liquid X; Scoop

HEROIN

A-Bomb (mixed with marijuana); Achivia; Adormidera; Antifreeze; Aunt Hazel; Avocado; Azucar; Bad Seed; Ballot; Basketball; Basura; Beast; Beyonce; Big Bag; Big H;

Big Harry; Bird; Birdie Powder; Black; Black Bitch; Black
Goat; Black Olives; Black Paint; Black Pearl; Black Sheep;
Black Tar; Blanco; Blue; Blow Dope; Blue Hero; Bombita
(mixed with cocaine); Bombs Away; Bonita; Boy; Bozo;
Brea Negra; Brick Gum; Brown; Brown Crystal; Brown
Rhine; Brown Sugar; Bubble Gum; Burrito; Caballo;
Caballo Negro; Caca; Café; Capital H; Carga; Caro;
Cement; Chapopote; Charlie; Charlie Horse; Cheese;
Chicle; Chiclosa; China; China Cat; China White; Chinese
Food; Chinese Red; Chip; Chiva; Chiva Blanca; Chivones;
Chocolate; Chocolate Balls; Choko; Chorizo; Chutazo;
Coco; Coffee; Comida; Crown Crap; Curley Hair; Dark;
Dark Girl; Dead on Arrival (DOA); Diesel; Diesel; Dirt;
Dog Food; Doggie; Doojee; Dope; Dorado; Down;
Downtown; Dreck; Dynamite; Dyno; El Diablo; Engines;
Fairy Dust; Flea Powder; Foolish Powder; Galloping
Horse; Gamot; Gato; George Smack; Girl; Golden Girl;
Good & Plenty; Good H; Goma; Gorda; Gras; Grasin;
Gravy; Gum; H; H-Caps; Hairy; Hard Candy; Harry;
Hats; Hazel; Heaven Dust; Heavy; Helen; Helicopter;
Hell Dust; Henry; Hercules; Hero; Him; Hombre; Horse;
Hot Dope; Hummers; Jojee; Joy Flakes; Joy Powder;
Junk; Kabayo; Karachi; Karate; King's Tickets; Lemonade;
Lenta; Lifesaver; Manteca; Marias; Mayo; Mazpan; Meal;
Menthol; Mexican Brown; Mexican Horse; Mexican Mud;
Mexican Treat; Modelo Negra; Mojo; Mole; Mongega;
Morena; Morenita; Mortal Combat; Motors; Mud; Mujer;
Muzzle; Nanoo; Negra; Negra Tomasa; Negrita; Nice
and Easy; Night; Noise; Obama; Old Steve; Pants; Patty;
Peg; P-Funk; Piezas; Plata; Poison; Polvo; Poppy; Powder;
Prostituta Negra; Puppy; Pure; Rambo; Red Chicken; Red
Eagle; Reindeer Dust; Roofing Tar; Sack; Salt; Sand; Scag;
Scat; Schmeck; Sheep; Shirts; Shoes; Skag; Slime; Smack;
Smeck; Snickers; Speedball (mixed with cocaine); Spider

Blue; Sticky Kind; Stufa; Sugar; Sweet Jesus; Tan; Tar; Tecata; Tires; Tootsie Roll; Tragic Magic; Trees; Turtle; Vidrio; Whiskey; White; White Boy; White Girl; White Junk; White Lady; White Nurse; White Shirt; White Stuff; Wings; Witch; Witch Hazel; Zapapote

HYDROCODONE
357s; Bananas; Dro; Fluff; Hydro; Tabs; Norco; Vics; Vikes; Watsons

KETAMINE
Blind Squid; Cat Valium; Green; Honey Oil; Jet; K; Keller; Kelly's Day; K-Hold; K-Ways; Special K; Super Acid; Vitamin K

KLONOPIN® (Clonazepam)
K; K-Pin; Pin; Super Valium

LSD
Aceite; Acid; Acido; Alice; Angels in a Sky; Animal; Backbreaker (mixed with strychnine); Barrel; Bart Simpson; Battery Acid; Beast; Big D; Black Acid (mixed with PCP); Black Star; Black Sunshine; Black Tabs; Blotter Acid; Blotter Cube; Blue Acid; Blue Barrel; Blue Chair; Blue Cheer; Blue Heaven; Blue Microdots; Blue Mist; Blue Moon; Blue Sky; Blue Star; Blue Tabs; Brown Bomber; Brown Dots; California Sunshine; Cherry Dome; Chief; Chinese Dragons; Coffee; Conductor; Contact Lens; Crackers; Crystal Tea; Cupcakes; Dental Floss; Dinosaurs; Domes; Dots; Double Dome; El Cid; Electric Kool Aid; Ellis Day; Fields; Flash; Flat Blues; Ghost; Golden Dragon; Golf Balls; Goofy; Gota; Grape Parfait; Green Wedge; Grey Shields; Hats; Hawaiian Sunshine; Hawk; Haze;

Headlights; Heavenly Blue; Hits; Instant Zen; Jesus
Christ Acid; Kaleidoscope; Leary; Lens; Lime Acid; Live,
Spit & Die; Lucy in the Sky with Diamonds; Mellow
Yellow; Mica; Microdot; Mighty Quinn; Mind Detergent;
Mother of God; Newspapers; Orange Barrels; Orange
Cubes; Orange Haze; Orange Micros; Orange Wedges;
Owsley; Paper Acid; Pearly Gates; Pellets; Phoenix; Pink
Blotters; Pink Panthers; Pink Robots; Pink Wedges; Pink
Witches; Pizza; Potato; Pure Love; Purple Barrels; Purple
Haze; Purple Hearts; Purple Flats; Recycle; Royal Blues;
Russian Sickles; Sacrament; Sandoz; Smears; Square
Dancing Tickets; Strawberry Fields; Sugar Cubes; Sugar
Lumps; Sunshine; Tabs; Tacatosa; Tail Lights; Teddy Bears;
Ticket; Uncle Sid; Valley Dolls; Vodka Acid; Wedding Bells;
Wedge; White Dust; White Fluff; White Lightening; White
Owsley; Window Glass; Window Pane; Yellow Dimples;
Yellow Sunshine; Zen

MARIJUANA

420; Acapulco Gold; Acapulco Red; Ace; African Black;
African Bush; Airplane; Alfombra; Alice B Toklas; AllStar;
Angola; Animal Cookies (hydroponic); Arizona; Ashes;
Aunt Mary; Baby; Bale; Bambalachacha; Barbara Jean;
Bareta; Bash; BC Budd; Bernie; Bhang; Big Pillows; Biggy;
Black Bart; Black Gold; Black Maria; Blondie; Blue
Cheese; Blue Crush; Blue Jeans; Blue Sage; Blueberry;
Bobo Bush; Boo; Boom; Broccoli; Bud; Budda; Burritos
Verdes; Bush; Cabbage; Cali; Canadian Black; Catnip;
Cheeba; Chernobyl; Cheese; Chicago Black; Chicago
Green; Chippie; Chistosa; Christmas Tree; Chronic;
Churo; Cigars; Citrol; Cola; Colorado Cocktail; Cookie
(hydroponic); Cotorritos; Crazy Weed; Creeper Bud;
Crippy; Crying Weed; Culican; Dank; Dew; Diesel; Dimba;

Dinkie Dow; Dirt Grass; Ditch Weed; Dizz; Djamba; Dody; Dojo; Domestic; Donna Juana; Doobie; Downtown Brown; Drag Weed; Dro (hydroponic); Droski (hydroponic); Dry High; Endo; Fine Stuff; Fire; Flower; Flower Tops; Fluffy; Fuzzy Lady; Gallito; Garden; Gauge; Gangster; Ganja; Gash; Gato; Ghana; Gigi (hydroponic) Giggle Smoke; Giggle Weed; Girl Scout Cookies (hydroponic); Gloria; Gold; Gold Leaf; Gold Star; Gong; Good Giggles; Gorilla; Gorilla Glue; Grand Daddy Purp; Grass; Grasshopper; Green; Green-Eyed Girl; Green Eyes; Green Goblin; Green Goddess; Green Mercedes Benz; Green Paint; Green Skunk; Grenuda; Greta; Guardada; Gummy Bears; Gunga; Hairy Ones; Hash; Hawaiian; Hay; Hemp; Herb; Hierba; Holy Grail; Homegrown; Hooch; Humo; Hydro; Indian Boy; Indian Hay; Jamaican Gold; Jamaican Red; Jane; Jive; Jolly Green; Jon-Jem; Joy Smoke; Juan Valdez; Juanita; Jungle Juice; Kaff; Kali; Kaya; KB; Kentucky Blue; KGB; Khalifa; Kiff; Killa; Kilter; King Louie; Kona Gold; Kumba; Kush; Laughing Grass; Laughing Weed; Leaf; Lechuga; Lemon-Lime; Liamba; Lime Pillows; Little Green Friends; Little Smoke; Loaf; Lobo; Loco Weed; Love Nuggets; Love Weed; M.J.; Machinery; Macoña; Mafafa; Magic Smoke; Manhattan Silver; Maracachafa; Maria; Marimba; Mariquita; Mary Ann; Mary Jane; Mary Jones; Mary Warner; Mary Weaver; Matchbox; Matraca; Maui Wowie; Meg; Method; Mexican Brown; Mexican Green; Mexican Red; Mochie (hydroponic); Moña; Monte; Moocah; Mootie; Mora; Morisqueta; Mostaza; Mota; Mother; Mowing the Lawn; Muggie; Narizona; Northern Lights; O-Boy; O.J.; Owl; Paja; Panama Cut; Panama Gold; Panama Red; Pakalolo; Palm; Paloma; Parsley; Pelosa; Phoenix; Pillow; Pine; Platinum Cookies (hydroponic); Platinum Jack; Pocket Rocket; Popcorn; Pot; Pretendo; Puff; Purple Haze; Queen Ann's Lace; Ragweed;

Railroad Weed; Rainy Day Woman; Rasta Weed; Red
Cross; Red Dirt; Reefer; Reggie; Repollo; Righteous Bush;
Root; Rope; Rosa Maria; Salt & Pepper; Santa Marta;
Sasafras; Sativa; Sinsemilla; Shmagma; Shora; Shrimp;
Shwag; Skunk; Skywalker (hydroponic); Smoke; Smoochy
Woochy Poochy; Smoke; Smoke Canada; Spliff; Stems;
Stink Weed; Sugar Weed; Sweet Lucy; Tahoe (hydroponic);
Tex-Mex; Texas Tea; Tila; Tims; Tosca; Trees; Tweeds;
Wacky Tobacky; Wake and Bake; Weed; Weed Tea; Wet
(mixed with PCP); Wheat; White-Haired Lady; Wooz;
Yellow Submarine; Yen Pop; Yerba; Yesca; Young Girls;
Zacate; Zacatecas; Zambi; Zoom (mixed with PCP)

MARIJUANA CONCENTRATES
246; BHO; Badder; Budder; Butter; Dabs; Ear Wax; Errl;
Honey Oil; SAP; Shatter; Wax

MDMA
Adam; Baby Slits; Bean; Blue Kisses; Booty Juice (dissolved
in liquid); Candy; Chocolate Chips; Clarity; Dancing
Shoes; Decadence; Doctor; Domex (mixed with PCP); E;
E-Bomb; Ecstasy; Essence; Eve; Kleenex; Love Doctor;
Love Drug; Love Potion #9; Love Trip (mixed with
mescaline); Molly; Moon Rock; Roll; Rolling; Running;
Scooby Snacks; Skittle; Slits; Smartees; Speed for Lovers;
Sweets; Vitamin E; X; XTC

MESCALINE
Big Chief; Blue Caps; Buttons; Cactus; Media Luna;
Mescal; Mezcakuba; Moon; San Pedro; Top

METHAMPHETAMINE
Accordion; Aqua; Batu; Blue; Blue Bell Ice Cream; Beers;

Bottles; Bud Light; Bump; Cajitas; Chalk; Chavalones; Chicken; Chicken Powder; Christine; Christy; Clear; Clothing Cleaner; Colorado Rockies; Crank; Cream; Cri-Cri; Crink; Crisco; Crypto; Crystal; Cuadros; Day; El Gata Diablo; Evil Sister; Eye Glasses; Fire; Fizz; Flowers; Food; Frio; G-Funk; Gifts; Girls; Glass; Go-Fast; Groceries; Hard Ones; Hare; Hawaiian Salt; Hielo; Hot Ice; Ice; Ice Cream; Jug of Water; L.A. Glass; L.A. Ice; Lemons; Lemon Drop; Light; Light Beige; Livianas; Madera; Meth; Mexican Crack; Mexican Crank; Miss Girl; Montura; Motor; Muchacha; Nails; One Pot; Pantalones; Peanut Butter Crank; Piñata; Pointy Ones; Pollito; Popsicle; Purple; Raspado; Rims; Salt; Shabu; Shards; Shatter; Shaved Ice; Shiny Girl; Soap Dope; Soft Ones; Spicy Kind; Stove Top; Stuff; Super Ice; Table; Tina; Truck; Tupperware; Ventanas; Vidrio; Walking Zombie; Water; White; Windows; Witches Teeth; Yellow Barn; Yellow Kind; Zip

MUSHROOMS

Alice; Boomers; Buttons; Caps; Champiñones; Hongos; Magic; Mushies; Pizza Toppings; Shrooms; Tweezes

OPIUM

Auntie; Aunt Emma; Big O; Black; Black Russian (mixed with hashish); Chandoo; China; Chinese Molasses; Chinese Tobacco; Chocolate; Cruz; Dopium; Dover's Powder; Dream Gum; Dream Stick; Dreams; Easing Powder; God's Medicine; Goma; Gondola; Goric; Great Tobacco; Gum; Hocus; Hops; Incense; Joy Plant; Midnight Oil; Opio; Pen Yan; Pin Gon; Pin Yen; Pox; Skee; Toxy; Toys; When-Shee; Zero

OXYCODONE

30s; 40s; Beans; Blues; Buttons; Greens; OC; Oxy; Whites

PCP

Ace; Alien Sex Fiend (mixed with heroin); Amoeba; Angel; Angel Dust; Angel Hair; Angel Mist; Angel Poke; Animal Tranquilizer; Aurora Borealis; Black Acid (mixed with LSD); Black Whack; Blue Madman; Blue Star; Boat; Busy Bee; Butt Naked; Cadillac; Cliffhanger; Columbo; Cozmos; Crazy Coke; Crazy Eddie; Cucuy; Cyclones; Detroit Pink; Dipper; Domex (mixed with MDMA); Dummy Dust; Dust; Dust Joint; Dust of Angels; Elephant; Elephant Tranquilizer; Embalming Fluid; Energizer; Fake STP; Flakes; Goon; Gorilla Tab; Gorilla Biscuits; Green Leaves; Green Tea; Heaven & Hell; Hog; Horse Tracks; Horse Tranquilizers; Jet Fuel; Juice; Kaps; K-Blast; Killer; Kools; Leaky Leak; Lemon 714; Lethal Weapon; Love Boat; Mad Dog; Mad Man; Magic Dust; Mean Green; Mint Leaf; Mint Weed; Mist; Monkey Dust; Monkey Tranquilizer; New Acid; New Magic; Orange Crystal; Ozone; Paz; Peace Pill; Peep; Peter Pan; Pig Killer; Puffy; Purple Rain; Red Devil; Rocket Fuel; Rupture; Scuffle; Sheets; Sherms; Shermstick; Space (mixed with cocaine); Spores; Stardust; STP; Super Grass; Super Kools; Surfer; Synthetic Cocaine; Taking a Cruise; T-Buzz; Tic Tac; Tish; Trank; Venom; Wack (mixed with cocaine); Water; Wet; White Horizon; Wobble Weed; Wolf; Worm; Yellow Fever; Zombie; Zoom (mixed with marijuana)

PERCOCEL (Acetaminophen and Oxycodone)

512s; Bananas; Blue; Blueberries; Buttons; Ercs; Greenies; Hillbilly Heroin; Kickers; M-30s; Percs; Rims; Tires; Wheels

PEYOTE

Black Button; Britton; Button; Cactus; Green Button; Half Moon; Hikori; Hikuli; Hyatari; Nubs; Seni; Shaman; Tops

PROMETHAZINE WITH CODEINE

Act; Drank; Lean; Purple; Purple Drank; Sizurup; Sizzurp; Syrup

RITALIN®

Kibbles and Bits

SYNTHETIC CANNABINOIDS

4-20; Abyss; Ace of Spades; AK-47; Amnesia; Atomic Blast; Big Bang; Blaze; Black Magic Smoke; Black Mamba; Blaze; Blue Cheese; Brain Freeze; Buzz Haze; Cherry Bomb; Chill; Chrome; Clockwork Orange; Cloud 10; Cowboy Kush; Crystal Skull; Dead Man; Devil's Venom; Dr. Feel Good; Dragon Eye; Earth Blend; Exodus; Extreme; Fake Bake; Fruit Candy Flavors; Funky Buddha; Funky Monkey; G-Force; GI Joe; Green Dream; Green Peace; Hammer Head; Helix; Hipster; Hysteria; Ice Dragon; Juicy Leaf; Jungle Juice; Just Chill; K2; Kaos; Karma; Kong; Krazy Kandy; Kryp2nite; Kush; Layer Cake; Limitless; Mad Hatter; Mile High; Mystique; Ninja; Odyssey; OMG; Pandora's Box; Phoenix; Pineapple Express; Posh; Potpourri; Pow; Rapture; Red Magic; Rewind; Scooby Snax; Sexy; Sky High; Snake Bite; Spice; Spike Diamond; Storm; Sweet Leaf; Synthetic Marijuana; Time Traveler; Top Gear; Train Wreck; Ultimate; Viper; Voodoo Child; Wazabi; Wicked; Wizard; Xtreme; Zero Gravity; Zombie

SYNTHETIC CATHINONES

Bath Salts; Bliss; Bloom; Blow; Blue Silk; Cloud 9; Drone;

Energy-1; Explosion; Flakka (Alpha-PVP); Gravel (Alpha-PVP); Insect Repellant; Ivory Wave; Jewelry Cleaner; Lunar Wave; M-Cat; Meow-Meow; Ocean Burst; Phone Screen Cleaner; Plant Food; Pure Ivory; Purple Wave; Recharge; Red Dove; Scarface; Snow Leopard; Stardust; Vanilla Sky; White Dove; White Knight; White Lightening; White Magic; Zoom

XANAX® (Alprazolam)

Bars; Bicycle Handle Bars; Footballs; Hulk; Ladders; Planks; School Bus; Sticks; Xanies; Zanbars; Zannies; Z-Bars

THE ART OF TRAPPING

A TRAPPER IN GANG parlance is an individual who partakes in drug dealing - usually at a local level – but in recent times many Trappers have become involved in county lines dealing. The term Trapper is believed to have originated in Atlanta, Georgia and refers to an area in the city called the trap where drugs were regularly sold. Locals then matched the word trap to rapper (on account of their status) to form the word Trapper.

Whatever the truth is behind the term, the one thing that isn't in doubt is the existence of Trappers in our society. I have engaged with a fair amount of them in my time, so here are a few stories relating to what life is like for them on London's streets.

I mentioned T in the Rice Crispies and Cornflakes chapter, so here is a quick resume of him and his activities. T was 15 years old when I first knew him, and always stood out in the academy on account of his distinctive Louis Vuitton clothing and expensive accoutrements that he would show off at every possible opportunity. To say that he wound the other students up would be the understatement of the year, as this facade was clearly being put on to mask some serious personal esteem issues. T just didn't get that, and the harder he tried to make friends, the more he got rejected. When the school questioned him about where he was getting all the money from he would just say that it was from a Saturday job, but you didn't have to be a genius to figure out that no teenage job pays that well.

I had already seen his phone, and his unique customer codes so I was well aware of what he was doing. One day a group of ex-gang members who were now working as intervention mentors dropped by the school to say hello to me, and to have a general catch up on life. T saw them in the car park and freaked out as he thought they were looking for him. When they left he couldn't wait to talk to me to get the low down on them, as he needed reassurance that he wasn't being targeted. I sat him down and basically asked him to be honest with me about what was really going on in his life. As he sat on the chair he was acting in a really skittish way, constantly looking around and nervously fidgeting with his hands. To put him at ease, I assured him that the guys in the car park were known to me, and that he had nothing to worry about from them. Which begged the question: who was he scared of?

After pausing to collect his thoughts, he confessed that he had got himself into a dodgy situation that was getting progressively worse by the day. He had essentially been groomed by older boys who had started off by being nice to him and giving him some cash, but of course wanted something in return. That something though - was trapping for them in and around the local area. And as if he didn't have enough problems, he had also agreed to rep for another gang in a different borough. When I pressed him further for more details he also admitted that things had got pretty bad at home on account of his dangerous lifestyle. His mother and father had reluctantly had to kick him out of their house after one of the gangs turned up with a view of   beating him up following a fall out with them. Finding he wasn't at home they attacked his father and mother instead and roughed up one of his sisters - so as to send him a message.

With nowhere to live, T temporarily moved in with his grandparents but that didn't last for long, on account of his girlfriend inadvertently letting the cat of the bag as to where he had been hiding out. Once the gang found out his new address they went straight around to the house and roughed up his grandparents – again to send him a message.

It was a pretty sad state of affairs, as he had now sucked his completely innocent family into the shadowlands of his dark world, and they were now essentially paying for his mistakes.

Although T was honest with me about his home situation, when it came to talking about what was going on within his own gang he was very vague, and at times evasive. I put it to him that he may have been creaming off more of the drug money, than he was due – as trappers of his age just don't get anywhere near the money that he was splashing about. I guessed I must have hit a raw nerve, as he got up at that point and walked off. A few weeks later I learned that he got really badly beaten up, and that he had left London to live with other relatives. I never saw him after that.

In another incident that occurred in a youth centre in West London, I had the job of mentoring a group of teenagers who had been associated with Trapping in and around the North-West London area. Because of the risk of them being seen with a gang intervention team we had decided to hold the meeting in a venue that was neutral. I had three staff assigned to me: two support workers, and a kind lady from a nearby Pentecostal church who usually helped us with food and refreshments. In advance of the meeting we agreed safety code words which would be used in the event of us feeling uncomfortable about any individual in the group. This is done to protect staff from groups that are hostile towards them, or where a change in the session is needed. It's probably not appreciated by those who work outside youth work, that there can be times when groups will single out one member of staff and subject them to either direct physical bullying or relentless verbal abuse. I have seen this happen all too often, and it is extremely uncomfortable to watch. Hence the reason I always protect my staff by pre-agreed code words.

Our session started off well with the group that we had, and all seemed to be going well until a youth from another group was suddenly dropped in on our session. Having a balanced group dynamic is really important as it reduces tension, and makes sessions more productive. Our late arrival had been bounced out of his group for disruptive behaviour, and it was hoped that he would be calmer in ours, but that was not to be the case. This session was particularly important and sensitive, as we were trying to get young people out of Trapping, and into something that was more beneficial to them. Our new addition was called R, and he was an absolute royal pain in the butt. He mocked the other attendees relentlessly about their compliance in the session, and even started to threaten them by means of showing their faces on snapchat. I could see my colleagues becoming increasingly anxious as this whole session was on the verge of kicking off.

My first priority was the protection of the good lady from the church, as I didn't want her placed in any danger

- so I directed her to the kitchen. At this time all the groups phones were on the main table, so nobody could use them. R was by now bragging about how much money he was making, and even flashed a bundle of notes from his man bag. He then started shouting that he would have an Audi as his new whip.

I just had to do something quick – but what? I then did something that could have back-fired badly but I had to chance it. Realising that everything was about to explode, I picked Rs phone up and thankfully he hadn't screen locked it. I then said" I bet that I could stop your trapping with just one message." I tapped in a message and then pressed send. R was curious, what did you just do? I replied, I sent your friends a little message, "Fedz jus busted me." With that he raised his two hands to his face and kicked a nearby chair in temper. He then shouted a tirade of abuse at me and stormed off through the fire exit door, with one of my colleagues close behind him. The rest of the group just fell about laughing, saying I cannot believe   you just done that…..are you mad? More amusing was the fact that R had left his phone behind in his hurry to exit. Eventually calm was restored and we just got back to our session. As for Rs phone, it didn't go off for the rest of the session. I cannot think why that would be?

As for R, our paths would cross again, but for some strange reason he was always wary of me.

My next Trapper, known as Y - probably taught me more about gang life and what it is really like than any other person that I can possibly think of. It was in the spring of 2018 that I found myself back in Gotham, only this time it was with a very different outfit. My initial thoughts were, my - how this place has changed since I was last here. I was assigned to a room on the 3rd floor of a building that looked out upon the burned out remains of Grenfell Tower. And although I never lost anyone in Grenfell, some of the students in this provision had, so when they entered my classroom they would always sit with their backs to it, on account of the sad memories that it brought back. Grenfell would always be part of my life also, but for very different reasons – as my brave little daughter had been one of the firefighters that had been involved in that terrible tragic fire.

My role in this provision was teaching English, computer skills and where and whenever possible - I would also mentor. At first it was all pretty standard stuff, students that had been expelled from schools and PRUs, or ones that couldn't get places – and then out of the blue I was assigned U.

U had been in the provision previously but had been expelled because of violence towards other students and staff. No school or provision would take him, but by law he was still entitled to an education. Eventually it was decided that because I was the only one that he didn't know, or have any history with – it would be me that had the dubious pleasure of teaching U, not in a school but in a secure Youth Offending Service building in Paddington, just around the corner from pretty little Venice.

On the day that I was due to meet U it was felt best that someone accompanied me as he could be very volatile according to previous teachers. L was to be my escort as he knew U really well, plus they got along. So that made sense. As our meeting approached I looked out of the armoured glass that adorned the camera covered bunker that passed off as the Paddington YOS centre, but U was a no show. 30 minutes later and still nothing, and just as 60 minutes were coming up, a hooded youth came into sight whose face I could not see. L under his breath whispered its U, and from there it was on. L introduced me, and off we went to a secure room for a chat. At first I said nothing, as I felt it was best for L to lay out the path for me.

Eventually the point came after hearing many war stories, that it was time for me to step in and interject an odd comment here and there. L mentioned that U loved talking about guns and warfare, so we clearly had something in common. After about an hour of talking we said our goodbyes, as from the next day it would be me taking the lead with a support worker assisting me.

The next day arrived and we were all sent to a secure room equipped with cameras and panic alarms. I like to work on the basis of trust, so I asked U do I really need these as I don't feel in any way that you are a threat to me. He responded no, you and me are cool – so from that day no panic alarms. As I talked to him I couldn't but help notice a big fresh knife wound on his left arm which still had stitches. I asked him what had happened and he explained that he had been walking down the street when two youth rushed him. One tried to stab him in the heart but he moved just in time – so the knife got him in the arm instead. U was enjoying recalling his war stories, and asked if I would like to go on a tour of his manor.

I replied yes, so off we went. Our first port of call was a catholic secondary school tucked away in a nice residential area. Intrigued with why we were here, U pointed to a security guard sitting in a deck chair outside the school lapping up the sunshine like a lizard on a rock. "Why do I need to see him I enquired"? "It's because of me that the geezer in the chair has a job" he replied. How so? "Because I used to terrorise all the kids in the school." With that he laughed, and off we went to our next port of call which was where he got stabbed. Looking around the quaint little street shops it was hard to believe that this was a gang battle ground. It made me regularly check my six, as being with U would also make me a potential target.

Our last stopping point was a wall beside a block of flats. Curious as to why I was standing here, U said look up at those holes in the wall, they are bullet holes from a skirmish a few months back. Whether they were or not I cannot say, but being around U was certainly going to be interesting.

Over the next few weeks that followed, our relationship started to strengthen. He would do work, and I would reciprocate by talking about any subject that he raised. U was clearly highly intelligent, and could articulate his points really well. At times we would forget the student/ teacher relationship and embark upon conversations that would be really interesting and topical. In the gang world if you cannot establish a relationship with your subject, than you cannot teach them. It's as simple as that.

Typically, I would ask U if he was good to do some work, and the answer would be either yes or no. If no he would explain why not. Normally it would be down to being arrested the night before, in which case he would explain what had happened. Damn those undies I would joke with him, as he would recall his arrest. What I always found amazing about U is that no matter how many times he got arrested he always spoke well of the police, and never talked about them in a derogatory way. He would later explain that one of his relatives was a senior police officer in Morocco, and that he had frequently offered to take him under his care.

One day he came into the YOS centre looking a little down, but initially wouldn't say what was bothering him. After a while he informed me that he had witnessed a lady laying on the ground after being shot dead outside her block of flats in Kilburn. He was clearly upset by what he had seen - especially the screams of her brother after he arrived at the scene. I talked him through everything and managed his grief to the point that he appeared more settled. He was clearly grateful and spudded me.

After a while he said I know you mean well trying to help me, but I cannot change my ways. He then opened his grey man bag and showed me bundles of cash that he had made from Trapping. There was probably about £700 in that bag, but it only represented a day or two worth of takings. He was clearly one of the more successful Trappers, as most of them don't earn anything like that.

A few days later, and we met up again. It was a Friday afternoon and all was going well with U work wise - as I had set him an English GCSE paper to do. Once finished I checked it over said great that's you done for the day. He then turned to me and said "Do you really have to go now, can we just talk" I said sure and then we went into the garden that was behind the YOS centre. U seemed grateful that I had stayed with him, and then without any prompt from me he just unloaded everything that he had bottled up.

He looked over at the young nursery children playing in the nearby school and said "you know Mike, I envy those children. They look so happy and have everything to live for. I remember a time when I felt the same." He then revealed that it was his cousin that had got him into a gang, which is sadly quite a common thing to happen. U then went on to say that" you probably think that all my drug clients are hood rats like me, but they're not." He explained that he regularly dropped packages off to schools, offices, Hospitals and even to law enforcement officers, but of course he never elaborated on who these people were, nor did I ask him.

He mentioned that all of his clients got a burn phone which was only for him and them, and that no names were used – only numbers. He mentioned that he felt no threat whatsoever from his clients, as to incriminate him, would incriminate them, so it was a no brainer that this particular risk was marginal. His main threat was the police and rival gang members. What surprised me with U was that during the short period that I had known him he had been arrested on 4 separate occasions for knife possession - yet had never been jailed. Indeed on one occasion he said to me, after this weekend you won't see me again as I'm definitely going to be sent down when I go to court next week. But to his amazement, and indeed mine he busted case and got let off on a technicality.

It was now July, and I was due to deploy to Australia for a military exercise that I was in charge of so my time with U was rapidly running out. On the last day that I saw him, I gave him a lift home and while outside his block of flats, as we said our farewells I asked him a blunt question. "U we have worked together for months now, and in that time you have never threatened me, never been rude to me, or ever been disrespectful in any way. Why"? He looked at me in a somewhat puzzled way and replied "From day one you talked to me, and not down to me, and at no point did you ever disrespect me, which is why I never disrespected you." It was interesting feedback and I have always valued it.

Barely days later and I was on a plane to Dubai, and from there on to Australia for my next adventure.

THE CITADEL

WHENEVER WE THINK OF a drug dealing house we will often imagine a squalid house or flat located in a deprived and run down part of the city. For the most part this image is valid as gangs frequently operate out of squats or abandoned industrial premises, as these are free to use, and easy to abandon should they get raided by the police. There are however some exceptions to this norm, and this one in particular is the most unusual and unique that I have ever personally known.

I have seen gangs use vans as mobile drug dealing hubs, I have known numerous recreational areas, underground car parks and tunnels to be used, but a public library? Well that was a new one for me, and even the police. This particular library was well known to me as a safe place to take young people for mentoring and intervention meetings, and never in all the times that I visited did I ever tumble the subliminal activity that was also going on right under my nose.

I have always been taught in the military world to look out for the unusual amongst the usual, and to be aware of what's going on around you. For the most part I am usually pretty tuned in and generally observant of things. But on this particular occasion - I did not see the wood for the trees.

The revelation that the library was being used as a drug hub occurred while I was carrying out an intervention with a young man called J who was heavily involved in the drill music scene, and by dint becoming precariously and increasingly close to becoming a victim of a rival gang. We could not meet in any school or YOS (Youth Offending Service) provision near his home on account of the danger he was in, as his Ops were monitoring him all the time. Meeting him would of course also put me and my work colleague Mr S in serious danger - as any attack on J - would include us as well - as we would be deemed associates, or in gang parlance: Paigons.

Before bringing J into the library, I had to carry out a quick recce to see if any other rival gang members or possible threats were present. This usually took a few minutes, but it was always time well spent. In the event of a possible problem we would abort the appointment and reschedule. On some occasions if I had a concern over an individual I would discreetly take a photo of them and show it to J to see if he knew them. Once these risk checks were carried we would enter the building and move to the far end, so that nobody walking past would see him through the windows. As an additional precaution he would always sit in a place where his back faced the main entrance, whereas I always positioned myself in a place where I could watch who was entering the area where we were seated. As they say better to be safe than sorry.

After finding ourselves a good position, a large group of elderly black men and women began entering the area of the library where we were, and a conversation between them and us quickly developed. They began to explain that they were part of the Windrush generation, and that they were visiting libraries around London to tell their personal stories to any young people that wanted to learn more about their journey to England, and what they experienced when they first arrived in cold rainy London. We gestured them to sit with us, and with that they commenced reeling off their tales of challenge and adventure.

J seemed to be fascinated with hearing their stories and asked if we could stay longer to hear more of them. I quickly agreed, as I had never seen him engage like this before. The gentleman that he was talking to introduced himself as George, and almost instantly we joked about how he looked like the American actor Morgan Freeman. His wife Cherie laughed and said " but him ain't got Morgan's money, nor a big flash house with a swimming pool." As we carried on enjoying their company George said to J that he was pleased to see a young black man like him and the others in the library trying to better themselves, and that it made him feel positive for the future. J shook his hand and said "thanks my brother that means a lot to me."

As George and Cherie walked away, J said "What a sweet man, but he has no idea why these other black youth are here." It was an interesting remark, so I asked him to explain what he meant by it. It was then that he started to inform me and Mr S that the library was a major drug hub for the local area, particularly the schools and colleges.

I suddenly became laser focused with everything that he was saying, as J was generally very coy about discussing anything to do with gang related criminal activities, on account of his connections with them. And yet here and now in this place he was describing an enterprise that we had no knowledge of. He started to explain that the small group of young school boys sitting in front of the computers in the research area were taking drug orders online from their users, and then passing them over to another group of boys located in a small area adjacent to them.

It was here where the orders were discreetly packed and then put into their designer Under Armour back packs. He then explained that from this point the back packs were taken downstairs and then given to a number of other young teenagers that were waiting outside with mopeds, featuring boxes that looked like those used for pizza deliveries.

I was absolutely fascinated with what he was telling me, as these teenagers would never have aroused any suspicion within me, as they just seemed like normal everyday school children. It was the perfect location, as I have never seen police in a library before, and I guess neither have they, otherwise they would not be operating from here. Also any police passing by would be unlikely to search them, as there were always plenty of young men walking around the area wearing hoodies and face masks that would make them far more likely to be targeted for a police search.

It was perfect cover, and I could easily understand why they had picked this location for their criminal activities. These teenagers could not have been any older than sixteen, while some seemed a lot younger. J said that they called the library the Citidel, which was really an odd name for a place that was the polar opposite of the words meaning, as it usually refers to a fortified area within a town or it can mean a fortress like structure built upon a rock. I had heard the name Citidel mentioned before in other interventions with other gang members, but I never knew what it referred to, but now everything made sense.

I could not but help feel that more powerful forces were at work here, and that these young roadmen who were cool with J, were just a clever front, and a distraction for some enterprise elsewhere that was even bigger in magnitude. Regardless of my views and thoughts it was an impressive operation, and one that clearly showed just how adaptable and resourceful gangs can be. It was intelligence gathering gold to me, and a lesson and reminder of why you must always pay attention and listen to what young people are trying to tell you, as just one sentence can be the key that opens a treasure chest of information.

O T

OT IS GANG SLANG for Out of Town and refers to Trappers dealing drugs outside their normal gang territory. I first became aware of the term a few years back while working in Gotham, but never really understood what it meant.

Eventually though It would all start to make sense after one particular day in which one of my students failed to turn up for his mentoring session. I asked him where he had been and he said that he'd gone O T to see his aunty in Birmingham. I let it go, until a week later the same thing happened – only this time his aunty was in Bournemouth. Erm I thought, me thinks something just ain't right in this picture.

Young U just did not strike me as the family visiting type, so I quizzed him more about his O T activities. "It's just stuff Sir" he replied. "Ok, like what sort of stuff?" I asked. I really wasn't getting anywhere with him, so one my colleagues L stepped in to enrich my knowledge. L was an ex- gang member who was now working as a mentor, and his presence was always welcome – as he filled in my knowledge gaps, when and wherever appropriate.

L was also very good at smoothing things with some gang members who were convinced that I was working undercover in the provision, which as you can imagine is not a good thing for someone who is trying to work with them, and not against them.

L eventually persuaded U to talk to me about O T and what it involved, without of course incriminating himself. U explained that dealing drugs around London was becoming increasingly difficult on account of all the rival gangs dealing, which meant that there was an oversupply in the market. That of course meant lower prices, for greater risk. To get around this problem, gangs began experimenting with supplying drugs to students attending colleges and universities in more rural settings. Coastal towns like Bournemouth and Brighton were particularly attractive, as they had large university campuses – so therefore lots of customers.

It was recognised in advance that most rural towns would already have someone insitu that took care of local drug supply, so strategies had to be figured out as to what should be done to negate the existing competition. The more entrepreneurial gangs took a pragmatic approach to the problem by entering into alliances and partnerships with the local dealers – as they viewed that as a win-win solution for all concerned. Essentially, the local campus dealers would now have a far wider range of drug product on offer, which would obviously boost their revenue. Whereas the benefit to the supplier was more stable and profitable markets, without the inherent risks associated with drug dealing in London.

The more aggressive London gangs had other ideas though. They would simply send a stooge into a college to identify who was the drug supplier, and once identified, they would be pushed off their patch - by either forceful persuasion or violence. Once neutralised the London gangs would move in with their style of operation.

Little did I know at the time, but I was in fact witnessing the initial grass roots of what would eventually become known as "County Lines" drug dealing.

County Lines

According to the National Crime Agency (NCA) County Lines is where illegal drugs are transported from one area to another, often across police and local authority boundaries (although not exclusively), usually by children or vulnerable people who are coerced into it by gangs. The 'County Line' is the mobile phone line used to take the orders of drugs. Importing areas (areas where the drugs are taken to) are reporting increased levels of violence and weapons-related crimes as a result of this trend.

NPCC definition of a County Line

The 2018 Home Office Serious Crime Strategy states the NPCC definition of a County Line is a term used to describe gangs and organised criminal networks involved in exporting illegal drugs into one or more importing areas [within the UK], using dedicated mobile phone lines or other form of "deal line". They are likely to exploit children and vulnerable adults to move [and store] the drugs and money and they will often use coercion, intimidation, violence (including sexual violence) and weapons.

Exploitation of young and vulnerable people

A common feature in county lines drug supply is the exploitation of young and vulnerable people. The dealers will frequently target children and adults - often with mental health or addiction problems - to act as drug runners or move cash so they can stay under the radar of law enforcement.

In some cases the dealers will take over a local property, normally belonging to a vulnerable person, and then use it to operate their criminal activity from. This is known as cuckooing.

People exploited in this way will quite often be exposed to physical, mental and sexual abuse, and in some instances will be trafficked to areas a long way from home as part of the network's drug dealing business.

Typically, a child involved in exploitation will not see themselves as a victim, or even realise that they have been groomed for criminality. Often they will see the police, school and social services as the enemy, so getting them to see the reality of their situation can be very difficult.

Initially, the police were very slow to appreciate the magnitude of county lines, as local forces don't have the manpower and resources that the Met police possess.

However, once the NCA got involved that picture changed, as they are geared up to deal with national crime networks. To be effective against county lines gangs you need to be able to spot unusual activities in your area.

Signs to look out for include:

- An increase in visitors and cars to a house or flat

- New faces appearing at the house or flat

- New and regularly changing residents (e.g different accents compared to local accent)

- Change in resident's mood and/or demeanour (e.g. secretive/ withdrawn/ aggressive/ emotional)

- Substance misuse and/or drug paraphernalia

- Changes in the way young people you might

know dress

- Unexplained, sometimes unaffordable new things (e.g clothes, jewellery, cars etc)
- Residents or young people you know going missing, maybe for long periods of time
- Young people seen in different cars/taxis driven by unknown adults
- Young people seeming unfamiliar with your community or where they are
- Truancy, exclusion, disengagement from school
- An increase in anti-social behaviour in the community
- Unexplained injuries

If you are a young person who is worried about your involvement, or a friend's involvement in county lines. A good option is to speak to an adult you trust and talk to them about your concerns.

You can also call Childline on 0800 1111. Childline is private and confidential service where you can talk to specially trained counsellors about anything that is worrying you.

Alternatively, speak to a children and young people's service like Catch 22. They work with children and young people of any age to help get them out of situations they're worried about, and have helped lots of children and young people involved in County Lines.

To be more effective against county lines gangs, the police are developing a more comprehensive strategy that brings in assets and personnel from other agencies.

Following recent criticism of its performance, this response was issued.

Law enforcement response

Tackling county lines, and the supply gangs responsible for high levels of violence, exploitation and abuse of vulnerable adults and children, is a priority for UK law enforcement.

Law enforcement collectively has been stepping up its response, working to identify and take effective action in areas of the country with the most significant problems.

To enhance the law enforcement response still further, a multi-agency county lines coordination centre has been established, bringing together officers from the NCA, police and regional organised crime units to develop the national intelligence picture, prioritise action against the most serious offenders, and engage with partners across government, including in the health, welfare and education spheres, to tackle the wider issues.

In addition to this response, in June 2020 it was announced that police will now seek to disable phones known to be used in county lines transactions. Senior police officers have been in talks with telecoms companies for quite a while now, trying to figure out the best way to disrupt drug dealing gangs.

Dame Cressida Dick, Britain's most senior police officer, said officers were working with the firms so that phones where it was glaringly obvious that they were being used by the gangs would be automatically locked to prevent them continuing with their drug dealing.

Gangs tend to favour older phone models that use pay as you go Sim cards. Some of these are known to be racking up hundreds of calls and texts per day, making them easy to track, trace and isolate. Dealers tend to be based in urban areas, whereas their customers are in more rural areas.

Dame Cressida also said: "It's glaringly obvious when

you look at the phone data what a device is being used for. It is a unique way of using phones like that. "We would say it is obvious to the companies that supply those devices. We will work with them and the Government and whoever necessary to continue to restrict the ability of county lines individuals to carry out their pernicious activities. We want to destroy the business model."

To further frustrate criminals, the police are also looking to restrict the use of anonymous pay-as-you-go phones. Under current laws, phones can only be blocked under a court order, but this has little effect on gangs as they simply go out and buy new ones. To get around this problem the Home Office are considering customers having to register personal details before being allowed to purchase a phone, or a SIM card.

Should these initiatives become reality, the impact upon gangs and their criminal activities will be immense, as phones are their main means of communicating. If the drug dealers in the city cannot communicate with their rural customers - their drug empires will simply collapse.

The National Crime Agency estimates that phone lines generate between £500 million and £1 billion every year for criminals, and that at any given time there are between 800 and 1,100 phones in action taking drug orders.

Up until March 2020, 1,300 people with connections to county lines were charged with some 2,000 offences, including 20 murders. The UK police currently target county line phone holders under the auspices of Operation Orochi.

Deputy Assistant Commissioner Graham McNulty said: " we set a very deliberate strategy of targeting the line holder. These are the people who often rarely leave

London, they avoid the risk of handling the commodity, getting hands on with the drugs themselves, but they co-ordinate the distribution of drugs across the UK. They exploit children and vulnerable adults, and they collect the profits at the end. These are the people who really are in the shadows, but they are responsible for a trail of misery and mayhem."

In one example given by the police, one line known as the Tommy Line, had a customer base of some 300 customers, and took 565 calls and text messages per day.

As for the future, I can see gangs making more use of drones in their rural operations, as they are becoming cheaper and more easy to fly on account of automated software. Also if they are compromised, it is very difficult to trace the operator unless you have very sophisticated tracking equipment available.

Drones of course have been used for supplying drugs and phones to prisons for some time now, and it is only a matter of time before there use becomes more widespread.

JIHADI-Gs

AT THIS PRESENT TIME there is no accurate data available as to how many gang members have become terrorists, or indeed how many jihadis have become gangsters. I can assure you though that it does happen, albeit rarely. I personally have only ever known two individuals that have got involved in terrorism, and both of those cases were some years ago.

The first case that I dealt with involved a young teenage boy from West London, who had recently arrived from Iraq under a refugee program. He had barely been in the UK a few months when he started spurting out extremely concerning views, that were not normal for a child of his age. Even if you made allowances for him coming from a war ravaged country, his comments and intentions were very specific, and dangerous.

In essence he wanted to receive military training in the UK, so that he could return to Iraq – to kill American troops!! There was zero chance of that happening around me, so I contacted a friend in counter-terrorism to make him aware of what we were dealing with. This was before the Prevent programme came into existence, so running him through the provisions safeguarding system would have achieved nothing.

As I was awaiting a response from my friends boss, my jihadi in waiting started bragging about how his cousins were going to kill many British people very soon. The other youths in our care, were horrified with his threats and started to feel uncomfortable around him. I too was getting concerned about his comments, so I decided to question him about who his cousins were, and where were they living?

As I talked to him, it became clear that he was very unstable, and that he could not be left along with anyone. What horrors he saw in Iraq, I do not know, but it was obvious that something had unhinged him. A few hours later, I got the call that I had been waiting for, and no surprise the word was he had to go – and as the French would say tout suite.

For months I heard nothing more, and then one day out of the blue I got a call from a senior officer in counter-terrorism. His call was just to thank me for the information that I gave them, and to say that it had led to a potential attack on a major shopping centre being foiled, as the two cousins had been very close to carrying it out. As for our subject who triggered the whole thing off, nothing was said about him.

Over the years I have frequently used this story as an example of why we have safeguarding and prevent training.

Most people that work with young people will thankfully never have to deal with such a situation. You must however always be open minded and observant as to what is going on, and what is being said. When I have talked to gang members during mentoring sessions about the possibility of them becoming radicalised, they have always looked upon the idea of it with absolute disdain. They will readily admit to being involved in criminal activities, but the idea of carrying out a terrorist attack is in their eyes totally unimaginable. Which of course is a good thing.

As for the other gang member that became a jihadi, although he was known to me in the provision, I never actually worked with him directly. I remember the day when we found out what had become of this miscreant after he had left us. It was just after our daily morning briefing when all the youths in the centre were laughing at some image on an ipad.

They gestured for us to come and have a look, so we all did. On the screen there was a photo of a young man on the back of a white Toyota pick-up truck complete with a heavy machine gun, set against a barren desert. Although he was wearing a black Durag on his head, you could clearly make out the face. It was U, and all I can say is thank god I never mentored him, as he was most definitely a lost cause.

There are of course parts of the UK where there is a very real threat of gangsters becoming jidadis, as some like the images that ISIS puts out promoting their cause. In some cases, there is even a synergy in images and music that I am sure are designed to seduce vulnerable young men into this type of life style. There is always a higher risk in diverse communities of youths becoming radicalised through extremism or dissatisfaction with how their lives are developing, and a groomer will spot that a mile away.

That's why we all need to be vigilante, and mindful as to who is influencing our youth.

CYBER GANGSTA'S

WHEN WE THINK OF GANGS, we normally visualize hooded youths hanging around street corners and estates, but there are some gang members who conduct their criminality in the shadows and behind closed doors. They are the cyber gangsta's, and they are part of an increasing number who do not want to be on the streets fighting over a piece of turf that may cost them their life.

For them, there are no knives or guns in their world, only the flickering screens of their computers.

My first introduction to gang related cyber warfare came about while I was working in Ladbroke Grove. The young man concerned was known amongst the local gangs as "Rainman" on account of the fact that he was autistic. He was an interesting young man in so many ways, not least because all of the gangs in the area knew him, and indeed hung out with him. So what did he have that gave him an all access pass into every gangs territory? The answer: His incredible database on unmarked police vehicles.

"Rainman", or R as I shall call him was of middle-eastern origin, and he had an obsessive interest in police vehicles. When I was first assigned to him, one of the first things that I needed to know was where did he get his information on the police vehicles? My initial concern was that there may have been some dark website that had surreptitiously obtained a police vehicle database. R assured me that wasn't the case, and got out his laptop to show me what he had on it. What I saw before my eyes was truly amazing. He had literally hundreds of images of police vehicles, along with spreadsheets showing the make, model, colour and registration of each vehicle. He also had lots of video that he had shot on his phone showing police vehicles racing through London on blues and twos.

At first I thought this was super creepy, but when I thought about it, was it really any different to someone plane or train spotting. I guess not. As I started to assess what he had on his laptop - all the dots suddenly started to join up as to why the local gangs had an interest in R.

As we talked he explained how his friends (the gangs) liked to look at his laptop or send him text messages with car registrations to look up. Although this information would initially seem really helpful to the gangs, what most of them had probably not realised is that the police move their unmarked fleet around, so that cars don't become too familiar in a particular area. These days they also tend to use a variety of different makes and models, so that brand associated usage is less likely.

As I got to know R, it became clear that he was no threat to anyone, and that he was completely harmless. I sometimes worried though that he might get exploited by the gangs for other things, like delivering drug packages, but from what he told me that had not happened. While working with R he would regularly fire dozens of questions at me about the police and the army, most of which I was able to answer for him without too much trouble. One particular question I remember him asking me related to why some marked police cars have yellow discs in their windscreens? When I told him that it indicated that they were carrying guns, his eyes lit up and a big smile appeared on his face. I so wish that I could please my other students as easily.

As I worked with R, I could see that he was noticeably improving academically, apart from in his reading, where he still struggled. As an experiment one day I gave him a green plastic sheet to put over the pages, to see if it made any difference to him. As he read he seemed more fluid, but there was still an issue. I then partly blanked off the green sheet, so that he could only read about ten lines at a time. The results were instant - as he could read fluidly now. I suspected that he was dyslexic, so I put in a recommendation for an assessment. Before leaving the provision I made some calls on behalf of R to try and get him into a government run programme that supports young people who are computer savvy. And he certainly was. There are not many people that you can call unique, but R was about as close as possible to that special club.

R was a pleasure to work with, but sadly the others that I encountered that were involved in cyber- crime were not so amicable. One that springs to mind was S who was a serial fraudster. His scam was setting up fake companies that exploited people looking to buy property overseas. Essentially he would intercept client to customer emails, and put in his bank details in place of theirs. Most people would fall for this scam, as they believed the money was going to the property company, as they had all their details. The lesson here is always pay by credit card if you can, as you will be protected by the banks.

Another scam that I became aware of while working

in Hammersmith, which I have to say was pretty clever -
involved very attractive young ladies handing out brightly
coloured key fob torches to car owners as they sat in
traffic. I guess that I must drive a crap car as I never got
offered one. It was only later that I found out what else
was inside the key fob that made this scam so successful.
The local gang who I suspect were in league with a high
level criminal network had planted small GPS trackers
in the key fobs, which instantly activated when the torch
button got pressed. After that they would track the car to
where it was parked up at night, and then remotely clone
the cars electronic key. Once done the car would be stolen
within minutes, and would end up either cloned in the UK
or broken down to be shipped overseas.

Gangs also have other uses for computers that include
the mounting of internet harassment and intimidation
campaigns against their rivals. These will sometimes
include the distribution of custom made drill videos that
taunt their rivals over previous violent confrontations, or
they advertise and promote future anticipated conflicts.

The cyber world can also host websites that gangs
have set up to promote themselves, and to identify the
territory that they control. I have seen some websites that
have been set up solely to sell drugs, but they are made
up to look like online games. Every customer gets an ID
that entitles them to buy credits for assets that supposedly
enhance the game. The assets however are all code words
for different types of drugs, and these highly innovative
websites are designed to get around the police clamp down
on county lines.

As gangs venture further into cyberspace, they are
becoming more and more adept at identity theft, fraud
and hacking. One of their latest scams involves exploiting
household intelligent electric meters as they give away their

owners patterns of life – making it easy for the robbers to target them.

In 2019 I attended a counter-terrorism expo, and while there one of the cyber security experts gave us all a talk on security and safety. One of the first things he said was if you have an intelligent meter that reports back to your supplier, you need to get rid of it straight away, as it can be hacked into. He also advised us all to get a RFID (radio-frequency identification) proof shielded wallet so that our credit cards couldn't get cloned.

Another lesson for us, and indeed for you - is change your passwords regularly as they can easily be hacked.

To illustrate this point, a young man gave us a presentation on laptop security. He said I'm not going to tell you my real name, so for the purpose of this presentation I will be called Sam. Sam had blonde hair, complete with a pony tail and wore a red chequered lumberjack shirt. He then went on to say that he worked for a government agency, and legally hacked foreign computers – but never mentioned which agency, or what countries he was hacking. He then took out £50 in cash and placed it on the table in front of him. He then issued a challenge to us. "I can get into every laptop in this room within 3 minutes, and if I don't succeed I will give this money to the person that has kept me out. At first nobody bit, and then suddenly an immaculately dressed gentleman got up and said I accept your challenge, as I don't believe that you will get into this laptop. Sam took his laptop and placed a USB like device called a duck into a side port, and then placed it down on the desk. He then invited its owner to sit in front of the screen and watch what appeared. As the seconds ticked by, the face of the laptops owner started to change as he could see his password appear on the screen. Sam asked him to confirm," Is that your password"? A very silenced voice replied "Yes." Sam then went on to say that his device analysed algorithms and the most common one is your password – so f…ing change it regularly, otherwise this will happen to you.

It was a good demonstration, and it most definitely had an impact upon me, and how I protected myself.

There were other cyber security demonstrations and briefings but they were classified, so I cannot discuss them.

So the lesson is do change your passwords regularly, and triple check anything that you do that involves computers, as there is always someone out there probing you.

NO FACE, NO CASE

"NO MATTER HOW CAREFUL you think you are, you will always leave a footprint of your activities somewhere – and that is how you will get caught." - M Ryan

If I had a pound for every time a gangbanger said "no face, no case" after they had been arrested by the police for a criminal act, I would be a very rich man. There seems to be a school of thought amongst gangs, that if you cannot identify my face, then you cannot prosecute me for anything. This misguided view was borne out of a misconception that prosecutors will drop a case against a suspect, if there is no visible image, or if a witness cannot pick them out in a line-up.

In most countries including the UK, a suspect is innocent until proven guilty beyond a reasonable doubt.

The idea of no face, no case is dependent on the fact that even when a suspect matches the exact description of the perpetrator – if no person saw the alleged transgressors face, or no camera captured it (no face), then there is usually reasonable doubt, which will generally mean a dismissal of the case (no case). In addition to this theory, there is also the assumption that if a third party witness of the crime refuses or fails to testify, then the case will be dropped due to a lack of definitive evidence. It is another example of no face, no case.

The term no face, no case is believed to date back to the year 2000, and is mentioned in a 2002 song by a rapper from South Carolina, called Pachino Dino. The song is about violent crimes, and in it the rapper mentions that he is not worried about being arrested because of no face, no case - as he is wearing a ski mask.

The phrase was also recorded in a 2004 Tennessee police interview with a suspect who incriminated himself by saying no face, no case when the police had not mentioned that the suspect was wearing a mask.

Eventually the phrase entered the legal system, and was commonly used by lawyers to refer to a witness who failed or refused to testify. This scenario was particularly applicable in domestic abuse cases where the witness is also the victim, and cannot be legally forced to face the suspect in court. This of course does not mean that the course will be dismissed.

Thanks to the advent of MTV and social media the expression no face, no case had become widespread, even if the legal implications still remained unclear.

Moving time forward to 2020, and the term no face, no case seems almost meaningless, as the police have so many other different ways to catch a criminal. Today, no gang member leaves home without a phone, which means that they can be tracked any time, day or night, and of course placed at a crime scene. We also have an abundance of CCTV cameras in London that can monitor human movements day or night, and in all weathers. In fact we have over 500,000 CCTV systems in operation that cover just about every main road and public place.

As a point of interest, London underground operates 15,516 cameras alone.

King's Cross and St. Pancras have 408 between them that monitor over 81 million people per year.

Other stations that like monitoring you include:

- Oxford Circus – 309

- Waterloo – 303

- Green Park – 210

- Elephant & Castle – 190

- Bank/Monument – 182

- Westminster – 177

- Piccadilly Circus – 175

- Wembley Park – 171

- Canary Wharf - 167

CCTV cameras tend to be installed on the basis of many factors, the most common being:

- Crime levels

- Transport links

- Footfall

There are however boroughs that have deployed more CCTV cameras than the normal average as they may different criteria that is based on local operational requirements. The London borough of Wandsworth for instance has more CCTV systems than Boston, Dublin, Johannesburg and San Francisco put together. This may surprise you, but in London you are likely to be captured on camera over 300 times a day.

Aside from safety reasons, CCTV is also very helpful in both preventing and indeed solving crime. In 2009 for example, 95% of the Metropolitan Police's murder cases involved CCTV footage that proved invaluable when collecting evidence for prosecutions.

Looking further into the future, the police will undoubtedly make more use of AI (Artificial Intelligence), as it is far quicker than the human eye. Current systems however are still very much in development, and will need to improve in accuracy before their usage becomes more widespread. Other technologies that I have seen being demonstrated at counter-terrorism events include cameras that can analyse body movements relating to your gait (manner of walking). We all walk differently, and even if we try to change our normal pattern to deceive a camera we can only do that for a short period of time. If you have a few minutes to spare, just watch how your friends or family members walk – you will see that all their walking patterns are different. This tool is particularly useful to the police, as it does not need to see any part of a perpetrators face in order to be able to identify them.

Another effective forensics science that is proving to be highly effective in no face, no case crimes is odorology – a technique that traces human scent by means of specially trained dogs. These dogs are incredibly effective, and can detect the most minute of scents at a crime scene. Also in development are biological smell sensors that can detect molecular compounds, such as explosives and drugs automatically as people walk through search gates or confined spaces. Once in service, they will reduce the need for random police stop and search's, as individuals can be specifically targeted for prohibited items - without hindering those that are innocent.

At this present time the most effective forensic

weapon for identifying a culprit in a crime is by means of a DNA (deoxyribonucleic acid) analysis test. DNA is the molecule that contains the instructions an organism needs to develop, live and reproduce. These instructions are found inside every cell, and are passed down from parents to their children. DNA is made up of molecules called nucleotides. Each nucleotide contains a phosphate group, a sugar group and a nitrogen base. The four types of nitrogen bases are Adenine (A), Guanine (G), Cytosine (C) and Thymine (T). The order of these bases is what determines DNA's instructions, or genetic code. Human DNA has around 3 billion bases, and more than 99 percent of these bases are the same in all people.

There are of course literally thousands of crimes that have been solved by DNA analysis, however one particularly interesting one that springs to mind occurred in Tottenham, North London on Saturday 3 February 2018, and involved the murder of 22-year old youth worker, Kwabena Nelson.

This is the official Metropolitan Police account of the murder:

> A man involved in a violent group attack on a youth worker in Tottenham has been jailed for his murder.
>
> Neron Quartey, 21 (22.03.1997), of north London was found guilty of the murder of 22-year-old Kwabena Nelson today, Thursday, 16 August following a trial at the Old Bailey which started on Monday, 30 July.
>
> Quartey, was sentenced on the same date to life imprisonment to serve a minimum of 26 years.
>
> Police were called at about 01:30hrs on Saturday, 3 February, to Kemble Road at the junction of St Mary's Close, Tottenham, N17, to reports of a stabbing.
>
> Officers attended along with London Ambulance Service and London's Air Ambulance and found a man,

later identified as Kwabena who is known as Kobi to friends and family, suffering from serious stab injuries. He was pronounced dead at the scene.

A post-mortem examination held at Haringey Mortuary on Monday, 5 February gave cause of death as hypovolemic shock and stab wounds.

The court heard that immediately before the murder, a black Honda Civic driven by Quartey, deliberately crashed into a grey Honda Civic being driven by Kwabena, in Kemble Road.

The occupants, carrying poles and knives, got out of the vehicle. Kwabena either got out or was forced from his vehicle, and he was attacked before the suspects ran off.

The court heard that the seriously injured Kwabena called police, and then a family member to tell them that he had been stabbed. Family members arrived at the scene, prior to his being declared deceased by a London Air Ambulance doctor who attended.

The Met's Homicide and Major Crime Command, led by Detective Inspector Jon Meager, launched an investigation.

The airbags in the suspect vehicle, which had been stolen 10 days prior, had been deployed, and investigators extracted DNA evidence from the driver's side. A DNA match came back for Quartey.

A number of knives, some broken, were recovered from the nearby area and some were later linked to the incident through DNA evidence.

Quartey was arrested on Friday, 9 February and charged the following day with murder.

He first appeared at Highbury Magistrates' Court on Monday, 12 February.

DI Jon Meager, from the Homicide and Major Crime Command said: "Kwabena was the victim of a sustained violent attack in which he appears to have been targeted. The reason is not known, but Kobi was not a gang member and it may be that he was mistakenly targeted by the defendant and his accomplices.

"He was outnumbered by a number of suspects with weapons, and the savagery of the attack meant that Kobi stood little chance and unfortunately succumbed to his injuries at the scene.

"His family have been left utterly devastated, and I would like to thank them for their assistance throughout the investigation.

"One person has been found guilty of Kwabena's murder, but we know from witness accounts that other people were involved. I would like to assure Kobi's family that we will continue to investigate and do everything we can to bring Quartey's accomplices to justice. We would urge anybody who has any information about the incident to come forward. It may be that you have heard Kwabena's murder being spoken about in the months since the killing, or you remember something about that night which may assist our investigation. Any information we do receive will be treated with the strictest confidence."

In a statement, Kobi's mother Serwah said: "Kobi was a son, cousin, favourite uncle, friend, colleague, best friend and my little boy. Snatched away from us in such a brutal and barbaric way. The young men, the cowards, who did this have now left a huge trail of devastation within my family. I wonder if they will ever realise this or just how much pain they have left us to cope with. I find every day a struggle. How could so few cause such devastation to so many of us. I take each day as it comes, sometimes I have to take each hour."

BUSTING CASE

WHEN I WORKED IN gang intervention I would frequently hear my students say I'm going to be "Busting Case" – which usually means: I'm going to be let off in court. This contrasts with the police expression I'm going to "Bust this Case" – which means, I'm going to solve it.

Gang members busting case seems to happen all too often, which raises the question: how effective is our youth legal system?

As an insider in the system, my job was to either discourage young people from joining gangs, or if they had already joined one – I was to do everything possible to minimise their criminal activities.

For the most part I was successful in my endeavours, when I had direct involvement and control over my students, but all too often that was not the case as some subjects just got ping-ponged from one provision to another. So sadly they fell between the cracks in the system.

On the occasions where I went to court as an advocate, I always made it clear to my students that my attendance was conditional upon them making a genuine effort to get out of crime. I certainly would not be writing them an ongoing get out of jail free card. When preparing a defence case, I would always have a plan that involved them engaging with their parents and schools, so that it led to a reestablishment of relationships and a pathway back to normality. I would also encourage my students to find an outside interest, such as cadets, sports or music – so that they had some sort of diversionary activity to keep them occupied in the evenings.

In recent years there has been a significant drop in youth prosecutions which of course is a good thing, providing that it is reflective of a drop in crime. In 2018 there were 4208 fewer custodial sentences handed down compared to 2008 – a massive fall of 73%.

These falls were apparently explained away as being due to a drop in the number of young people entering the justice system for the first time, as opposed to a general liberalisation of sentencing that had brought about these lower numbers. Whatever the truth is, crime certainly hasn't dropped in London from where I'm sitting, as I see the effects every day.

There are certainly more organisations and charities that are carrying out wonderful work in the way of diversionary activities. But there is still lots of crime, so why hasn't that translated into the justice systems figures. My personal view is that due to significant shortages of police officers, a lot of petty crime is not being investigated, which means the perpetrators are getting away with it.

There is also what I call carousel justice, which is where young people get put in the youth justice system - go to court and bust case - and then go back to committing crime, knowing that they will just keep going around in the same loop.

On the rare occasions where someone does get a

custodial sentence, the detention periods tend to be very low, which serves little purpose – as the young people that are put away will not get access to any long term rehabilitation programmes that could turn their lives around. This is not a good state of affairs as it means that they are highly likely to reoffend again once they have been released back into society.

When dealing with gangs, the problems become ever more complex as you have to define an individual's role within a gang, and indeed if their group is a gang or a collection of young people who hang out together.

The 2009 Act defined a gang as consisting of at least three people; using a name, emblem or colour or has any other characteristic that enables its members to be identified by others as a group; and is associated with a particular area.

In 2015 it was simplified so that a gang is now defined as having one or more characteristics that enable its members to be identified as a group by others.

Minister for Preventing Abuse and Exploitation Karen Bradley said:

Gang and youth violence has a devastating impact on the young people who get caught up in it, as well as their families and communities.

It is not an issue that any one agency or government department can tackle alone. It requires the police, teachers, social workers, housing officers, youth workers, employment advisers and many others working together, and sharing information in order to safeguard vulnerable young people and target the most violent.

Due to the changing nature of the way gangs operate we have updated the definition of a gang to ensure injunctions remain effective. We have also made it easier for courts to grant injunctions to prevent gang-related drug dealing and protect individuals from this kind of activity by expanding the scope of gang injunctions.

JOINT ENTERPRISE

ANOTHER CONTENTIOUS LEGAL ISSUE is that of joint enterprise – which is defined as follows:

Criminal law generally only holds offenders liable for their own actions but, under the doctrine of joint enterprise, a person may be found guilty for another person's crime.

Simple association or accidental presence during a crime is insufficient for a charge under joint enterprise. A suspect must knowingly assist or encourage the crime and agree to act together with the primary offender for a common purpose. For example, the driver of a getaway vehicle can be charged with robbery under joint enterprise even if an accomplice actually perpetrated the crime.

I have included a chapter on Joint Enterprise in this book, simply because it is one of the most controversial subjects in UK law. I fully understand why the CPS (Crown Prosecution Service) has such a law on its statute, as gang related crimes and individual culpability can often be very complex affairs.

So as to gain a better understanding of the process that

the CPS has to go through in order to bring about a Joint Enterprise charge. I have included this Crown Prosecution Service lawyers guide as a reference.

Charging group assaults

Where a death or serious assault occurs at the hands of a group or gang, prosecutors should seek to determine the exact role played by each suspect and select charges that differentiate the roles.

However, prosecutors should be mindful, when selecting charges, not to overly complicate the presentation of a case. This includes a consideration of the directions of law that the indictment will require as a result.

In homicide cases, it is not always possible to identify who are the killer(s) or principal offender(s) and who are the secondary parties. R v Jogee confirms that it is not necessary to prove whether a defendant is a principal or an accessory (provided he is one or the other), and in a multi-handed assault it will often be the case that no-one can say whose hand did the act which proved fatal. What is necessary is that someone (identified or not) is shown to have committed murder or manslaughter.

In such cases, it is permissible to prosecute the participants to the offence as principals, without necessarily differentiating roles. However, alternative charges may be put on the indictment, to allow the jury to convict D of a lesser offence, where it is not satisfied that D was responsible for the more serious offence.

The following example demonstrates how charge selection may be approached in this type of case. The actual charges selected will depend on the particular evidence against each suspect.

Example

Group A chases group B, and someone in group A attacks and kills V, who is a member of group B. Some of group A carry and use knives, others inflict harm without the use of a weapon. It is not clear who inflicts the fatal injury, which is a stab wound to the heart. Not all of group A is present at the moment of the final fatal attack, and not all of those who are present at the final attack assault V.

Possible charges

Murder: against some or all of group A, on the basis that those charged:

- Killed with intent to kill or do GBH; or
- Intentionally assisted or encouraged one or more of their group to intentionally kill or do GBH to any member of group B; or
- Conditionally intended to assist or encourage one or more of their group to intentionally kill or do GBH to any member of group B, if it is necessary or should the occasion arise.

Although proof of D2's knowledge that one or more of the group carried knives will be evidence regarding D2's intention, proof of such knowledge is not necessary in order to prove the requisite intent. In accordance with the 1861 Act they may all be charged as principals. In cases where a charge of murder is put on the basis of conditional intent, or where proving the requisite intent of D2 may be problematic, it may be appropriate to put an additional charge of manslaughter on the indictment. Note that in appropriate cases the judge is likely to leave manslaughter as an alternative verdict for the jury: if a jury is not satisfied that D is guilty of murder, it may find D guilty of manslaughter (s6(2) Criminal Law Act 1967).

Manslaughter: in some group assaults resulting in the death of V, this may be an alternative charge to murder, on the basis that D is a party to a violent attack on another but without an intent to assist in causing death or really serious harm. Manslaughter may be charged, regardless whether D had knowledge that one or more of the group carried a weapon.

Violent disorder: as an additional charge to murder or manslaughter, to allow the jury the opportunity to convict on a lesser offence, should they acquit of a homicide offence.

Part 2 Serious Crime Act offences: as an alternative charge to murder, against those who texted or posted messages on social media sites, encouraging others to join in the proposed attack on Group B.

Conspiracy to cause grievous bodily harm or conspiracy to murder: an additional charge against those who were involved in planning the attack beforehand.

Culpability will be further differentiated on sentence, when the judge will take into account the role played by D in relation to the offence(s) for which he is convicted.

Charging murder or manslaughter in group assaults without a weapon

Deaths caused by groups (or by individuals, whether identified or not, within a group) where no lethal weapon is carried or used require careful consideration of the mens rea of the individual participants.

Whereas there will often be no doubt that someone has committed a murder in cases where a lethal weapon is used, other cases are more problematic. The issue to be determined is whether at least one person acted with the mens rea for murder ie with an intention to kill or to do GBH. Fatal injuries may, in some cases, be evidence of such an intention. In other cases, death may have resulted where the intention of the participant(s) to the attack was no more than to cause some, but not serious, injury. In such circumstances, manslaughter, not murder, would be the correct charge.

In many cases of this kind, a central issue will be whether a particular D realised that the group were out to cause really serious injury, or might well do so if the occasion arose, and therefore the requisite intent for murder may be inferred (Jogge, 92-95); or did the D simply join in a violent attack, intending to cause only some harm, but the violence escalates and results in death? (Jogee, 96)

In such cases, when assessing the evidence, prosecutors should take the following approach:

Is there sufficient evidence that one of the assailants (although not identified) committed murder as a principal ie killed V with intent at least to cause serious bodily harm? If not, murder charges would not be appropriate.

If there is sufficient evidence that one of the assailants committed murder, consider, in relation to each D who participated in the incident the following questions:

Murder

- Was D the killer who acted with intent to kill or do GBH? or

- Did D intend to encourage or assist the intentional infliction of serious bodily harm? or

- Did D conditionally intend to encourage or assist the intentional infliction of serious bodily harm, if the occasion arose?

- If so, the appropriate charge is murder.

Manslaughter

- Did D intend to encourage or assist only the infliction of some harm (falling short of serious bodily harm)? or

- Did D conditionally intend to encourage or assist only the infliction of some harm, if the occasion arose? or

- Did D participate by encouragement or assistance in any other unlawful act which all sober and reasonable persons would realise carried the risk of some harm (not necessarily serious) to another?

- If so, the appropriate charge is manslaughter.

- Lesser or alternative offences may also be charged.

- Recording the basis for charging decisions

In multiple offender cases, the basis on which each defendant is charged for each offence should be clearly set out in the charging decision, recorded on the MG3 form. Where possible, the following information should be included:

- Whether the D is charged as a principal, an accessory, or as either a principal or an accessory.

- The role played by the D. For example: assisting or encouraging the offence; assisting the offence despite not being present at the scene; procuring the offence.

- The same information should be recorded whenever charges are amended during proceedings.

- The role of each D should also be made as clear

as possible in the case summary or opening note.

Serious Crime Act 2007 offences

Part 2 Serious Crime Act 2007 (SCA) offences of encouraging or assisting crime (ss 44-46) abolished the common law offence of incitement.

Since SCA offences are inchoate in nature (the substantive offence does not need to occur), they can be used where it is not possible to charge someone as a secondary party. These include the following situations:

1. No substantive offence is committed. Secondary liability does not arise.

   Example

   D2 supplies a jemmy to D1, believing that D1 will use it to commit a burglary. If D1 does not in fact commit a burglary, D2 cannot be liable as a secondary party to the burglary. Nor can D2 be liable for conspiring with D1 to commit a burglary, unless there is an agreement to do so. D2 may nevertheless be charged under s45 SCA, for encouraging or assisting an offence.

2. D2 does an act capable of encouraging or assisting D1, but the act does not in fact provide encouragement or assistance: there is no connecting link between D2 and D1's act.

   (Note that although secondary liability may not require a causative link between D2's actions and the offence or D1's involvement, it does require that D2 assisted or encouraged D1.)

   Example

D2 emails / tweets / posts an entry on Facebook encouraging others to commit an offence or a number of offences, such as public order offences. D1 does not read D2's communication but nevertheless commits the offence(s) that D2 encouraged. D2 performs the actus reus of a SCA offence by the act of posting / tweeting etc, regardless whether D1 receives the communication or acts upon it.

Charging common law offences or Serious Crime Act 2007 offences

Although the SCA offences are inchoate, their wording also allows them to be used where a substantive offence is committed. Therefore, there is a clear overlap between charging someone as a secondary participant and the SCA offences.

Prosecutors should be alert to cases that present the possibility of charging either as a secondary participant or a SCA offence.

Note that where an SCA offence is charged, the penalties are the same as that for the reference offences that D2 encourages or assists D1 to commit: s58 SCA.

The following should be noted in relation to the overlap between charging either as a secondary participant or a SCA offence:

D2 gives assistance to D1, not knowing the precise offence that D1 will commit. For example, D2 drives D1 to a pub, not knowing which offence D1 is to commit, murder, robbery or an offence against the person. D1 murders V. D2 could be charged as an accessory (R v Jogee ; DPP for Northern Ireland v Maxwell), or with a s46 offence. However, the mens rea for the s46 offence is arguably stricter, and therefore more difficult to prove:

In R v Jogee the court clarified that it is enough that the offence committed by D1 is within the range of possible offences which D2 intentionally assisted or encouraged D1 to commit;

S46 SCA requires D2 to believe that one or more of a number of offences will be committed (although he has no belief as to which). See also s47 for the further mens rea required for a s46 offence.

Where the evidence is inconclusive as to whether D2 acted as a principal or an accessory, but it must be one or the other, he may be charged as a principal (see above); however, he also may be charged with a SCA offence: s56 allows a charge where it is proved D2 committed the inchoate offence or the anticipated offence, but it is not proved which. In these circumstances, D2 should be charged as a principal, as D2 will then be liable to conviction and sentence as a principal or as an accessory, depending on the evidence that emerges during trial.

By virtue of section 118(1) of the Criminal Justice Act 2003 a statement made by a party to a common enterprise is admissible against another party to the enterprise as evidence of any matter stated. Such evidence may be lost if a SCA offence is charged.

There may however be circumstances where it is not possible to charge a substantive offence on the evidence available. For example, where D2 has a viable claim that he is not liable as a secondary offender due to:

An overwhelming supervening act by the principal; or

D2's withdrawal from the joint venture before the offence was committed; or D2's encouragement or assistance faded to the point of mere background by the time D1 committed the offence.

In such cases a prosecutor should assess how the defence is likely to affect the prospects of conviction. In many instances, it will be proper to charge D2 as an accessory and for these live issues to be decided by the jury. In some cases however, prosecutors may conclude that the evidence sufficiently supports D2's defence, and therefore charging a SCA offence will be more appropriate (liability for the SCA offence will not be affected by the lapse in time; and in cases involving an overwhelming supervening act, D2 may still be liable for encouraging or assisting a different offence to the one committed by D1).

Charging an offence under s46 Serious Crime Act 2007

An offence under s46 SCA can be charged where D does an act capable of encouraging or assisting the commission of one or more of a number of offences, believing that one or more of those offences will be committed but he has no belief as to which.

In R v Sadique [2013] EWCA Crim 1150 the court held that the count on which the defendant was convicted was not bad for duplicity nor defective for uncertainty, but was appropriately charged and fell within the proper ambit of the s46 offence. The particulars of the count alleged:

Omar Sadique ... between the 1st day of January 2009 and 8th day of June 2010, supplied various chemicals to others, such supply being capable of assisting two or more offences of supplying/being concerned in the supply of controlled drugs of both class A and B, believing that such offences would be committed and that such supply would assist in the commission of one or more of those offences.

The indictment also included three alternative counts, alleging offences of assisting in the supply of: class A drugs only; class A or B drugs; and class B drugs only. The court commented that the trial judge's directions to the jury, which asked them to consider each count in turn, and allowed them to convict on only one count, represented sensible management designed to achieve a fair trial.

It is therefore not necessary to include separate s46 counts on the indictment for each offence identified. However, alternative counts may be included, as in the instant case.

Participating in the activities of an Organised Crime Group

Section 45 of the Serious Crime Act 2015 creates an offence of Participating in the activities of an Organised Crime Group. The CPS legal guidance on prosecuting offences under this Act can be accessed here.

Charging Conspiracy

In cases where there is no substantive offence, or where there is insufficient evidence that D participates in the substantive offence, but there is evidence from which an agreement to commit an offence can be inferred, a charge of conspiracy may be appropriate.

The essential element of the offence of conspiracy is an agreement by two or more persons to carry out a criminal act. Even if nothing is done in furtherance of the agreement, the offence of conspiracy is complete.

Statutory conspiracies are charged under section 1(1) of the Criminal Law Act 1977, and are triable only on indictment.

Where a conspiracy is charged, evidence in furtherance of the agreement / common enterprise may be admissible against another party to the enterprise: section 118(1) of the Criminal Justice Act 2003.

SEND IN THE ARMY

WHENEVER WE HAVE A crisis in London, be it the London riots of 2011, or the George Floyd BLM (Black Lives Matter) protests in 2020, one thing you can guarantee is that when things turn violent there will be calls to send in the army.

Generally the British Army tends to stay out of public order matters – as law enforcement is the job of the police.

There are only exceptional occasions where the army gets called in to take over a police incident. The last one that I am aware of took place in 1980, after six armed men took over the Iranian Embassy on Prince's Gate in South Kensington – taking 26 hostages in the process. For several days there was an intense stand-off between the gunmen and the Metropolitan police, which all came to a head when a gunman executed one of the hostages, and threw his body out of the embassy. Fearing more executions the police commander transferred responsibility of the crisis over to the SAS (Special Air Service), the UK's elite special forces unit - on account of the fact that in those days the police had no armed officers that were trained and equipped to mount a CRW (counter- revolutionary warfare) hostage rescue operation.

Once the army assumed command of the situation they launched Operation Nimrod, and within minutes the world witnessed on their TVs one of the most efficient and effective military operations ever mounted. The sight of ninja like warriors abseiling off the roof and into the buildings windows was the stuff of legends. During the 17-minute operation, they rescued all but one of the hostages, and killed five of the six hostage-takers.

Following the Iranian Embassy siege, the Metropolitan police started to develop its own counter-terrorism capability that involved high level training featuring Special Forces and other high end military assets, such as RAF Chinook helicopters.

It would be many years later before the elite police CTSFO (Counter Terrorist Specialist Firearms Officer) teams got their chance to prove themselves. The opportunity came on 5 June 2017 when 3 terrorists in a hired van ploughed into pedestrians on London Bridge, and then embarked upon an orgy of violence in nearby Borough Market killing 7 people and injuring 48. Within eight minutes of the 999 call, and 50 rounds later - all three terrorists were dead. By any measure, this was an incredibly swift and effective response, and one that put our armed response teams into a totally new league.

It's not common knowledge, but on the night of the attack, an SAS unit known as "Blue Thunder" landed on London Bridge in an unmarked AS365N3 Dauphin (Dolphin) helicopter – its mission to hunt down any terrorists that may have evaded capture during the police response.

Prior to these two incidents, the only other time where the army assisted the police was during the London riots of 2011, and that was only with accommodation and transport.

So why do I mention the army in a gang warfare book? There are actually several reasons. In recent years following all the terrorist attacks, many people have started to join up the dots concerning murder rates in London, and have noticed that gangs kill far more people than terrorists. Families who have lost loved ones often feel that the police seem to be almost powerless against the rise of gung culture, yet at the same time – the very same police force is extremely efficient at taking out terrorists.

The argument of using the army against gangs, will not stand – as there has to be a total breakdown in law and order before that would ever be considered. The last time such an event occurred was in Northern Ireland, in August 1969, when - following days of sustained sectarian violence between the dominant Unionist Protestant majority population and the Catholic nationalists (republicans) minority population - a crisis erupted that eventually led to days of rioting that simply overwhelmed the RUC (Royal Ulster Constabulary) to the point that they were unable to perform their duties. This failure resulted in the deployment of the British Army. Eventually in 1998, almost thirty years later they were withdrawn, and the conflict that was generally referred to as "The Troubles" was now over – leaving a trail of pain and suffering that cost the lives of more than 3,500 people, of which 650 were British Soldiers. A further 50,000 were also injured.

The Troubles have made the UK deeply cautious of how it conducts itself with regards to internal security - and the thought of involving its army in potential conflict with its citizens in London - would seem unimaginable.

The army however can play a very valuable role in supporting organisations that are trying to work with young people that are crime vulnerable. As I mentioned earlier in the book, I headed up a military styled programme that's remit was to inspire young people to achieve to their maximum potential. Our team consisted of military personnel, army cadets, youth workers, gang mentors, social workers and a team from the Metropolitan Police's TSG (Territorial Support Group). On one of the many occasions where I ran the programme, we took our 30 plus team along with some 50 youths to the wilds of Sennybridge camp, which is located in Wales.

This particular type of army base is called a battle camp – as it is simply a place to eat, sleep and shower in between military exercises.

The young people that we had with us were drawn from all over London, which created its own set of problems – as many were hard core gang members. Hence the reason we had a TSG unit with us, complete with a riot equipped carrier vehicle. During the day our young people carried out obstacle course training, map reading, first aid, command tasks and adventure training. Being on an active military base, there was always lots happening – ranging from RAF Chinooks and Merlin's landing to rapid vehicle deployments of heavily armed SAS teams. This was really hard core stuff for our young people to see, as nothing like this would be seen in London.

Most of the time we came up with really good high quality activities, but on occasions some were not so bright. One example that springs to mind concerns the TSG. In their infinite wisdom they decided to teach some of the gang members riot reaction drills using long and round shields. At first it was going really well, until some eejit in police uniform gave the gangbangers missiles to throw at his fellow officers. You can imagine the joy that they got from this, especially when they thought of all the times that they had been subjected to a stop and search. Eventually I brought these proceedings to a close and gave my police friends a little advice as to what we could do with them, and more importantly what we couldn't.

In my case, my orders were pretty flexible so I had a lot of latitude in what I did – apart from weapons, where my mandate totally forbade me from allowing gangbangers any access or instruction on any type of weapon . I am sure you can understand the reasons for this directive.

While in Sennybridge, I worked alongside a great colleague, Capt Chris Booth who sadly is no longer with us. He used to joke with the gangbangers, "The kinder ones amongst you will say that I look like Freddie Mercury out of Queen, while the unkind amongst you will say that I look like Adolf Hitler." After that speech they all called him Adolf!!

Later that evening one of the American Special Forces commanders who was on the base asked to see me. The captain of the US 75th Ranger Regiment was already known to me, and extended an invitation to us to attend their final FTX (Field Training Exercise) that night, as they were about to deploy to Afghanistan to fight the Taliban. I made some calls, and the answer was yes – subject to a huge amount of paperwork involving risk assessments and health and safety directives. So here we were now about to witness the nearest thing to war, without actually going to one. Prior to our departure to the training area, I briefed the gangbangers and my staff about my expectations and requirements from them – as any mistake or act of inappropriate behaviour would result in us being bounced off the exercise instantly.

We formed up in a large convoy that consisted of military landrovers, armoured vehicles, minibuses and of course the police carrier. It was now pitch black, and the only lights to be seen were small red convoy lights that enabled us to follow each vehicle. The lead guys had NVGs (Night Vision Goggles), so for them there was no lights. As our 20 vehicle convoy drove onto the training area, the excitement of the young people was growing by the minute. As we sped through the forests, and zig-zagged along the dark and dusty roads, the young people in the back, as well as the staff were experiencing what we call high speed tactical driving. We eventually reached our RV point, and everyone was escorted to a small ridge beneath a hill where they were contained within a taped off sterile area.

Everyone, including the adults were given ear defenders and made to sit down in this place, as it was the safest place to be. Just as everyone's eyes got accustomed to the darkness, a salvo of parachute flares were fired into the night sky and temporarily illuminated the area immediately in front of us. As everyone took in this amazing spectacle, two heavy machine guns located behind and above us opened fire with red tracer rounds. Tracer looks like laser bursts, and the sight of thousands of them whizzing above our heads every minute into the night sky was truly amazing to see. As everyone clapped and whooped, a platoon of US Special Forces, along with fire teams from the RAF Regiment who were located in trenches just in front of us opened fire with assault rifles, light Minimi machine guns and underslung grenade launchers on to targets strewn across the valley ahead.

The whole firefight lasted for about 25 minutes, but the legacy of that evening will last forever in the minds of all who attended.

GOLDEN HOUR

IN PRIMARY SCHOOLS THE term Golden Hour refers to a period during the week when children come off their education time table and enjoy an hour of fun packed activities. In the gang world however, the term Golden Hour is completely the opposite in meaning – as it refers to the critical period of time that you have to live – following a stabbing or shooting – and the more of that hour you use up, the less likely your chances of survival.

For many years now I have run first-aid programmes in all the schools and special provisions that I have worked in – as I believe it to be a vital life skill. My own personal view is that every child should be taught first-aid, as their intervention in a medical incident could make the difference between life and death. Only recently, a young man that I taught first aid tried to save the life of a 20-year old man who had been stabbed on board a train at Hillingdon Station. Sadly despite his best efforts, and those of a doctor who he was assisting, the young man died. Despite being very upset by the tragedy that he had just witnessed, he helped treat a number of female passengers who were suffering from shock. I was very proud of his efforts and submitted a recommendation for him to be officially recognised by one of the leading humanitarian organisations.

So just how bad is the current level of stabbings in London? In February 2019, NHS figures showed that hospital admissions for youths assaulted with knives or sharp objects was up by almost 60%. In fact teenagers accounted for more than 1,000 admissions to hospital – their wounds usually being sustained as a result of a knife assault.

Admissions for all injuries caused by an assault with a knife or other sharp object have gone up year on year, and show no sign of letting up.

Commenting on these tragic admissions Duncan Bew, the clinical director for major trauma and surgery at King's College hospital in London, said: "We have seen this upward trend ourselves and it's very concerning. It's heart breaking that so many young people are coming to such harm.

"We see victims of knife crime from the age of 10 or 11 upwards, though the big increase we've seen in recent years has been in those aged between 10 and 20, and especially 13 to 17. Violence is a spectrum. We treat young people who have suffered a single, individual stab wound, perhaps to a limb, and also those who have suffered more than 10 knife injuries all over their body."

Responding to this alarming upward crime trajectory Sarah Jones, the chair of parliament's all-party parliamentary group on knife crime, said: "A 60% rise in young victims of knife crime is an abhorrent indictment of our failure to grip this epidemic. The NHS is right to warn of the human cost of knife crime and to highlight the benefits of youth workers in some of our hospitals. But the health sector needs to take more of a lead, fund this type of work more widely and put in place a comprehensive public health approach to tackling youth violence."

Martin Griffiths, a consultant trauma surgeon and lead for trauma surgery at the Royal London hospital, said his hospital saw on average two stabbing victims a day. "You never forget the sound a mother makes when given the devastating news that her child has died," he said. "I see the wasted opportunities of young people stuck on hospital wards with life-changing injuries."

Knife crime affects all ages but especially young people. The overall number of victims of all ages who ended up in hospital after being stabbed rose from 3,888 in 2012-13 to 4,986 last year, a near 30% rise.

John Poyton, the chief executive of the charity Redthread, which works to reduce youth violence, said the NHS's establishment of a network of regional major trauma networks in 2012 had increased the chances of young stab victims surviving.

"Violence is a predictor of wider health inequalities and knife crime victims admitted to major trauma wards are just the tip of the iceberg. We know that young people attend their local A&E four to five times before being admitted with a more serious, life-threatening injury,"

"We must urgently invest in NHS support for all young people caught up in all forms of violence if we hope to reverse this trend and safeguard our young people." He said.

Prof Chris Moran, national clinical director for trauma, NHS England, said: "Violent crime destroys lives, devastates families, and diverts doctors' time away from other essential patient care.

"Changes to NHS trauma services have saved an extra 1,600 lives in recent years, but hospital visits linked to

knife crime and other violence is a major cause for concern
and puts extra pressure on our expert staff.

"The NHS Long Term Plan sets out more improvements
to emergency care services across the country, with more
people able to get faster urgent care without the need for
an overnight stay in hospital.

The NHS are clearly playing their part in reducing
future knife casualties, by working with organisations that
have close working links to gangs. There are sadly those
who are contributing to knife crime by knowingly selling
sharp items to young children that are clearly under age.
In response, the NHS recently put out this statement "far
too many young people are able to buy knives on the high
street, and we need councils and retailers to work together
to stop this."

The NHS warning about the rising human cost of
knife crime comes as government confirms it is considering
tougher laws for people carrying a weapon, following a
series of high profile incidents involving this type of attack.

Indeed, many high street shops are breaking the law
by selling knives to young people, with eight out of 10
retailers in one part of the country found to have done so.

Figures published recently by the Office for National
Statistics show an 8% increase in the number of recorded
knife crimes in the year ending September 2018, with
violent crime overall rising by 19%.

Health service data show that there were 4,986
instances where people were treated for knife or sharp
object injuries, many of whom will need long-lasting care
for both the mental and physical impact of their trauma.

Commenting on this upsurge a consultant said " It's
a lot, but looking after people is what we do and we're
rightly proud of our hospital teams as world-leaders in the
care that we give. "But it doesn't stop with us. A stabbing

has relentless repercussions that stretch far beyond the victim.

Since 2013, the NHS working in partnership with charity St Giles Trust have successfully reduced retaliation violence and the number of young people returning with further violent injuries, down from over 45% to less than 1%. Research shows that a targeted approach by the community may help break the cycle of youth violence."

The recently published NHS Long Term Plan for the health service set out improvements to emergency care.

It will build on progress achieved by the creation of a shake-up of trauma services.

Major trauma centres, introduced in 2012, have improved care so that around 1,600 more people survived severe and complicated injuries than would previously have done so.

In 2017/18, 4,986 admissions to hospital were a result of knife or sharp object assault injuries. People aged 20-29 accounted for more than 1,900 episodes of consultant care – an increase for this age group of 24% since 2012/13.

Cases involving all young people – those aged 10-29 – made up nearly two-thirds (60%) of all admissions.

TREATING A STAB WOUND

Hopefully you will never have to treat a victim of a stabbing, or ever have to witness one of these vile acts. But sadly, if you live in London the chances of both are quite high. So what should you do? If you see a stabbing in progress, ring 999 immediately, give your location and the number of perpetrators involved, and then leave it to the police.

If you come across someone who has been stabbed - and the perpetrators have gone - phone 999 and request an ambulance and police assistance. If the perpetrators are still on scene, move away to a point of safety and then call 999.

If safe to do so, and you are feeling confident enough to try and help. If the casualty is still standing get them to lie down. Try and calm them down as this will help slow blood loss. If the knife or sharp object is still in the wound – DO NOT REMOVE IT – as that needs to be done by qualified medical personnel in hospital. If you can slow down the blood loss by means of covering the wound with a clean piece of clothing please do so. I say that as I am assuming you will not be carrying a first aid kit. If you can do so – apply pressure to the dressing or improvised bandage, as that will slow blood loss. If other people are near you – get them to help you. Finally, and this is important to remember. Before that ambulance arrives, you are the person that is keeping that victim alive – and you cannot be held legally responsible for what you have done, as you have acted in good faith.

When you get a moment, do download the SJAB (St John Ambulance Brigade) first-aid App as it has lots of great medical advice.

TEACHERS AND PREACHERS

GOOD TEACHERS PLAY A vital role in a young person's life, as it is through their guidance that a positive pathway through life is defined. Over the years I have worked in numerous schools and provisions where I have seen both good practice, and sadly some not so good practice. When we all think of our own childhoods and the teachers that taught us, I guarantee that the only names that we can remember will be those of our favourite teachers, and indeed those that we despised.

I must confess that every now and again I do wonder what category my former pupils will put me in. I do know in one school where I taught English, over 300 children signed a petition asking the head of the school to find me, and get me back teaching in the school. I must confess I was gobsmacked when I learned of this petition, as it was then that I realised just how much impact I was having on their lives. In times gone by, I've received cards, letters and paintings – but a petition, that was a new one for me. So why me? As a teacher I have always given 100% to my students, all day, every day and all year long.

You just cannot be half-hearted if you are a teacher, as all your pupils are relying on you to be there for them. I often think that if god ever gave me a special gift – it has to be with working with young people, as I have always connected with them.

In one of my schools I used to run an afternoon problem solving surgery during prep time. It was designed to cover anything from how do I do this homework Sir to I'm in the doghouse at home – what do I do? I had to categories of resolution – one in front of my desk, and the other in the corridor.

One day in class I noticed that one of my Ukrainian students M seemed unduly quiet. I asked him what was wrong, and he said "Sir, can we talk outside. We went into the corridor, and I said "ok, what's going on"? My student then blurted out that he had borrowed his dad's laptop for homework and inadvertently discovered his porn stash. Yikes!!! I then pointed out to him that even if you find your dad's porn stash – you don't find it, if you get my drift. It's what you might call a professional courtesy.

He was now in the doghouse with his dad over finding his private stash, plus he was in trouble with his mum for looking at porn. But as I said to him, no matter how much trouble you are in with your mum – your dad is going to get absolute hell from her. We both laughed about the situation, and after spudding me, off he went back into the classroom. M was so pleased with my advice that he told all his mates, which in turn led to them turning to me for advice with regards to problems that they were having out of school with local gangs.

At the time I was completely unaware of the fact - as were the rest of the other teachers - that a local gang was targeting our pupils as potential recruits and drug customers. This information would never have come about had I not had such a close relationship with my pupils. I think this is a quality that is often forgotten by my fellow teachers who often view their job as just being them and us.

If you really want to have a good relationship with young people, you must be able to connect with them, otherwise you risk becoming alienated from them. I see this too often in schools where teachers berate their students at every opportunity possible, which eventually leads to a teacher – student breakdown. Indeed I remember in one school where I taught, witnessing a student teacher having a complete breakdown in class with her pupils who simply would not listen to her. The poor lady was in absolute tears and I really felt for her, as she was at the end of her tether with the class.

When I walked in to assist her, the class all cheered and said "great Mr Ryan's here now so we can kick her out." That class got a piece of my mind, as I viewed their behaviour as bullying. I eventually calmed them down, and spoke to the student teacher, and advised her as to the best way to handle a class like that. I obviously had a massive advantage over her, as I had worked and taught in some of the most violent schools and provisions in London, so this class were lightweights in comparison. As I always say to disruptive classes "if you see bullying – step up, and stop it – as one day it could be you that is the victim."

Nipping bullying in the bud is really important in schools, as it can escalate rapidly if not checked. Remember whatever you tolerate, you accept. And if you accept bullying you run the risk of creating a fertile recruiting ground for gangs.

Which is exactly what happened in an Academy where I worked.

I started my contract with this school in September 2017, and at first all seemed to be going well. The school used a staggered start system, so that new pupils had a chance to settle in before the arrival of the older children.

Including me, there were 19 new staff – that included mentors, support workers, therapists and of course teachers. All seemed enthusiastic and raring to go, so what could possibly go wrong? The answer: just about everything!!

The new children were no problem, as they were still settling in. It was when the older children arrived that the problems started, or should I say continued – as they had known issues from the previous term. My first day with the year 11s, and I witness a girl grabbing a young female teacher by the throat, and subjecting her to an assault that was truly vicious. Thankfully, she was pulled away quickly by the support staff and restrained until she calmed down. The teacher concerned was badly shaken up – but still carried on. The following day, and three assaults on staff occurred. How many there were on pupils I have no idea. As the weeks went by, assaults on staff and pupils became a daily occurrence.

Most assaults would involve just punching and kicking, but some did involve weapons. I remember at the time thinking, what part of my interview did I miss, where they mentioned that the school had a massive problem with bullying and violence? Indeed not helping matters, was the fact that the school only suspended violent pupils for one day, as they did not want to lose any local authority premium pupil revenue. One of the admin staff told me that when she first started working at the school there would only be a big fight once a term, then it went to a monthly event, and then after the summer break it jumped to being weekly – and here we were now at multiple fights and assaults every single day. In fact, I cannot recall a day when there was no fights. It was such a crazy place to work.

About half way through my contract, I was seriously starting to question myself as to why I was still there – as I had no shortage of job offers - on account of all the special needs qualifications that I held. By nature I am not a quitter, so I was determined to see my four month contract out – come hell or high water. My other colleagues however were rapidly starting to quit, as many of them had suffered significant injuries. When I broke it down there were only actually about 14 pupils who were causing all the problems, so the situation could have been easily resolved if remedial action had been taken by the senior leadership team. However they would not entertain the idea, as pupils meant money, so it was never going to happen.

One day during a lull in the school day, one of the therapists who I got on really well with informed me that she was leaving, as she did not feel safe in the school. She then went on to say that she was convinced that the school was deliberately putting all the aggressive and violent children together so that they become impossible to place in a normal school on account of their off the scale behaviour. She was a very bright girl, and one who clearly knew a lot more sensitive information than me. So maybe she was right.

Out of the group that was violent, I was aware of eight who had known gang affiliations. They were particularly aggressive, and would frequently leave class and go around as a group attacking any random pupil or member of staff that they encountered. To counter this, I would always make sure that the coast was clear before leaving a locked classroom – as they could be hiding in any number of alcoves or camera blind spots. I also laid my classroom out in such a way that only one individual could attack me at any time, as the gap between my desk and the massive portable white screen that I used would be too narrow for a group. One on one, I can handle myself comfortably – but 8 against one - no chance.

I was pretty obsessive about personal security, and always tried to be a couple of steps ahead of any adversary – as that's what keeps you alive. One evening while on my way to a staff meeting I learned that our maths teacher had been seriously injured by one of the gang members, and had sustained a fractured eye socket after being beaten unconscious, and thrown down the stairs. I was deeply angered by this totally unjustified attack, as the injured teacher was a decent compassionate man that would never have done anything to provoke this. He was simply in the wrong place, at the wrong time. As for the thug that carried out this cowardly attack he was arrested by police and charged with assault. I later learned that he was allowed to return to the school!!

In another attack that I witnessed, two pupils attacked the sports teacher at the same time, and before I intervened all I can remember seeing was this poor man standing still being punched and kicked with tears rolling down his cheeks, as they subjected him to a beating. One of them pulled his glasses off and deliberately trod on them. At no point did he try and defend himself, as he was worried that he might get sacked if he retaliated. It was a sickening thing to witness, and one that I do not want to see again.

There were literally dozens of incidents like this that continued to occur, and I was beginning to get concerned that I was becoming inured to the daily violence. It was December now, and I was only three weeks away from finishing my contract. But the daily madness still continued, so I needed to stay sharp. They say that the nearer to the end of a combat tour you are – the more vulnerable you become. This however was a school, so I should not have been thinking in that way. And yet I was.

Although I was counting down the days, I was still very much alert to any potential dangers that were ahead. One of the gang members who was both a trapper and a gang banger came into the school one day armed with a tin of oven cleaner which he sprayed on any teacher or pupil that was within his range. That wasn't the worst part, as once he sprayed you he then tried to set fire to you by means of a fire lighter that he had. Essentially he had a portable flame thrower. As he went about this nonsense, in the company of two support staff, who were struggling to disarm him, World War 3 commenced.

In front of our fire starter, some idiot had opened two classrooms filled with rival gang members who instantly attacked one another. As this madness was being quelled, in the nearby computer room a boy with learning difficulties had exploded into a rage – and had commenced chucking chairs at all the Apple Mac computers and windows that were in the room. A couple of staff were trying to restrain him, but he was too strong for them. As one tried to grab his arm, he head butted them and then punched them in the face. It was utter carnage. As this madness was going on, I had restrained one youth and put him on the floor so that he couldn't hurt anyone. I had also pulled his hood down over his head so that he couldn't spit at me. They were a charming bunch. As I looked around at the battle that was taking place in front of my eyes, and one that now involved every member of staff in the school, I noticed an unfamiliar face in the melee.

It turned out that this poor guy had come for a job interview, and was so horrified with what he saw that he walked out of the building and never returned. What a smart guy.

As for me, I was now down to my last three days but the threat level was still high. We had just had our school open evening, and only 8 parents had turned up for it. Yet, when we had held the school Christmas dinner for our pupils and their parents – over 170 turned up!!! That just about summed up everything for me. By now it had been announced to the pupils that I would be gone within a few days, so there were some sad goodbyes, as there were a lot of decent children in the school that I liked.

One of them was in tears when he heard that I was leaving, and I felt really bad for him, as we had got on really well. I can still remember his words "why is it that every time in my life when I meet someone that I actually like and connect with they leave"? I must admit that was a painful one for me, as I liked C a great deal. Before walking away, C said to me "Sir, watch your back as R is looking to attack you before you leave." By coincidence, my boss and some other mentors had also warned me, so I knew that I had to remain cautious right until the last minute.

At this point despite all the violence that I had witnessed, and all the skirmishes that I had been involved with, nobody had actually been able to attack me. As a precaution though, my boss cancelled my last few lessons and told me to work out of his office for the last few hours.

As I filed my final school reports, I observed on the CCTV one of the more violent gang members skulking in the corridor with his fists clenched and his hood over his head. You didn't have to be a genius to figure out where he was heading. The door opened and in walked this hooded thug. I said to him "I hope you haven't got any silly ideas about attacking me"? He responded "you're the only teacher that I haven't punched", and with that he threw a punch at me with his right arm. I blocked him, and with my free right hand I shoved my palm straight into his chest which sent him flying backwards on to the desk and computer behind him. As he got up, he raised his fist again and then had another go at me. I anticipated his attack and blocked him again, and responded by a double chest thrust which sent him backwards and on to the floor. I made it clear to him, that he had now had his two warnings, and that they're wouldn't be a third. He heeded my warning and then began smashing up the room out of frustration. As he did so, my boss walked in and unfortunately he got assaulted instead. Eventually other staff members arrived, and as quickly as it had started it was all over in a flash.

As I left the school, I looked over my shoulder to look at it for the last time. Vowing never to return. I had survived unscathed, and it was now time to move on. Out of the 19 who had started out with me in September, only 3 had survived with me by December. The rest sadly got assaulted, or they left before they became victims.

I still keep in touch with a number of my former colleagues who worked at the school with me, and we all agree that this was at the time the most dangerous and challenging school in London. Bar none.

SILVER BULLETS

OFTEN WHEN WE TALK about gangs and crime in London, one of the most common expressions used when we discuss possible solutions is "what is the silver bullet that will solve this problem"? A silver bullet is a description for an idea or solution that will provide an immediate or extremely effective solution to a specific problem or difficulty, especially one as complex as gang warfare. It is widely accepted that no such solution exists, as this particular subject is immensely complicated. That means we have to tackle the problem on many fronts, and attack it from all sides.

So where should we start our journey towards the ultimate solution to the gang problem in London? If you take a problem at its most basic level, the best way to deal with a problem - is to not have a problem to solve. Which in the case of London means educating young people as early as possible about the dangers of gang life.

We are of course talking about primary school children – as they are now being increasingly targeted by gangs, as potential drug mules. Talking to children in their late teens about gangs is way too late, as you have to nip the problem in the bud as early as possible. Essentially, by educating them - you are inoculating them against the deadly virus of gang culture. And that is exactly the way that you should look at this issue, as it is a potential health problem.

SCHOOLS OUT

The single biggest factor that I have witnessed that contributes massively towards young people embarking down the wrong road - is the action of expelling children from school – often for the most simple and pathetic transgressions. I totally get that if a child is violent and aggressive towards a member of staff or indeed a fellow pupil they should be removed from the school – as a clear message needs to go out that such behaviour is totally unacceptable.

But expelling a child because they played up in maths, or they were a bit cheeky to a teacher in the playground – is not in my opinion, grounds for expulsion. I have of course worked in state schools, where children are disruptive in class, which can at times be really frustrating, as it interferes with the other pupils learning. To get around this problem, when I was teaching I would place all those who wanted to work in one part of the classroom, and then set them work that I would supervise. As for the rest who wanted to be disruptive, I would just firefight from one table to another until I settled them down.

I have always held the view that whatever level of disruption a pupil is at - once you expel them, and cast them away to a PRU or a PPP their behaviour is only going to get a hundred times worse. As in order to survive they have to either match or outperform their fellow students – or they risk being bullied.

Another unacceptable practice that some schools undertake is that of off-rolling. Off-rolling is the practice of removing disadvantaged and struggling pupils from the school roll - usually before they take their final exams – so that their poor results are not included in the schools Ofsted statistics. Once off-rolled, pupils will usually struggle to find other schools willing to take them on, which often results in them hanging out with other children who are in the same situation – making them perfect targets for gang exploitation.

So what would I do to solve this problem? I can tell you exactly what I would do as I have raised and discussed the subject many times over the last five years. If I was Education Minister? I would make every secondary school set up a hub within its grounds – that specialised in supporting children with learning or behavioural difficulties. They would operate to a customised time-table that de-conflicted with the main school – and staffing would consist of well trained, highly motivated staff that had the children's best interests at heart. Every child in the hub, would have their specific learning difficulties and behavioural issues identified and then rectified – at which point they would be returned to the main school. So simple – so why don't they do that? You tell me, as I know this concept already works – because I have used it in a number of schools where it has been a great success.

So what else can we do to divert young people away from gangs and crime? My personal advice would be to encourage them to join either sports or uniformed youth organisations – as they can offer some truly amazing opportunities for young people. I am of course biased – as I coach football and teach young Army Cadets. I cannot even begin to imagine how many young people's lives that I have diverted – as it must be literally thousands by now. I must of course stress, that the vast majority were always on a positive path – but needed a bit of guidance now and again - whereas the others, well let's just say that they were most definitely not on the right path and needed intense support.

Indeed, I have some young people who are currently serving in my cadet unit who were in the dim and distant past serving gangs members and through lots of hard work by me and my fellow Army Cadet instructors we have now turned their lives around. One believe it or not, is now a serving police officer – and doing extremely well by all accounts. There are of course numerous other organisations that are also doing great work with young people, and each and every one of them is performing a vital role. The more young people you turn around – the more you will continue to turn around – as many of them will become either staff or volunteer mentors. And so the circle of life continues.

One other programme that I created in order to turn former gang members around and help them rebuild their lives involved me developing bespoke courses in Prisons and Young Offenders Institutions that were designed to train and prepare young men for their prison release. Essentially, they would spend four months being trained in: youth work, mentoring, young people's mental health and first-aid. The idea being that they would leave prison on a Friday - spend the weekend with their family – and then on the Monday they would start a gang intervention mentoring job that would help turn other young people's lives around. Friday would of course be a very important day -as they would get their first pay cheque.

The prison service and the Courts absolutely loved the concept and were more than happy to introduce it – but as usual the argument came up, just who is going to pay for it?

At the end of this book, I have provided details of a

fund raising campaign that I have set up to address this problem. I very much hope that you can support it.

And finally, and in my humble opinion - the most effective antidote against gangs is strong community. Where I live we have a really close community as well as a highly effective neighbourhood watch scheme - so anyone acting suspiciously is quickly picked out and challenged. Like all boroughs in London, we have had our fair share of problems in the past, however since the introduction of our community led neighbourhood watch scheme there has been no crime of any significance.

So my suggestion would be for you to do the same thing, as nobody knows their own community better than you. By all means involve other organisations or individuals that can help and advise you, as many will have valuable experience gained from other community projects. If you have a particular problem with gangs and anti-social behaviour in your area, you should consider inviting local councillors, community leaders, Head teachers and of course the police to your meetings – as you all have a vested interest in making your community a safer place to live.

In one part of London where I worked on a gang intervention programme, local parents would turn out every night as a group and patrol their estate. Any young children still out on the streets after dark would be escorted home, and their parents advised of the potential dangers that may befall them from gangs operating in the area. Such techniques are incredibly effective if used with care and good planning, as it sends out a message to the criminals that you are not willing to put up with their anti-social behaviour. I have even known some communities to put up professional looking road signs that say: Reserved for drug dealers only or designated drug dealing site. Other signs also warn the criminals and their customers that they are being filmed and photographed as they go about their business.

Please be careful if you are filming or photographing criminals, as they tend to be camera shy for some strange reason!! If you do see anything dodgy or concerning please call the police, and leave it to them as they are trained and equipped to deal with these situations. It could even be the case, that the police have an undercover surveillance operation in place, and that they are gathering evidence. So please bear that in mind.

For those of you who are really keen to support your local community, you can apply for community support group funding from your local council. Grants can be as high as £10,000 so good luck with your applications.

FIVE – O

"We need social bridges between our communities – and not social chasms"
M RYAN

THE POLICE ARE KNOWN by many different names in the gang world, ranging from Feds to Five – O, as well as a plethora of other names that are not printable. So what do our gangs actually think of the police, and the way that they operate?

This question was actually posed to a large number of gang members that I worked with over a period of months, and their answers helped me to understand just what needs to be done to transform the Metropolitan Police from its current traditional mind set into a forward thinking highly dynamic organisation that is reflective of the needs of the people that it serves.

When asked about stop and search, the teenagers in my group where surprisingly understanding of the need for this controversial police tactic, as many of them felt that when used appropriately it is an effective tool for reducing knife crime. They also commented upon how police officers carried out stop and search. Some said that the police had treated them fairly and respectfully, while others felt that the police had been rude and heavy handed.

When questioned about what police units they feared the most, they cited: armed response, the TSG and Scorpion anti-bike units.

When asked about ordinary rank and file police officers, they said that most treated them well, but they had no respect for them - as they felt that they were weak and powerless.

When discussing prison sentences, all agreed that current tariffs are too low to serve as any form of deterrent. They also mentioned that the chances of getting arrested, convicted and sentenced were minimal.

When asked about BAME (Black, Asian and Minority Ethic) police officers, the views were very diverse. Some said it wouldn't make any difference to them, whereas others felt that having more BAME officers would make them feel more trusting of the police, as most officers that they interact with tend to be white.

When asked about police officers carrying guns, most felt that all frontline police officers should be armed, as it would serve as a deterrent.

At this present time the Metropolitan Police is going through some truly challenging times, and there are no quick solutions to any of them. On average 85 police officers get attacked every day in the UK which is a very high figure in comparison to other police forces in Europe. The reasons behind these appalling and sickening attacks are complex, but most agree that our unarmed police are simply seen as easy targets, which is why the assault rate is so high. Of particular interest is that to the best of my knowledge, no armed officers have been attacked in the line of duty. Indeed not helping matters is the fact that the perpetrators of these heinous acts have little to fear from the law.

Commenting upon these assaults the Home Secretary

Priti Patel said "I'll back the police and help bring an end to these shocking acts of violence."

A Government spokesman added "Being attacked should never be part of the job for our courageous police officers, who put themselves in harm's way to protect us – that is why we supported the Assaults on Emergency Workers Act, which means judges must consider tougher sentences for assaults on emergency workers."

Another issue that the Metropolitan Police needs to address, relates to its officers ethnic breakdown. At present 13.4% of the force identifies itself as BAME, which in comparison to other UK forces that only average 6% it would appear that they are doing really well. However London has a population that is made up of 40.2% BAME citizens, so there is still more to do in order to gain parity.

Another change in policing that urgently needs to be addressed relates to the use of technology. The Metropolitan Police tends to be reactive rather than proactive – and that needs to change.

Bearing in mind how many CCTV camera systems we have in London, we could easily adapt them to be intelligent observers. For example, if an individual is riding his scooter around the streets in a suspicious manner, the AI (Artificial Intelligence) cameras would pick this up and vector a police unit to observe and monitor them. They could then decide if a stop is needed, or that it is an innocent action.

We already use intelligent monitoring of individuals by means of Electronic tags – or tagging as it is most commonly known. So the precedent is already in place. The UK currently uses ankle tagging to monitor curfews and conditions of court orders, and operates two different types of Tag:

- Curfew tags
- Location tags

A Curfew tag is used to check if you're where you're meant to be during curfew hours. IE your home. If however you're not in your designated curfew area an alert will be sent to a monitoring centre.

A Location tag is used to record data about your movements at all times, and monitors:

- If you are going into areas that are prohibited by a court or prison order
- If you are going to appointments or intervention programmes that are part of your conditions
- If you are sticking to your curfew

This information can be used by a monitoring officer to report either good behaviour or negative behaviour – so it is a tool that can both potentially clear or convict an individual of suspected wrong doing.

When I worked with gang intervention, I remember dealing with one slippery individual who had removed his tag by means of washing up liquid, and then placed it on his pet dog - so that it moved around. Unfortunately for him, a member of his family took the dog for a walk in to a curfew prohibited area – which of course dropped him in it.

METROPOLITAN POLICE SERVICE V NYPD (NEW YORK POLICE DEPARTMENT)

So how does the Metropolitan police compare with the NYPD – America's most effective police force?

Unfortunately, the short answer is not very well. New York City has a population of 8.399 million (2018) whereas London's population is around 8.982 million (2019). So they are very comparable in terms of size. NYPD uniformed police strength as of 2018 stood at 38,422 which is higher than the Metropolitan Police - whose current uniformed strength stands at 32,104 (2019). But here's the kicker. The NYPD has a smaller budget than the Met, and yet it can field over 6,000 more frontline officers – who have through a ruthless no tolerance policing strategy driven crime down to the point that it has now half of that of London's.

These figures are not secret, nor is the NYPD policing strategy. We have in fact over the years sent numerous police commanders and senior political figures over to New York to see how their police force operates, but little or nothing ever seems to change or get implemented after these visits.

When I lived in New York, I was always amazed at just how well the NYPD harness cutting-edge technology into everyday policing, and we could clearly learn a lot from them. Here are a few examples of their typical kit:

- Smartphones for all police officers
- Tablets for patrol vehicles
- Super strong pepper spray
- Escape hoods
- Belt-worn trauma kits
- The Domain Awareness System – this pools live streams of data from multiple sources
- CompStat 2.0 – this provides officers in the field with access to updated and interactive, real-time crime pattern analysis and mapping software

- Body camera technology that records enforcement encounters
- Shot Spotter technology – this identifies, records, locates and reports gunfire

This technology is incredibly effective, and give officers on the ground total situational awareness at all times. For example if a suspect is reported in a neighbouring street, officers can instantly tap into every CCTV camera system in that area to gain further information. This system also allows access to non- City run CCTV systems such as those operated by private home owners and the local business community.

Suspects can also be run through facial recognition systems that can track their movements throughout the city without making them aware that the police are on to them.

It is now 2020, so the Metropolitan police needs to start embracing modern technology and new methods of policing.

POLICING IN THE 21ST CENTURY

Over the many years that I have spent working with gangs, I have often thought long and hard about what I would do to reduce gang culture and violent crime if I were appointed Commissioner of the Metropolitan Police Service. So here are my thoughts on the subject.

The first thing that I would do is drag the organisation into the modern world of technology and forward thinking – as that will make it more efficient and effective.

As a democratic country - we operate a "policing by consent" policy – which is a good thing. Policing by consent indicates that the legitimacy of policing in the eyes of the public is based upon a general consensus of support that follows from transparency about their powers, their integrity in exercising those powers and their accountability for doing so.

This system has been with us for a long time now - and as good as it is - it does need updating. At this present time, almost half of all Londoner's are from the BAME community, and there are many within this social strata who feel that they are over policed yet under protected – so we must get them onside. The police should be seen as guardians of the community, and not warriors amongst it.

In order to achieve that we need a seismic shift in current police culture, and one that will see us return right back to basic community policing. This is an aspect of policing that we used to do really well, and decades later I can still remember my local beat officer who was called Gordon, and I will tell you more about him in the 3Rs chapter. As a point of interest, can you name an officer at your local police station? Yep, thought not.

We all live in communities – some good, some bad – but without a personal stake in them, nothing is ever going to change. We must encourage greater ownership of our communities through partnerships with local government and the police. If we can get it right at grassroots level, the chances of young people drifting into gangs and crime can be greatly reduced, or in some cases even eliminated.

In London at this present time we have a serious shortage of police officers, and although the Government has embarked upon a massive recruiting drive, it will be some years before the Metropolitan Police recovers the 5,000 officers that it lost on account of austerity measures. Also not helping matters in this recruitment drive, is the fact that almost 100 police stations have been closed down in the last decade – which begs the burning question, where will all these officers be based?

By now I am sure you will have joined the dots up that help you understand why London has so much gang crime, and also what needs to be done to resolve it.

AREA SUPPORT GROUPS

To address the problem of local officer shortages, I would set up two ASGs (Area Support Groups). One to operate north of the river Thames (ASG N), and the other to the south of it (ASG S). Each ASG would comprise of 150 officers that would be trained, resourced and equipped to operate independently of other units. ASGs would be set up with their own unit assets that would comprise of an:

- Armed Response Team (ART)
- K-9 – Dog team
- Traffic Management Team (TMT)
- Patrol officers
- Community Engagement Officers (CEO)
- Gang Intervention Team (GIT)
- Scorpion Tactical Team (STT)
- Covert Operations Team (COT)
- Specialist Search Team (SST)

There are 32 boroughs in London, so the ASGs would be assigned to each one for a guaranteed 28 days per year. The remaining days would be used as contingency reserve and for block leave. The rationale behind the ASGs is high visibility and community engagement – both of which are in short supply at this present time. ASGs would only be deployed in each borough for 7 day periods, as any longer would negate their operational effectiveness.

ASG borough usage would be by means of mutual agreement, with priority giving to boroughs with higher crime rates. When deployed to boroughs, ASGs will come under local command, and will be tasked according to local priorities. Their presence would significantly increase the number of visible officers operating in a given area – which would reassure residents and deter gang activity.

SPECIAL PATROL FORCE

In addition to the Area Support Groups, I would also look to set up a Special Patrol Force (SPF). The SPF would be an elite unit comprising 300 armed officers, equipped with high end patrol cars and light armoured vehicles. Their operational tasking would be counter-terrorism and gang intervention - the two biggest killers in our society.

The purpose of the SPF is deterrence – as current conventional police units are just not robust enough to undertake this role. The SPF would patrol London – both overtly and covertly – as that would make life very difficult for gangs and terrorists.

So as to create a more intimidating look, all SPF vehicles would be black in colour – complete with low visibility markings. SPF uniforms would be similar to those worn by counter-terrorism officers – as they are more reflective of the unit's perceived role.

Having a fully armed Special Patrol Force on London's streets 24/7 would I believe significantly reduce knife and gun crime – as gangs and terrorists know that they will never win a firefight against a highly trained well-armed police unit.

GANGS VIOLENCE MATRIX

FOLLOWING THE LONDON RIOTS in 2011, the Metropolitan Police in response created the controversial Gangs Matrix.

Launched in 2012 the Gangs Violence Matrix (GVM) is a database of suspected gang members, and it is used as a risk-management tool for the purpose of preventing serious violence. Amnesty International however does not believe that the Gangs Matrix is legal in its current guise, or that it helps the fight against gang crime.

According to the Metropolitan Police, the Gangs Violence Matrix (GVM) is an intelligence tool that is used for the identification and risk-assessing of gang members across London who are involved in gang violence. It also seeks to identify those that are at risk of victimisation.

Ultimately the aim of the matrix is to reduce gang-related violence, safeguard those exploited by gangs and prevent young lives being lost.

So how does the matrix work?

The GVM measures the harm 'gang nominals' (people who are named on the matrix) pose by scoring them based on evidence of them committing violence and weapons offences, any police intelligence relating to them having access to weapons, or them being involved in, or at risk from, gang violence.

From these scores every individual is graded as Red, Amber or Green (RAG rating) denoting the level of risk (victim) or harm (offenders) they present. This rating enables the police to identify the most violent or at risk gang members and then work with other partners to prioritise the response.

The GVM also identifies gang members who have been repeat victims of violence and also those that need support in order to safeguard them from becoming further victims. Diverting them away from gangs is also a priority.

Some of the key benefits of the GVM are that it:

- Identifies gang members in London and prioritises the current most violent gang subjects
- Identifies gang members who have been victims of violence and are at risk of becoming further victims of violence
- Aids the prioritising of resource allocation and methods of intervention
- Highlights possible gaps in activity or intelligence on violent gang subjects

Every locally based Basic Command Unit (BCU) in the Met has their own matrix. These are combined to produce a single matrix across London to provide an assessment of the risk gang nominals pose. All locally based BCUs also share data with their partners to enable a multi-agency approach to tackling gangs in London.

How are names added to the matrix?

When assessing whether someone should be included on the matrix the threshold is: 'Someone who has been identified as being a member of a gang and this is corroborated by reliable intelligence from more than one source (eg, police, partner agencies or community intelligence).'

They will only be added to the matrix if they fit this definition.

A 'gang' is defined as a: 'relatively durable, predominantly street-based group of young people who:

1. See themselves (and are seen by others) as a discernible group, and

2. Engage in a range of criminal activity and violence.

    They may also have any or all of the following features:

 • Identify with or lay claim over territory
 • Have some form of identifying structure feature
 • Are in conflict with other, similar gangs

This definition is distinct from – and should not be confused with – other criminal structures, such as organised crime networks, which merit a different policing approach.

How many names are on the matrix?
The number of individuals on the GVM changes daily. As of February 2020 there were 2,676 names on the matrix – which represents a 31% decrease following a review of GVM criteria.

How do you get off the matrix?

Individuals' names are removed on a regular basis, over 4,000 have been removed from the GVM since its inception in 2012.

Here are some examples of why individuals' names are removed from the matrix.

- There is evidence they have exited gang lifestyle.

- They are engaging in a diversion program for a period of time (6 months) and haven't come to police notice since that engagement started.

- They have not come to police notice for a significant period (12 months).

- They have moved away from London and are no longer believed involved in gang criminality within the Metropolitan Police Area.

Who uses the matrix?

The GVM is used in the Met by a number of police officers and staff in roles with a relevance to gangs. Information from the matrix is shared with partners to make sure there's a multi-agency approach to tackling gangs.

This can include mentor schemes, help with education, employment, re-housing and more. Local partnership meetings take place at a borough level where gang nominals and others are discussed to achieve these ends.

Statutory partners will differ in each London borough/BCU but will include CSPs such as the local authority, Youth Offending Service, National Probation Service, Community Rehabilitation Company, health, education and more.

Under the Crime and Disorder Act 1998 the police have

a responsibility, working with CSPs, to formulate and implement strategies for reducing crime, disorder and reoffending, and will share information with CSPs to facilitate such strategies.

Partners are selected based on their ability to provide relevant information about individuals that can help in positive interventions to move them away from gangs and criminality.

There are of course always two sides to every story.

If London had a low crime and murder rate, the Gang Violence Matrix would probably not exist. However as we all know that is not the case so it remains in place.

There are aspects of the GVM that are very good, and these clearly benefit the Met police as well as society. But in a comprehensive review of the GVM carried out by the Mayor's office it was deemed that almost 500 individuals should be removed from the database - as there was little or no evidence to link them to criminal gangs.

The Mayor of London, Sadiq Khan, who was previously a humans rights lawyer announced that his review had made the GVM more up-to-date, more evidence based, and more focused on those most likely to commit violence.

The review also resulted in a significant reduction in the number of BAME young men who prior to the report's findings had appeared on the GVM database.

Another area of contention related to the number and types of organisations that had access to the database – which led to multiple and serious breaches of data protection laws. Following the review access has now been reduced to a far smaller group of organisations – and they are reviewed regularly.

Commenting on the review, The Mayor of London said "The perceived cloak of secrecy around the Gangs

Matrix led to genuine community concerns, which is why I promised in my manifesto to carry out a thorough review to help restore trust and confidence in the way it is used. We are now seeing real progress with the Met acting on all recommendations.

Our review showed that the Matrix is a necessary enforcement tool for reducing violent crime in London, but it's also vitally important that the police continue to evaluate and communicate how it is used."

3Rs

"Everyone dies – but not everyone lives"
M RYAN

BACK IN THE DAY, the term - the 3Rs meant: reading, writing and arithmetic. Today however, its use in the gang world means: right person, right place and right time. So what does that actually mean in the real world? When we think over our lives, we all at some point or other have had someone that has impressed us, or maybe had some form of positive influence over us.

If you can think of lots of examples in your life, then you are very lucky indeed. That sadly is not the case for some in our society. When I was a teenager, and in the Air Cadets there were countless people that gave up their time for me, and my fellow cadets. And in doing so, they kept us out of trouble and on the straight and narrow. That's why decades later I do exactly the same thing for our young people, as I want to inspire and encourage them to make the most of their lives.

There are of course super influencers, and they are a very rare breed. One that comes to mind for me is Gordon, my local police beat officer who dates back to when I was a teenager. Not to put too fine a point on it, but Gordon was absolutely amazing, and the Met police would do well if they introduced an army of Gordons to police our communities.

What made Gordon special was his ability to work with young people at every opportunity possible - one of his favourite haunts being the Odeon cinema in Northfields, West London. Unlike today where you have literally hundreds of TV channels to choose from, in my day we had a lousy 3!! So to make up for it, every Saturday morning we would all descend upon the Odeon to watch a feast of cartoons and movies.

On the front doors would be fat Barry, who was always stuffing himself with chips, plus his female partner in crime who was a proper fierce Irish woman – armed with a tongue that would cut a hedge. Standing near them to keep order, was of course our hero Gordon – who greeted every young child as they entered the cinema. Sometimes he would hand out leaflets detailing nearby youth organisations, while on other occasions he would mark bicycles with ownership tags.

I don't think any of us ever knew Gordon's surname, I guess it just didn't seem important to know that as everyone knew who Gordon was – including our parents!! As a teenager I never needed Gordon's help, however when I was 21 I did.

It was shortly after I bought my first car - a Mk 1 cherry red 1969 Ford Capri 1600 GT - that I had to call the police, on account of some low life stealing the radio out my car. Shortly after my call, who should turn up – it was Gordon of course - as he was still our beat officer. Gordon took all my car details, and then made a kind offer to me that would today seem unthinkable. He informed me that he would be off shift in a few hours, and that if I could get a car alarm between now and then, he would install it for me.

As amazing as this sounds, hours later he did turn up in his jeans and bomber jacket, and true to his word he installed my car alarm. I remember my mum making him bacon sandwiches and giving him numerous mugs of tea as a thank you.

I cannot even begin to tell you just how much that kind gesture meant to me, as Gordon did not have to do that, and yet he did. He was a proper old school copper, and I so wish that the Met Police had modern day equivalents of him, as they would almost certainly bring our communities closer together.

For me, Gordon was my 3R.

As you can probably imagine after reading some of the stories in this book, I have met and worked with some truly fantastic people who do wonderful work with our young people every day, yet seldom get any recognition for it. Some I can identify, and others sadly I cannot on account of the sensitive work that they do in gang intervention.

One particular person that always sticks in my mind was a black police officer called C who was attached to my Outreach Programme in Wales. On the first day of the programme it was always customary to run a meet and greet session – so that everyone got to know who was who. As the officer in charge of the programme I wore my army uniform while making the introductions, while our attached police personnel wore civvies.

We went to lunch, and sitting around my table were 10 young men who were from different boroughs in South London. As I talked to them and discussed the forthcoming programme, one of the boys said I am so glad that I have you as a leader, and not one of those feds. I asked why he felt that way about the police and he rattled off a plethora of reasons for his disdain of them.

I then asked him how he felt about all the others around the table, and he said that he was cool with them. "That's interesting I commented, because one of these guys is a police officer." With that he jumped on the table, and started demanding to know which one. C with a big smile on his face then stood up and produced his warrant card.

My man on the table was by now looking horrified, as he had spent the best part of an hour joking with C and spitting lyrics we him. Not to be outdone, he pointed at C and shouted to everyone "look at this guy – he's five o, he's five o. As he shouted he put one hand up in the air with five fingers showing, then changed his fingers to an o shape. It was a very funny thing to witness, and as a little experiment I put both of them in my team for the rest of the week.

The results of their interactions would have made for great TV, but alas we had no camera crew with us. What I found particularly interesting about our gangbanger and police officer partnership related to how they viewed one another once they accepted that they were both young men with a surprising number of outside interests in common.

By the end of the programme, both men had found a new level of respect for each other's point of view and choice of lifestyle – and from where we had started out from that was a massive improvement.

Another Outreach story that I have relates to an amazing gang intervention worker called Leon, who was attached to my team during a programme that was being run in Devon.

Leon was a very athletic guy, which was just as well as he accompanying me on a 4 day hike through the wild country of the Dartmouth Tors. As we moved through the barren, and yet pretty countryside, our motley crew of gangbangers and roadmen were bitching like crazy about their expensive creps getting ruined. They had all been issued with walking boots, but for some strange reason they had all taken them off and swopped them for their obscenely expensive designer trainers.

After walking for several hours we came across an enclosed field with a large sign saying "beware of the bull." You would have thought that sign would have been enough to deter our gangland friends, but no they decided to ignore it. The field where they had ventured looked like a muddy scene from a WW1 battlefield, so what possessed them to enter it I will never no. As they cautiously picked their way through the mud, one of the idiots called out "don't worry about the bull, it will only chase you if you have a red top on."

A few minutes later and that theory had been well and truly proved wrong, as now we had a gang posse running like mad through the mud trying to reach the fence where we were formed up. It was hilarious to watch, especially the vista of gangbangers watching their trainers being sucked off their feet and sinking into the quagmire around them. Eventually they made it over to us, albeit somewhat muddy and soaking wet.

Leon, and one of the attached TSG police officers gave them all a good rifting for their nonsense, and from that point on, it was walking boots only.

As we reached the final leg of our hike we across a large farmhouse complete with stables. Just in front of the stables was a large field that contained around 14 horses that were out grazing in the sun. The group asked if they could stroke the horses, and I said yes. As Leon and the rest of our team supervised the group, the owner of the farm came out and said hello to us. She then asked if the boys would like to help her feed the horses, an invitation that was just to kind to pass – so I accepted.

Sometimes in life you have a golden moment, and this certainly was one of those rare moments. As Leon and I watched the boys feed the horses, you could see a visible change in their attitude. Right now there was no aggression, no shouting – just calmness, and wonderful displays of kindness. I have seen this before when working with equine programmes that have been designed for violent children, and they do work. Horses are very sensitive and can detect aggression instinctively, which is why they back away. However if they sense calmness they will be responsive towards you.

The lady who owned the farm had a really good way of approaching the boys, and showed them what to do without causing any embarrassment to them. She had a real gift for working with young people, and both Leon and I joked about hiring her, as she would have been a great asset to our programme. We eventually left the Farm, but not before saying a big thank you to the wonderful lady who had given us all a very special afternoon.

Some days later, an incident occurred where Leon's presence on the programme proved invaluable.

When working with gangs or crime vulnerable children on Outreach programmes, there is always a debate about whether to do the class based activities first, and then the field based ones – or is the best way the other way around. For me personally, its field based activities first – always and every time.

These are my reasons:

1. When you take someone from a London borough out to a wild and remote place they are unsettled and disoriented initially – so you have the upper hand.

2. By getting them off the operating base as quickly as possible – they cannot form alliances with rival gangs, or attack rival gangs.

3. Also by getting them off the base quickly – they can only bond with their team members and directing staff, which is exactly what you want to happen

4. Once in the field the participants become more compliant, which means when you return to base – they are far easier to manage.

For my colleagues who had remained back at base, life had been absolute hell for them while we had been away - as a number of gang members had formed alliances and were now attacking rival groups.

To put a stop to this, I filled one barrack accommodation block full of gang participants, and then sealed off the building. Outside the block we had TSG police officers in attendance who had sealed off the perimeter to prevent anyone from either sneaking into the building or sneaking out.

Inside the block were all the remaining staff, who were supporting me in an amnesty weapons search. I had given every person in the building 20 minutes to put any weapons that they had into the shower block. After that they would be subjected to a police search, and would of course face the legal consequences of having possession of an offensive weapon.

After 20 minutes I entered the shower block with Leon and by the main shower curtains there were about 20 weapons of various sizes, including knives, knuckle dusters, martial art stars and baseball bats. There was also a crudely manufactured swinging mace that had been made out of a tennis ball that had been pierced with nails.

Because they had all been compliant, and due to the fact that the search had taken place under an amnesty - no further action was taken. All things considered it was a good result.

The following day we had a very unpleasant incident to deal with that involved a female psychologist and a number of gang members. They had grabbed her by the arm and verbally abused her while she was doing her rounds – so she was understandably very upset. When Leon saw what had happened he stormed off to their room to confront them about what had just happened. The second he stood in their doorway the room just fell silent – which says everything about Leon's influence and control over them. Eventually, they decided to fess up to him and were duly disciplined as a consequence.

As for our psychologist, she was fine and took no further action against the gang members that had been involved in the incident. She also to her credit apologized to Leon for an earlier comment that she had made about him, where she questioned the wisdom of having non-professional staff as mentors.

I think it would be fair to say that nobody on that programme was more effective than Leon – as he walked the walk, and talked the talk.

He was an outstanding 3R.

If you are ever wondering just how much effect a good 3R can have on a young person's life – then read this account by Roadman A.

ROADMAN A

2018 had just begun, GCSEs were just around the corner, everyone was looking forward to Prom and Graduation, and one of the high achieving Prefects had just been arrested for having a Meat Cleaver in his bag. This is the story of how my life changed forever.

=Thursday after school, I get a panicked call from one of my best mates saying he was about to get in a physical altercation with a group of boys who had previously assaulted him on the Tube. He told me to bring a weapon and with no second thoughts I rush home and grab the biggest thing I could find, a Meat Cleaver with the handle taped red. Where I live, stabbings are common and I didn't want to lose my friend so I wanted to protect him. I feared for our lives. But as I'm running to the park where he was, he called me telling me it's all over and that I shouldn't bother as it's not worth it. Now the realisation sets in, I've got a meat cleaver in my bag. This is dangerous. What if I'm caught?

I go to meet a friend to talk with him, eventually spending the rest of the night out with him smoking and drinking. I get home quite late, I'm worn out. I leave my bag on the side along with my school uniform ready for the next day. It's now Friday morning and I wake up quite late. I get dressed, grab my bag and rush to school, completely forgetting about the meat cleaver in my bag...

My period 1 lesson was RE. He said to the class that he could smell cannabis, and that there would be bag searches. At this moment I got paranoid and searched my own bag, and saw the red taped handle and the shimmer of the 7 inch blade. I'm shitting bricks.

My bag gets searched during my Period 2 English lesson by the head teacher. He was accompanied by two police officers and by this point my dad was called in. The realisation sets in as I'm taken out of circulation for the rest of the day and sent to the Police Station for an interview.

They told me that it shouldn't result in a conviction and it would only be a referral to the Youth Offending Team, which gave me some comfort as my aspirations were to become a Lawyer. A couple of weeks passed and I get a charge sheet sent to me, summoning me to Willesden Youth Court with 2 counts of Possession of an Offensive Weapon, scheduled for the day of my Physics GCSE exam. At this point I've been banned from school premises and sent to an alternate provision tuition academy which only taught Maths and Science.

Weeks go by and I'm teaching myself the entire syllabus. I was determined to get all of my GCSEs. At this point I was depressed and needed an adrenaline rush, so I stole a moped. I got caught because my passenger did not have a helmet. I got arrested and spent a night in custody, did my interview and then got a second court date.

I did my GCSE exams in a meeting room isolated from everyone else. I knew I had to get something out of this, so I worked as hard as I could to get my qualifications. In between of all of this were court appearances. In total, I had been referred to maximum sentence Youth Referral Order (12 months), 1 year driving ban, and amassed more than £700 in fines.

These convictions stick, meaning they will show up on an enhanced DBS. This makes getting a job as a Lawyer difficult, or any job that requires an enhanced DBS. All sixth forms in my area turned me down on this basis, and I had to watch all of my friends get their licenses and driving while I'm walking like a mug. I had a driving ban before it was even legal for me to own a car.

If it wasn't for the Army Cadet Force, I would not be here today. I am a Sergeant at the moment and that means I am one of the most senior cadets there, so I spend my time delivering training and organising the structure of a parade night. My NCOs are fantastic and they help the unit run like clockwork and outside of cadets we are all good mates. They have helped me get through depression and having issues with the law. Since joining the ACF I have achieved many great things and have exceeded myself in every way possible. A career in the Army is something I now seriously consider. If it wasn't for the adult instructors dragging my arse through demotions and promotions, breaking me down and then building me back up again, I would have continued to spiral down a lowlife path, probably in prison, in hospital, or in a grave. They have inspired me to become a better person and to turn my life around for the better, and everyone who knows me will tell you I have really worked hard to get where I am today.

I was always told that my greatest enemy is myself. I always do great things but I somehow consistently do stupid things to cancel it out. The ACF and the YOT team have helped me manage my behaviour and do better as a member of society. I am forever indebted to their work.

RATTING OUT

RATTING OUT IS A term that is normally used to
describe someone who has gone against the gang code
of silence - where they have revealed either incriminating
or embarrassing information about their gang, or an
individual gang member. In their eyes it is the ultimate
betrayal, and yet it happens every day.

No gang member is ever going to admit that they have
ratted to the police, or a rival gang – as that would be a
death sentence for them.

Gangs clearly get information about their rivals from
someone who is in a place of trust – otherwise how would
they know where to find them? The police of course, also
have their own sources within the gang world – as that's
how they gain intelligence.

At any given time, there are gang members who are
questioning their loyalties to their respective gang, for a
whole variety of reasons. For example, some may feel quite
comfortable about being involved in low level crime – but
do not want to be involved in any violence. There will
also be those who joined a gang because of a friend or a

relative, and now find themselves older and wiser – with better life choices on the table.

These are indeed difficult predicaments – so for those who want a way out, there are thankfully plenty of organisations that can help make that happen.

If you are in a gang you cannot just announce one day that you are leaving, as you would in a job, as that just isn't going to work. You would without a shadow of a doubt put yourself in a very difficult situation, and one that could possibly open yourself up to reprisals and bullying - so it's definitely a good idea to say nothing until a safe and viable option is on the table.

According to a case worker at St Giles Trust, a charity that supports people affected by gang-related violence. "At any one time, I usually have two clients that need to move because of gang activity. But some only want a move so that they can hide and then pop back up again. Many of them are still at it with the gang activity. For the move to be successful it has to be that they want to completely get out of gangs."

If you are seriously considering getting out of gang life, one of the best organisations to contact is London Gang Exit.

The London Gang Exit (LGE) programme was commissioned by MOPAC (The Mayor's Office for Policing and Crime) and is specifically designed to help young Londoners who are gang nominals, as well as those who are being exploited by gangs.

To be eligible for referral, the young person should be:

- Aged between 16-24 and associated with or involved in gangs
- At significant risk of harm from gang activity, (such as violence or exploitation), a risk to

themselves, or pose a risk of harm to others motivated to end their gang involvement.

- They must also be willing to work with the LGE service.

If the above option is not viable for a gang member, there are other organisations in London that can offer support. For reference I have provided a list of supportive organisations at the back of this book.

COVID – 19

AS I WAS WRITING this book, a crisis from out of absolutely nowhere torpedoed my world - and I would guess yours to – that is unless you're living on a remote island. I am of course referring to the Coronavirus pandemic, or COVID – 19 as it is now more commonly known.

Just prior to the Governments national lock-down in March 2020, I was working in a quirky little school in Staines, Surrey that helped support young people that are temporarily out of mainstream education. As every day passed by, my car journey was getting quicker and quicker – on account of the diminishing airport traffic.

However at the same time the amount of passenger aircraft that were parked up by the aprons and runways was growing by the day. In the final days of my time at the school, I remember looking at a big sign saying welcome to Staines – which made me for some strange reason think of Ali G and his infamous Staines massive. As I thought about gangs, I started to wonder how the lockdown would affect crime in London. My initial thoughts were that it would drop significantly on account of fewer people being on the

streets, equals less people to rob, and with more people
working from home, or on furlough that would mean
less burglaries – and fewer gangbangers on the streets
would mean less stabbings. So there was a positive side
of lockdown.

As I thought about it further from a drug dealing
aspect, if all of Europe's borders were closed, and there
were no ships sailing, and aircraft flying – how would
the drugs market get supplied? The short answer was
no, it wouldn't get supplied – which meant higher drug
prices. While conversely, because nobody was travelling
fuel prices had plummeted. So lockdown was definitely a
case of win or lose depending on what side of the tracks
you were on.

Eventually the police started to confirm what I
had already suspected, which of course was good news
for Londoners. This is a list of positive outcomes from
lockdown:

The price of drugs doubled – on account of limited
supply

Violence in London was down by 79%

Stabbings and shootings were down by 50%

Gang members self-isolating, were easier to catch

No public transport meant gangs had to use their own
cars – so police were able to spot them easier.

One other particular positive consequence of lockdown
related to some gang members reflecting on their criminal
lifestyle, and deciding that it was time to quit and live a
more positive life. In other cases gang members that had
been living a fast life style now had to live a slow one,
which meant less crime for them.

Despite the fact that gang crime had decreased
significantly under lockdown, the Met Police as a response

decided to go into overdrive and launch an all- out attack on gang crime. With almost every gang member in London on lockdown – they were sitting ducks. The police also used Violence Suppression Units to target 1000 known gang members and prolific criminals.

Some just received warning letters, whereas others were on the receiving end of targeted police search raids. Gangs and criminals however are extremely adaptive, and will constantly react to changing environments and threats.

At the time of writing I am aware of a massive cyber war on social media between rival gangs in London – which will clearly end in bloodshed at some point in the near future.

I sincerely hope that I am wrong, but after years of working with gangs I know how they think and operate – and pandemic or not, they will resume their gang warfare as soon as a convenient opportunity presents itself.

CONCLUSION

IF YOU HAVE MANAGED to reach this point in the book, well done. I must confess that I never set out to write so much, but gang warfare is a complex subject. The more I wrote, the more I needed to add – as you either tell the whole story, or you tell no story.

Every time I finished a chapter, I realised that I needed to add another one to explain all the constant changes and evolutions that were taking place - even as I was writing.

However the biggest story to impact upon me, and I am sure you was COVID-19. In fact even today I am still processing all of its known effects, and those that I perceive will affect me, my family and friends in the future.

There will also be implications for both the gangs and the police, and it's only over time that the long term effects of this pandemic will begin to be understood and appreciated.

I hope "Raised to Kill" has given you a better insight and understanding of London's gang warfare problem, and what needs to be done to resolve it.

I also hope that some of you reading this book will

become mentors or supporters of gang intervention programmes, as we need good people to act as role models.

If you are in a gang and you are reading this book, I hope you see where it will all lead to. Although you may not have been shot or stabbed, I guarantee at some point in time you will get hurt by either one of your rivals, or one of your own. That's gang life for you.

If just one person reads this book and decides that they want to give up on gangs, and just pursue a normal young person's life - then I will be a very happy man.

If however you have read this book, and then decided that a gang life is for you, I will have totally failed in my endeavours to help you and other young people live a life that is both rewarding and fulfilling.

I sincerely hope that is not the case.

Take care, and stay safe

AUTHORS APPEAL

AS I MENTIONED EARLIER in the book, I have set up a programme that has been designed to help young people get out of gangs and into real jobs. If you would like to support my efforts, and those of the Human Dynamics Group - please kindly donate to Mike Ryan at justgiving.com

Thanks in advance for your support.

USEFUL CONTACTS

If you are a young person, or a parent and you need support, please check out the following charities and organisations for help and advice:

Action for Children – actionforchildren.org.uk

Anxiety UK – anxietyuk.org.uk

CALM – thecalmzone.net

Centrepoint – centrepoint.org.uk

Childline – childline.org.uk

FRANK – talktofrank.com

Hope Again – hopeagain.org.uk

Hub of Hope – hubofhope.co.uk

Kooth – kooth.com

Me and My Mind – meandmymind.nhs.uk

Mencap – mencap.org.uk

NSPCC – nspcc.org.uk

NHS Go – nhsgo.uk

No Panic – nopanic.org.uk

OCD Youth – ocdyouth.org

On My Mind – annafreud.org/on-my-mind

Papyrus – papyrus-uk.org

Refuge – refuge.org.uk

Relate – relate.org.uk

Rethink Mental Illness – rethink.org

Safeline – safeline.org.uk

Samaritans – Samaritans.org

Shelter – shelter.org.uk/youngpeople

The Mix – themix.org.uk

Time to Change – time-to-change.org.uk

Victim Support – victimssupport.org.uk

Voice Collective – voicecolleactive.co.uk

Women's Aid – womensaid.org.uk

Young Minds – youngminds.org.uk

Young Stonewall – youngstonewall.org.uk

Youth Access – youthaccess.org.uk

GANG SUPPORT CONTACTS
Abianda – abianda.com

Catch-22 – catch-22.org.uk

Gangsline - Gangsline.com

KIKIT – kikitproject.org

NSPCC – nspcc.org.uk

Redthread – redthread.org.uk

St Giles – stgilestrust.org.uk

Printed in Great Britain
by Amazon